Fish and Fishe
of Kintyre, Lochfyneside,
Gigha & Arran

Fish and Fisherfolk
of Kintyre, Lochfyneside, Gigha & Arran

ANGUS MARTIN

Previous books by Angus Martin also published by House of Lochar

The North Herring Fishing
Herring Fishermen of Kintyre and Ayrshire

Cover illustration: John Ramsay's *Adoration* of Carradale, heaving up trawl
off Whitestone, Kintyre, c. 1983. *Photograph by Lachlan Paterson*

British Cataloguing in Publication Data
A catalogue record for this book is available
from the British Library

ISBN 1 899863 97 4

© 2004 Angus Martin

All rights reserved. No part of this publication may be reproduced,
stored in a retrieval system, or transmitted, in any form or by any means,
electronic, mechanical, photocopying, recording or otherwise,
without the prior permission of the publisher.

Typeset by XL Publishing Services, Tiverton.
Printed in Great Britain by Bell & Bain, Glasgow
for House of Lochar, Isle of Colonsay, Argyll PA61 7YR

Contents

List of illustrations — vi
Introduction — vii
Acknowledgements — ix
Oral Sources — x

Leac Bhuidhe — 1
Four Inshore Fishermen — 10
Seine-netting — 16
Crustaceans — 26
Saithe and Lythe — 50
Cod — 58
Haddock and Whiting — 70
Hake — 78
Flatfish — 84
Skate and Ray — 96
Other Species — 101
Scallops — 124
Silvercraigs — 137
Kames — 150
Food — 156
Childhood — 164
Women in the Fishing Community — 179

Appendix — 188
Glossary — 190

Amendments to previously published books — 193

Index — 195

Illustrations

Map: Kintyre, Arran, Lochfyneside and Gigha   *page xii*

Photographs (following page 52)
1. Leac Bhuidhe, 2003.
2. Robert Wylie, New Orleans, 1972.
3. Dick Gillon, Southend, c. 1960.
4. John 'Knuckler' Robertson, Campbeltown, 2002.
5. Swedish seine-net boats moored at the New Quay, Campbeltown, c. 1925.
6. The seine-netter *Gleaner* of Peterhead.
7. Colin and Jock Campbell seine-netting on the *Silver Quest* of Carradale, c. 1958.
8. Captain George McSporran casting with bamboo rod at Southend, c. 1933.
9. Salt Pans village, 1835.
10. A Gigha fishing crew, c. 1925.
11. Skipper Willie McBride, Pirnmill, on his skiff the *Ella*, Lochranza, c. 1922.
12. A basking shark, taken in the prawn-trawl of *Silver Spray* of Tarbert, c. 1970.
13. Campbeltown fisherman, William 'Oakie' Gilchrist, with sturgeon, c. 1920.
14. Duncan Graham, Peninver, with 42lb salmon taken at Ugadale, c. 1978.
15. Duncan and Maggie Campbell at the crofthouse, Silvercraigs, c. 1925.
16. Donald MacVicar at Low Kames, Lochfyneside, 1983.

Line Drawings
The images of Crab, Crawfish, Lobster, Prawn, Scallop and Squid were specially drawn for this book by Bob Smith, Linlithgow. All the others, which are also not to scale, are from wood engravings in *A History of British Fishes* by William Yarrell, 2nd edition, London, 1841.

Introduction

Although I fished for several years, in the late 1960s and the '70s, in all the books I have written about fishing, I have resisted the temptation to include my own (albeit modest) experiences, believing that a work of history should not be used as an autobiographical vehicle, though an autobiography might be used as a vehicle for history. Since, however, this is likely to be my last book on fishing, I feel that I should say something about what fishing means to me. That the industry fascinates me and that I admire its practitioners – the 'old-timers', at any rate – is obvious, I think, in all that I have written, but my personal perception of fish has altered radically and I'll go straight to the end of my experiences, to 1977, when I crewed on the *Intrepid* of Campbeltown.

One Monday morning, I boarded the boat and began readying the trawl for shooting. Hauling the cod-end clear of the boat's stern, I found a small crab cowering in the scuppers, still alive. I put it straight back into the sea, wondering if it would survive its ordeal, and wondering, too, what it had done to deserve that ordeal. Some weeks later, at the Grips, when the last haul of the week came up, on a Friday afternoon, there was a big haddock – the only one – in the cod-end. He was still alive and I debated with myself whether I should release him or take him home and eat him. I ate him.

Thereafter came nightmares of fish that I had to save from death, and I began – to the unspoken consternation of my skipper, Willie MacDonald – returning to the sea all living fish whose chances of survival I judged to be good (something I had always done anyway with small, unmarketable fish, flats particularly). When the *Intrepid* was sold later that year, I came ashore and have never returned to sea, even for a day, on a fishing-boat. Some months after leaving the fishing, I stopped in the middle of eating a dish of spaghetti bolognese and never put meat into my mouth again. Nor do I now eat fish in any form.

I recount these experiences not to present myself as some kind of moral paragon, but to explain that I had suddenly begun to see fish and all other living creatures as individuals worthy of compassion and respect. At a time when the Scottish fishing industry is increasingly dominated by multi-million pound boats with massive catching power, it might be pertinent to remind ourselves that fish aren't merely tonnage for market.

Historically, the drift-net fishermen who opposed ring-netting and pair-trawling, and the line-fishermen who opposed otter-trawling and seine-netting, were no doubt concerned primarily with protecting their own livelihoods from the competition of more efficient operators, but it is also true that they feared for the fish stocks on which their communities had for generations depended, so conservation is no novel concept.

That many species are locally depleted to the point of commercial non-viability is undeniable, but the generality of fishermen are reluctant to admit that over-fishing and indiscriminate destruction of small fish – notably in small-meshed prawn-trawls – might be primary causes. They will cite water-temperature changes, the depredations of seals, the Chernobyl nuclear disaster of 1986 and other forms of pollution as possible causes, but shrink from accepting at least a part of the blame.

Yet, the apportioning of blame is pointless now. The damage has been done and it remains only to administer remedial treatment, as far as that is possible, though I suspect that certain stocks of bottom-living fish are locally extinct. Seabed conservation-zones may be one measure, restriction of small-meshed nets another, but the decimation of fishing fleets – which proceeds rapidly under European Commission governance – is, I fear, likely to be the most effective measure, bringing with it the demise of many long-suffering fishing communities.

Angus Martin
Campbeltown, January 2004.

Acknowledgements

There were many people, both living and dead, without whose knowledge and assistance this book would not have been possible. I thank all contributors and also: Murdo MacDonald, Archivist, Argyll & Bute Council, Lochgilphead, for his invaluable supply of documentary material; Iain Henderson, Ardnamurchan and Machrihanish, and Michel Byrne, Department of Celtic, University of Glasgow, for advice on Gaelic words; Lachie Paterson, Carradale, and George McSporran, Campbeltown, for assistance with sourcing and copying illustrations; Moira Burgess, Glasgow, Bob Smith, Linlithgow, Tommy Ralston, Lundin Links, and Lachie Paterson who most helpfully criticised the penultimate draft from their differing perspectives; Jim Tarvit, Anstruther, for his assistance with determining boats' registrations; James Kinnear, Marine Laboratory, Aberdeen, for advice on species identification; my wife Judy, for computing support skills; finally, Georgina Hobhouse, editor at House of Lochar, for without her faith in the trilogy of mine which she and her colleagues published, it would probably never have appeared.

Oral Sources

Female contributors are identified by maiden surname in text, but also by married surname below.
* denotes that the informant is deceased
+ denotes full-time/part-time fisherman

    Alistair Beattie*, Southend, b 1906
    Chrissie Black (Mrs George McGregor) Dalintober, b 1908
    Kenny Brown+, Tarbert, b 1967
    Ronnie Brownie+, Carradale, b 1943
    Archibald D Cameron*, Southend, b 1894
    Jessie Campbell* (Mrs Colin MacBrayne) Silvercraigs, b 1892
    Maggie Campbell*, Silvercraigs, b 1899
    Archibald Carmichael+, Tarbert, b 1914
    Willie Colville, Machrihanish, b 1930
    Robert Douglas, Campbeltown, b 1925
    Cecil Finn+, Campbeltown, b 1936
    Robert Gillies+, Campbeltown, b 1948
    Archibald Graham+, Peninver, b 1923
    Bill Harvison, b Lamlash, 1944
    Eoghann Henderson*, Gigha, b 1924
    Katie Jackson (Mrs Jimmy Prentice) Tarbert, b 1924
    Mary Jackson (Mrs Peter Brown) Tarbert, b 1930
    Teddy Lafferty, Campbeltown, b 1934
    Angus MacAlister+, Gigha, b 1917
    Archie MacAlister, Tarbert, b 1935
    Archie MacAlister+, Gigha, b 1955
    Carol McAulay (Mrs Jimmy Crossan) Dalintober, b 1923
    Mary MacBrayne, Campbeltown, b 1922
    Annie McBride* (Mrs Eddie Martindale) Carradale, b 1911
    Ellen McBride (Mrs David Oman) Carradale, b 1908
    Margaret McBride (Mrs Cliff Harvison) Pirnmill, b 1918
    Isobel McCallum* (Mrs Robert McInnes) Stewarton, b 1929
    John McConnachie+, Carradale, b 1932
    Turner McCrindle+*, Maidens, b 1902
    Donald MacDonald*, Gigha, b 1891
    James Macdonald+, Campbeltown, b 1925

May McDougall (Mrs Johnny McMillan) Carradale, b 1917
Neil McDougall, Carradale, b 1940
Peter McDougall+, Tarbert, b 1941
Dugald MacFarlane+*, Tarbert, b 1899
Hugh MacFarlane+*, Tarbert, b 1884
Mary McGeachy* (Mrs Duncan Blair) Dalintober, b 1910
Duncan MacInnes+, Eriskay, b 1925
Donald McIntosh+*, Carradale, b 1893
Nan McKay (Mrs Alex McMillan) Dalintober, b 1923
John McKerral+, Peninver, b 1937
Donald Macleod, Castleton, b 1937
Willie McMillan, Drumlemble, b 1934
Archie MacNeill*, Muasdale, b 1906
Betty MacNeill, Gigha, b 1929
Duncan MacNeill+*, Gigha, b 1899
Mary MacPhee (Mrs Archie Lang) Machrihanish, b 1943
Hugh McShannon*, Southend, b 1901
George McSporran, Campbeltown, b 1949
Willie McSporran+, Gigha, b 1936
David McVicar+, Drumlemble, b 1949
Donald MacVicar*, Kames, b 1898
John McWhirter+*, Campbeltown, b 1886
Henry Martin+*, Dalintober, b 1891
Jean Martin (Mrs Joe Crowther) Dalintober, b 1918
Denis Meenan+, Campbeltown, b 1926
George Newlands+*, Campbeltown, b 1902
Archie Paterson+, Carradale, b 1925
Lachie Paterson+, Carradale, b 1956
Tommy Ralston+, Campbeltown, b 1935
Davie Robertson+, Campbeltown, b 1922
Lawrence Robertson+, Campbeltown, b 1935
Robert Ross+, Tarbert, b 1926
Neil Short+*, Campbeltown, b 1917
Bob Smith, b 1928, West Fife
Neil Thomson+*, Muasdale, b 1904
Billy Wareham+, Campbeltown, b 1936
Margaret Watson (Mrs Duncan McIntyre) Southend, b 1923
Willie Watson, Muasdale, b 1943

Published sources used in this work will be found in the notes and references at the end of each chapter, where *Campbeltown Courier* and *Argyllshire Herald* are abbreviated *CC* and *AH*.

Inveraray
LOCH FYNE
Furnace
Minard
Lochgair
Kames
Achnaba
Lochgilphead
Ardrishaig
Silvercraigs
Otter
Loch Long
Kyles
BUTE
Rothesay
Tarbert
Loch Caolisport
Lagan
Sgolaig
Ettrick Bay
Inch
Cumbraes
KINTYRE
Skipness
Claonaig
Cock
Garroch Head
GIGHA
W Loch Tarbert
Crossaig
Lochranza
Ardminish
Tayinloan
Cath Sgeir
Cara
Pirnmill
Garradale
ARRAN
Muasdale
Brodick
Machrie Bay
Lamlash
Holy Isle
Bellochantuy
Drumadoon
Ugadale
Peninver
Ayr
Machrihanish
Leac Bhuidhe
Drumlemble
Davaar Island
Campbeltown
Lodan
Auchenhoan
Brig
Ru Stafnish
Feochaig
Southend
Arranman's Barrels
Mull of Kintyre
Glemanuill
Sanda Island

Leac Bhuidhe

This book begins where fishing itself must have begun – on the seashore, where our ancestors found abundant food. Not only were limpets, mussels, oysters, winkles and cockles abundant, they were also constant. The gathering and preparation of shellfish, however, are monotonous, time-consuming tasks and those hunter-gatherers must have quickly recognised the potential of fish as a superior resource. Perhaps that potential was realised providentially – when fish were driven ashore by predators or trapped in tidal pools – but human ingenuity would soon have taken over and traps constructed, spears fashioned, nets woven and hook and line assembled. Commercial fishing, as now understood, was far in the future, however; fishing was a subsistence occupation, one of many in the lives of coast-dwellers, and would remain so for countless individuals even as the sea filled with the boats of those who had chosen fishing as their economic mainstay.

On 7 August, 1937, the *Campbeltown Courier* reported a 'thrilling rescue' at Machrihanish. Alex McShannon, Lossit Cottages, had entered the water, at 'a spot known as The Lake', for an 'afternoon swim', got into difficulties and been rescued by Malcolm Thomson, 'a swimmer of repute' who plunged in fully clothed. This is undoubtedly the same incident that Willie Colville, in May 2003, spoke of – when 'Alex Shennock' was 'pulled oot the pool at the Lake…' From the *Courier* report, one would assume that Alex had been swimming in the sea, but he was actually cooling off in a deep natural pool – 'a great place for a dip', as Willie said – in the rock known in Gaelic as Leac Bhuidhe and corrupted into 'The Lake'.

That rugged promontory lies between the Galdrans and the rounded headland of Tòn Bhàn, which features at extreme left of William McTaggart's famous painting of 1895, *The Coming of St Columba*. On 26 May, 2003, I walked to the Lake, with a friend George McSporran and his son Sandy, to renew my acquaintance with the place. There wasn't, in truth, much to renew. I'd looked at it many times from above, but had been down so seldom that had it not been for a particular encounter there, decades ago, I might have doubted I'd ever set foot in it. On that day, I chanced upon a man lying at a rock-hole, patiently watching its depths. His name was Davie McVicar and he was hunting lobster and crab. He demonstrated the rudiments of the technique, after which I resumed my walk; but I never forgot that encounter, and, looking back on it now, I realise that I might have seen a similar procedure enacted there had I lived 500 or 5000 years ago.

Revisiting the place in 2003, my strongest impression was that no one would go there without good reason. It consists entirely of a jumble of mica schist boulders, some of them massive, and the biggest of them – containing the bathing pool – at the seaward extremity. Though the whole point is referred to as 'the Lake', that rock alone gives the place its name, *Leac Bhuidhe* – Yellow Slab – for it has a flattish, if tilted, surface, parts of which appear yellow from seaweed encrustation.

Above the bouldered shore, that day, primrose, bluebell and seapink splashed their colour amid the outcrops of lichen-dappled rock; there were fine views south to Tòn Bhàn and the Irish coast, and north to Machrihanish Bay, surmounted now by a string of stately, if inescapably alien, wind-turbines, their blades revolving placidly; both on our way there and back, we disturbed a peregrine falcon from its perch beneath the clifftop; but all that was capped by the appearance, close inshore, of a school of bottle-nosed dolphins plunging northward.

I find the Lake inhospitable and cannot imagine spending an entire day there, but it was formerly a convenient and popular picnic place for many Machrihanish and Drumlemble families. Camping, however, is impossible there and it was visited only as a day's outing. An additional disadvantage was the scarcity of fresh water. Mary MacPhee first went to the Lake as a girl with her father, Alick, a miner at Machrihanish Colliery. She recalled a 'lovely wee well' being dug out and lined with light-coloured stones – 'so that people wid see it wis a waterin place' – above high water mark to the north of the Lake, but it was frequently found to have been 'trampled' by wild goats. Mary's brother-in-law, Davie McVicar, remembered water being carried into the Lake from the little burn that runs off the cliff at the Doos' Cove (Pigeons' Hollow) still further north. In Davie's time, water would be filled into National Dried Milk tins en route to the Lake. The first task, on arrival, was to gather driftwood and make a fire for brewing tea, milk tins serving also as billy-cans.

The anchor

Tea-making and cooking took place on the south side of the Lake at a rock face variously known as the Kitchen, Devil's Kitchen, Cookhouse or Galley. A National Dried Milk tin also served as a permanent container for tea, sugar and powdered milk, individually wrapped in miners' oil-cloth. Close to the Kitchen, there is a huge anchor lodged amid boulders. That immovable relic belonged to the *Madelaine Ann* of Dundalk, Ireland, wrecked on 22 December, 1904, with the loss of her master, James McCourt, and crew of four – Patrick and John McCourt, James Kennedy and an unnamed boy – during a storm which climaxed in 100-mile-an-hour winds.[1] Nearer the sea was the Table Rock, by which Leac Bhuidhe – the 'yellow slab' itself – was also known, and where the snares and bait were prepared and picnics enjoyed. There were four rock-holes there, another at the Kitchen, and a few others – 'hard to fish' – nearer the sea.

The Lake is, in fact, a rather dangerous place owing to its Atlantic exposure. As Willie Colville remarked: 'It's naw a place for anyone tae go roon on their own.' Children generally were barred from the north side in case they got 'waashed off'. Scares were not unknown even among adults. One regular there, an ex-Royal Marine, Neil 'Beela' Thomson, was almost swept off a fishing rock one day when a wave 'came up oot o naething'. To reach that rock, careful timing was required to cross a channel; and, once out on the rock, there was a danger of being cut off if a 'bound' started up and the channel became a 'ragin torrent, like a river in spate', as Willie put it.

Mary MacPhee recalled, at the north end of the Lake, a 'danger spot' where the children were warned never to go. One day, her father said that he was going over there for half-an-hour – probably he had seen signs of fish – and told Mary and her siblings: 'Lift yer head every five minutes an make sure A'm there.' He did catch some fish there, but when he turned to come back he disappeared from sight in a surge of broken water. Having returned safely, he asked Mary: 'Did ye see that?' – 'Uhuh,' she replied. 'If it hadn't been for a lump o white campion, I wis gone,' he said. He had grabbed it when the wave struck him, and it held. He always wore leather boots at the Lake and wouldn't allow the children to be there unless barefoot or wearing boots – 'wellies', being slippery, were prohibited.

Rock fishing

Dangers notwithstanding, there was good fishing to be had there. Bamboo poles were used as rods; bait was eel-tail lures or limpets, the latter bound to the hook using sheep wool pulled from fences. Lythe, up to 12 lbs in weight, could be caught, and some of these would be cooked on the spot. There was a huge cast-iron frying-pan kept at the Lake, and, when lythe were taking, Alick MacPhee would shout: 'Get the fryin-pan out!' That old pan – which came from the MacPhee family's earlier home, Lochsanish Cottage, and which would be scrubbed regularly in salt-water using a sandy-rooted clump of grass – could hold four or five fish, gutted and cleaned in sea-water and 'so sweet' when fried. Sometimes there would be a pot of potatoes already boiled, 'and that wis yer dinner there'. If fish were being caught, visitors got their share. Most of the regulars had their signals – a certain whistle – and by the time the newcomer had arrived down, fish were frying and the kettle had boiled again. Nothing was wasted. Surplus fish, at the end of the day, would be carried back to Machrihanish and Alick MacPhee would distribute fillets among neighbours.

Willie McMillan, of Coalhill, Drumlemble, began going to the Lake as a schoolboy, to try his hand at snaring crab and lobster, but didn't rod-fish from the rocks until older. If he caught two or three lythe to string and carry home to Drumlemble, he was satisfied. These would be boiled and the flesh mixed with mashed potato to make fish-cakes. Townsfolk, as he remarked, could go 'doon the quay an get a rasher', but in Drumlemble 'ye dinna get fish for nothin'. After he left school, in 1949, he began camping with friends at the south end of the Galdrans, close to the Lake. They had no tent, but slept under a split wool-bag, wrapped in an old blanket and wearing an extra jersey to keep out the nocturnal chill.

Willie Colville recalled the excited cry, one day, of Willie Allan: 'A've caught a creggach!' This was a ballan wrasse (p 105) – 'rid as hell' and 'armour-plated' – which Willie Allan obviously prized, because it went straight into his bag to be carried home. A native of Gigha, he worked on farms in the Laggan and married a Drumlemble woman, Lizzie Galbraith.

Limpets

Equipment used for catching crabs and lobsters was simple: a bait-bag or -string and a snare. The snare – or *snig* – was a loop of copper wire attached to a length of fence-wire. The bait-bag, a piece of netting weighted with a stone, could also be attached to fence-wire. Limpets were always readily available as bait. These would be strung together – perhaps a couple of dozen of them – on a length of twine, which was lashed to a flat stone; then the whole assemblage was fastened to a length of fence-wire.

Limpets were knocked off the rocks using a smooth stone about the size of a hammer-head. There being no beach at the Lake, these stones were picked out of the pools and, after use, could be left on Table Rock for the next time. Their 'pedigree' must go back to the prehistoric 'elongated stones with bevelled ends... known as *limpet hammers*', whose true function continues to provoke debate among archaeologists. In *Scotland's First Settlers*[2] it is remarked that '... the need for such a weapon to attack the harmless limpet has been questioned'. The Lake bait-gatherers, I suspect, would have entertained no such doubt. The limpet is notoriously difficult to dislodge. As Willie Colville remarked, 'Ye'd tae knock them quick', because there was no second chance, and to attempt the operation without a tool would have been senseless. In Davie McVicar's experience, limpets on exposed Atlantic coast – such as the Lake – are tougher to dislodge than limpets living in calmer waters, and maybe tougher eating too!

As a young girl, Mary MacPhee invariably gathered limpets by the hundred from the rocks around Bun an Uisge – 'Waterfoot' – where the stream, generally now known as the Goats' Burn, enters the sea at the south end of the Galdrans Bay. Using a stone – 'a kinna round one that wid fit yer hand' – it was vital to knock the limpets off with the first blow 'or ye don't get them at all'. She became a 'dab hand' at the business. 'Ye got it on yer first swoop,' she recalled. 'That wis a game; that wis fun.' With knives, the men would cut off the very tip of the shell and then string the limpets, on a loop of shot-firing wire, for carrying to the Lake. At that time, when the colliery at Machrihanish was flourishing, those miners who frequented the Lake invariably carried a roll of that variously coloured wire, which was also used for making the snares. When the Lake was reached, the limpets would be unstrung and placed in a tin filled with sea-water, to keep them fresh; but as Mary remarked: 'The poor wee limpets wid be dead, right enough.'

Of limpets, Willie McMillan remarked: 'They wirna the easiest things tae take off.' If, however, a blow smashed the shell but failed to budge the sucker-like foot, the job could be finished with a 'sailor's knife', which was a big black-handled tool containing both a heavy blade and a spike for rope-splicing. Campbeltown being a wartime Naval base, many of these knives were in circulation among the civilian population and were particularly coveted by boys. Willie acquired his through an aunt, Janet Brown, who lived at the time in Clochkeil Cottages and occasionally had Royal Navy officers billeted there.

Hunger pangs

Davie McVicar has boiled Lake limpets in a billy-can and eaten them to relieve the pangs of hunger. 'Yer jaws wir sore chowin them,' he recalled; but the hunger that intensifies during an active day in the open air knows few restraints, and, as he remarked: 'If ye're gonny be hungry, it's roon there ye'll be hungry.' The old people made limpet soup with onion or watercress. As a girl, Mary MacPhee and several of her companions boiled limpets in a billy-can, but they were all sick after their feed and got 'such a row' from the adults, who suspected that the limpets hadn't been properly cooked. Mary and her friends also gathered winkles in the Galdrans and cooked them too in billy-cans. Somebody had a pin keeping up his trousers, and that was used to dig the meat out of the shells. She didn't care for winkles either, but her maternal grandmother, Mary Ann Glen (née McGeachy), would ask her to bring home three or four dozen big winkles and make oatmeal-based 'wilk soup' with them. In May, when gulls were laying at Tòn Bhàn, eggs could be gathered. Willie Colville once cooked an omelette of gulls' eggs and wilks, which resulted in an outbreak of particularly offensive flatulence! Willie McMillan also ate the Tòn Bhàn gull-eggs. They were too strongly flavoured for his taste, but if there was some milk available, he'd scramble them to render them more palatable.

Willie Colville and Don Thomson went one day to the Lake, not intending to stay long because the weather wasn't good. Don had brought a dozen fresh herring with him as bait. He and Willie duly baited three or four holes and waited for the action to begin; but they 'never saw a thing'. They were enjoying themselves, though, because 'it turned oot a colossal day... a burning hot day'. Having brought only 'a couple of slices o breid' with them, they were also becoming very hungry. In desperation, they hauled up the bait-bags, removed the fish, threw them into the embers of their fire and ate the crispy herring. 'Ett the bait, an there wir naethin wrang wae it – not a thing wrang wae it!' Willie recalled.

At the age of 11, Willie McMillan was allowed to go to the Lake, which became a frequent destination for him and his friends, Donald McVicar, Jock Kerr, Archie Kerr, Willie Deans, Tommy Paterson, Donald Nimmo and 'Mecky' Allan. They went by Mingary, and on their way they'd try 'the douse' – diving on and killing a rabbit. 'The place wis moving wi rabbits at that time,' Willie recalled. Having reached the Lake, wood would be gathered and broken up for a fire, and the rabbit – which had been gutted and skinned on the hill – would be stewed in a pot along with the few potatoes which each of the boys carried in their pockets, and perhaps turnip and carrots lifted, in passing, from a field. While the holes were being baited, the stew would be simmering in the Kitchen, where cutlery and plates were secreted for the use of visitors; afterwards, everything was religiously cleaned and returned to the rock-shelves. Sometimes the boys would carry hard-boiled eggs with them. These would be gathered the day before, around farms where hens were 'laying out', and boiled at home.

Fishing the holes

The Kintyre-born gamekeeper and naturalist, Dugald Macintyre, was first attracted to the notion of catching lobsters when, rod-fishing on the Atlantic coast of Kintyre, he observed them moving about on the sea-bottom. Individuals would occasionally tackle baits, but, the hooks being 'too large to enter their mouths', he instead baited a 'small minnow triangle' with herring or (preferably) rabbit liver 'and caught a good many lobsters that way, including some monsters'. The lobsters having a habit of carrying off the bait in their claws, 'to be successful in hooking them one had to *see* the bait enter their mouths'.

In an effort to catch more lobsters, Macintyre rigged himself a gaff. The big hook was lashed to the 'steel ramrod of a rifle', which was itself lashed to a long bamboo shaft. His lure was a muslin bag filled with a 'skinned and squashed rabbit' or herring heads and guts, which he set down at the turn of the tide in a spot where 'the scent of the bait was quickly carried down a long stretch of rugged coast'.

'One evening,' he recalled, 'four lobsters of immense size were seen coming to the bait at the same time, and one after the other came straight up tide from the open sea on the scent of the bait. Each was gaffed just as it grabbed the bait, without the smallest difficulty, for lobsters are only armoured on their backs; their under parts are soft enough.'[3]

I asked Davie McVicar to comment on these accounts, and his opinions were much the same as my own, that gaffing is certainly practicable but that catching lobsters by baited hook, though arguably feasible, rather stretches credulity. Macintyre's stock as a naturalist has declined to such a degree, it has to be said, that his books are scarcely ever mentioned now. While the bulk of his observations are unquestionable, some appear tainted, with the passage of time, by a suspicion of exaggeration or too great a willingness to draw conclusions which a more rigorously analytical observer might hesitate to draw. Also, his fondness for turning out fictionalised vignettes of the lives of the creatures he observed has tended to detract from his more serious essays in natural history.

Patience, more than any other quality, was required when fishing the Lake rock-holes. Crabs might be snared round a claw, but not lobsters, which would cast the claw and escape. Likewise, an attempt to snare a lobster's tail by direct action was invariably futile – as soon as he would feel the assault, he'd dart off. The surest method of taking a lobster was to position the snare behind the tail and give the bait a jerk; the lobster, startled, might then back into the snare.

Davie McVicar's 'best day' at the Lake resulted in eight lobsters, all of legal size, which were divided among his companions. The sport was, indeed, communal, and if there were several parties fishing, they would watch one's another's pools for movement. Davie has seen two lobsters cautiously watching each other from different parts of a pool, only their antennae visible and neither inclined to approach the bait. 'Their tells,' he said, 'wid still be below the rock. Ye nee'na bother tryin tae snare them. Ye'd go away hame that night and they'd still be there.' Willie Colville recalled the 'hell of a sunburn' that fishers were subject to when lying shirtless watching the holes.

Girls too participated, and Mary MacPhee caught her share of crabs and lobsters, lying for an hour at a time on the rocks. Once the tide turned and began to come in again, the prey would appear. Often the only sign of a big lobster would be its antennae protruding from a rock crevice. Egg-bearing lobsters were always returned to the pool – that was the accepted rule. The big *croobans* – crabs – were 'devils tae catch because they wid snap their nipper off'. Latterly, there were very few sizeable crabs to be caught at the Lake, but Mary fished – and returned – the small ones just to 'keep up the tradition'.

When Willie McMillan took his sons, William and David, to the Lake for the first time, around 1976, his younger son, David, pulled out a lobster within half-an-hour. It was a case of 'beginner's luck' and it was also, Willie believes, the last lobster he saw caught there. In the summer of 1998, however, David – home on holiday from England – snared a giraffe in one of the pools. It wasn't, of course, a real giraffe, but a hardwood carving. The base was gone and the legs worn to points, but the neck, surprisingly, remained unbroken. Willie took the ornament home with him, intending to repair it and mount it on a suitable piece of driftwood, but so far it remains as it was when pulled from the rock-hole in which it mysteriously came to rest.

Fishing equipment was originally secreted in rock shelves at the Kitchen, but latterly it became necessary to carry it there because either it had gone missing or had been abandoned in the holes. The bamboo rods were also left there for the use of anyone, but, latterly again, there would be the 'odd stupid buggar that went roon an damaged the lot', as Willie Colville complained. Davie McVicar recalled it as 'really a grett deh oot'; but as Willie reasoned: 'There wisna much else ye could dae on a Sunday because ye couldn't get a drink. That's wan reason. The other reason – ye hanna the wherewithal either!' [Willie Colville, Willie McMillan, Mary MacPhee, Davie McVicar, 2003]

I know of no place like the Lake, where fish, crabs and lobsters can leave the open sea and enter a complex of interconnected tidal passages and pools. Since, with the exception of a brief account in my own *Kintyre: The Hidden Past* (1984)[4], there is absolutely no historical record of the Lake as a fishing place, and, furthermore, no oral traditions going back further than a couple of generations, it is impossible to say with certainty that the Lake's resources were exploited over a period of centuries, let alone millennia; but it seems unlikely that such a rich source of food escaped the notice of our ancestors.

Before our society, in the latter half of the twentieth century, acquired its dependence on mass-produced and packaged foodstuffs, imported from all over the world for sale in supermarkets, ordinary folk had to get food wherever they could find it. For many families, in any case, there was little enough money to spend on food, so the pot had to be filled with whatever could be caught in the wild, whether legally or illegally.

In the not so distant past, all coastal communities – including those of shepherds and farmers – had particular fishing rocks.[5] These rocks were often named, and some of the names have survived. At Machrihanish, Creag Dhomhnuill Mhóir – Big Donald's Rock – was one such fishing place, and Dan Mann's Port – an inlet on the north-east side of Mill Bay – likewise commemorates an individual 'said to have been in the habit of fishing from this place'.[6] Donald Mann, a 28-year-old farmworker recorded at Kilkivan in the 1841 Census of Campbeltown Parish, may well have been that rock fisherman. George McSporran in 2003 recalled, from his father, three named rock fishing locations along the Keil shore of Southend: east to west, Islaymen's Port, Gardener's Rock (below Keil House, later School) and Graveyard Rock (below the cemetery).

Such rocks are now seldom used, and, if used, are accorded their ancient function not from necessity, but for reasons of sentiment or leisure. Likewise, the Lake no longer serves to fill empty bellies and may wait forever to become again a resort of hunters with instincts attuned to phenomena our prehistoric ancestors would have recognised.

References and Notes
1. A Martin, *The Kintyre Magazine*, No 38, p 28.
2. C R Wickham-Jones, *Scotland's First Settlers*, London 1994, p 93.
3. D Macintyre, *Highland Gamekeeper*, London N D, pp 80–2.
4. Edinburgh, reprinted 1999, p 151.
5. A Martin, *Kintyre Country Life*, Edinburgh 1987, pp 168–9.
6. *The Place Names of the Parish of Campbeltown*, Campbeltown 1943, pp 14, 16.

Four Inshore-Fishermen

Robert Wylie

The salmon- and lobster-fisherman, Robert Wylie, lived with his wife, Marjory, a schoolteacher, in the secluded cottage of New Orleans, at the foot of a beautiful wooded glen with views eastward to Arran and the Ayrshire coast. Robert, born in 1890, was a son of Thomas Wylie, joiner, and Marion Merrilees. An uncle, Robert Wylie, was a noted boat-builder in Campbeltown. Marjory belonged to the Rae family (p 62) and appears in the Campbeltown Census of 1891 as a baby of 14 days at New Orleans with her parents, Donald, 'Salmon Fisher', and Maggie Rae, who latterly occupied the cottage west of New Orleans. Beside that dwelling – now named 'Fisherman's Cottage' and rented to holidaymakers – may still be seen a windlass for hauling boats ashore and a stone-built fire-place with iron cauldron and chimney, for melting tar and preparing the 'cutch' solution in which ropes and cotton nets, etc. were steeped to preserve the fibre.

Archie Graham got to know Robert Wylie when, having sold his ring-netter the *Margaret Rose* in 1958, he took up lobster- and salmon-fishing. Robert had been about Sanda Island in his younger years and had known Archie's maternal grandfather, Charlie Cameron, so the relationship began on a sound footing. Robert helped Archie 'tremendously' at the start, not least with his intimate knowledge of the coast, and gave him invaluable advice. One of his sayings that Archie never forgot was: 'It's all one how good a fisherman ye are, yer net's got tae be in the right place.'

To obtain a smoother passage, his advice was 'Get in as close as ye can', when 'contrairy' conditions – perhaps wind and tide in opposition – were encountered off headlands; and it was his wise practice, with south or south-westerly wind, to take the ebb tide south along the Kintyre coast and return with flood, because, as Archie explained, 'If it was bad going down, it was generally no worse – and sometimes better – coming back with the wind and tide together.'

'A spade was a spade with Robert,' Archie recalled. There were times when the old man was approachable and times when he was best left alone. If his bees were swarming, it was advisable not to go near him because 'he was as cross as the bees'. If denied a sound night's sleep, Robert tended to be irritable, and Archie once fell foul of him on that score. Archie had a salmon net set near New Orleans and had attached a couple of floats to its end. These metal balls had 'worked together' during the night and had been knocking constantly, and when Archie later met the old man, he was told emphatically: 'These bloody floats have been chucklin all night – separate them!'

During one season, Archie was fishing lobsters off the Arranman's Barrels, where creels were inclined to stick in shipwrecks. Six of his creels were thus immobilised. He told Robert, who said that he would accompany him on the first good day. When that day came, Robert equipped himself with a small home-made grappling-iron and a length of creel-rope with a round stone lashed to it. In six or seven fathoms of slack water and with the boat hauled tight on the rope of the first jammed pot, Robert dropped the stone and began probing. 'That's the arse of it now,' he announced. 'Drop the creeper now, Archie, and drop it on the other side. Have ye got a grip of it?' – 'I think so.' – 'Pull up.' – 'Up came the pot,' Archie recalled. 'We recovered these six pots as quick as that.' [Archie Graham, 2003]

Robert Douglas, who was reared on Knockbay Farm, first met Robert and Marjory in about 1950 through a shared interest in bee-keeping. Thereafter, the younger Robert was a fairly regular visitor at New Orleans. It was there that Robert Wylie explained how he and Marjory had got started on the hobby. He had been talking to the farmer at Feochaig, Jackie MacIntyre, about bee-keeping and Jackie said: 'You can have some of mine!' Robert walked the four miles to Feochaig to discover that the bees lived in a barrel, which was to be cut in half. 'This,' Robert Douglas speculated, 'must have been worth seeing, for they'd have to keep the smoker going constantly to keep the bees subdued, and the wax and honey would stick to the saw. Anyway, they managed it and Robert carried the half-barrel home on his shoulder. His words were: "What a trauchle it was to carry these bees home."' Next day, however, he noticed that very few bees were coming and going, and, when he investigated, he discovered that most of them had gone back to Jackie's half, where the queen was!

When, as a young man, Robert Wylie was in the Royal Navy, his ship docked in a Middle Eastern port and the entire crew was invited to dine with a local sheikh; but some of the officers expressed a preference for embarking on a fishing trip and talked Robert into accompanying them. At which point in the story Marjory remarked: 'Fancy missing out on the chance to see the grandeur of a sheikh's palace when you could go fishing any old time!' – 'Ach weel,' Robert replied, 'when ye're young ye don't think aboot they things.' [Robert Douglas, 2003]

Angus MacAlister worked two seasons, 1936 and '37, for Robert at salmon 'pole nets' (p 119). Robert was having difficulty finding assistance with the three nets he operated along the Ballimenach and Auchenhoan shores, and 'reached' Angus, who was living in a bothy at Auchenhoan Farm. At six o' clock in the evening, after Angus had finished his Estate duties, he would walk over the hill to New Orleans and help Robert with the nets until one or two in the morning. 'He insisted on payin me a pound a night,' Angus recalled. 'It wis more as A wis gettin for a week's wages.'

At the end of the salmon-fishing season, which was his real money-earner, Robert would turn to lobster-fishing, and, when winter ended that occupation, he would take piece-work at fencing, drystone-dyking and hill-draining. As he explained to Angus: 'A'm no needin tae do it, because three months in the year keeps me, but A canna be lyin for nine month idle. A waant tae keep masel on the go.' Angus's summary of Bob: 'A very nice man, a hardy man – he called a spade a spade.' [Angus MacAlister, 2003]

Teddy Lafferty first met Robert Wylie, whom he knew as 'Bob', when he became a 'Coaster' in the early 1950s. A Coaster was a week-end rambler and camper belonging to an unorganised but nonetheless exclusive band of individuals which frequented the Learside coast south of Campbeltown. Bob didn't take to every passer-by, and was wary of groups of walkers, but he took to Teddy, perhaps because the young man was unassuming and a natural listener.

As Teddy said: 'He wis good tae listen tae, Bob.' Teddy, however, wasn't always eager to be detained; often, his strongest urge was to keep moving and reach his destination. In the winter, though, New Orleans often was his destination on a Sunday morning, and he was content to sit at the big fire in Bob's cottage and drink tea while the old man puffed on his pipe and told his tales of the sea. Teddy always took a lemonade bottle filled with milk for Bob and Marjory, whose trips to town were infrequent.

Bob told him that he always released the 'berried' lobsters – egg-bearing females – knowing that other less scrupulous fishermen would catch them later and keep them, which annoyed him. Bob also described his wood-gathering trips to the Bloody Bay, south of Auchenhoan Head. With tide and weather both suiting, he would row his punt to the bay and lash the biggest pieces of driftwood together to form a raft, on to which he would load the smaller bits. Then he would tow the raft to New

Orleans and carry the wood up the beach to the cottage. 'It took ye a long time,' Bob said, 'but there wis nae hurry for it.' In 1973, his last year of life, Bob gave Teddy a comb of honey and asked him to return the wooden frame for next year's sweetness; but he was dead when summer came round again. [Teddy Lafferty, 1981, 2003]

Dick Gillon

Richard 'Dick' Gillon was born in Southend of parents – John Gillon, fisherman, and Margaret Cowper, daughter of James Cowper, fisherman – who originated in County Antrim, Ireland. When he was compelled to vacate the Lifeboat House at Dunaverty, the farmer at Machribeg, James Barbour, gave him the use of an old cottage in the woods at Keil, where he lived until his son, John, a captain in the Merchant Navy, installed him in a modern caravan.

Two boats belonging to Dick were registered for fishing, the *Midge*, an old vessel, 18 ft overall length, replaced in 1904 by the 25 ft line-skiff *Lizetta*. She was built by James McDonnell in Greencastle, County Donegal, and delivered to Dick in the Sound of Sanda from the Clyde-bound Londonderry steamer. She ceased fishing in 1937.[1]

Dick engaged in every mode of inshore fishing, but in Hugh McShannon's estimation, he was a 'great line-fisherman'. He had a wheelbarrow from which he would sell his fish through the village. His speared flatfish fetched a 'big price' and the line-caught 'red cod' (p 61) – 'so appetisin-lookin… ye couldn't resist buyin them' – were in great demand. When Hugh, in the years before the First World War, sailed with Dick to the fishing, he received £1 a week, a grand wage for a schoolboy. [Hugh McShannon, 1982]

As a girl in Southend, Margaret Watson and her friends, the sisters Cissie and Elsie Barbour from Machribeg Farm, would accompany Dick on nocturnal fishing trips in summer. They usually fished with rods for lythe and gleshans in Machribeg Bay, and Margaret remembered going home across the golf-course with a string of fish at half-past midnight under a shining moon. Dick was fond of bridge and would call for a game at her parents' house or at the house of her uncle, Alex Watson, or at Seaview where Mrs Janet Reid lived; but 'he would overbid to get playing the dummy hand every time'. [Margaret Watson, 2003]

Captain James Taylor in Southend once introduced Dick to an English visitor, saying: 'This is one of our local characters.' With that, a tramp, whose nick-name was 'Tobermory'*, came along, prompting the visitor to ask: 'Is this another of your local characters?' Dick, displeased, at once replied: 'No, he's a common visitor like yourself!' On another occasion, a visitor asked him: 'And do you mend your nets in the winter?' – 'Aye,' Dick replied. 'And what do you do in the summer?' the visitor continued. 'Answer questions from damned fools like yourself!' was Dick's answer. [Isobel McCallum, 1983]

Dick's sense of humour could be misconstrued as sarcasm; his beliefs and opinions were often both unconventional and vigorously held; and his intelligence sometimes produced surprises. When, for example, a local sea-captain, George McSporran, visited him in the 1930s, before leaving to take up a job harbour-dredging in Iraq, Dick produced a copy of the Koran and advised him on those tenets of the Moslem faith which would impinge on his residency.[2] Dick died on 17 March 1963, aged 92.

*A minister's son, John MacLean. Intelligent, and convivial with those whom he respected, he began tramping to find work 'until the call of the road got a hold of him and he couldn't stop'. [Angus MacAlister, 2003]

Neil Thomson

Neil Thomson was born in Muasdale in 1904. His father, Hector, was a fisherman and his mother, Janet McCallum, a dressmaker until she became postmistress at Muasdale. She and Neil, who was an only child, delivered mail in the village and beyond. Neil – who was always referred to as 'NPO', for 'Neil Post Office' – delivered the mail on his Norton motorcycle, and it was not unknown for him to 'put on a show' by standing on the seat of the motorcycle when driving through the village. He also fished lobsters and turned, as many part-time fishermen did, to rabbit-catching in the winter. Willie Watson remembered seeing him 'leaving on his bike with hundreds of snares tied in bundles around his shoulders etc., heading for farms where he would be employed to kill off the rabbits, a major pest to anybody growing crops'.[3]

Neil had Gaelic; indeed, he was one of the last native speakers in Kintyre. In his youth, there were very few folk in and around Muasdale who wouldn't address him in Gaelic, but, as he said, 'It died away very quick.' He had an extensive knowledge of local place-names and their meanings in Gaelic and knew old tales, of the type seldom, if ever, heard in Kintyre now. Some, which he heard in Gaelic from his grandfather, were known as *ùr-sgeul*, which Neil defined as 'bedtime stories'. One such was set at Creag Ruadh, where a 'grinding stone', for milling corn, could be heard at times revolving 'without anybody with it'. The old man who lived there when asked about it would say: 'Yes, I hear it of'en enough, but I've never come on it goin.' For two or three nights after a birth, several young men would sit with the baby in case an attempt was made to spirit it away and leave a changeling in its place. 'The glens,' Neil said, 'had more stories. Civilisation dinna touch them as quick. If we could call it civilisation. Sometimes ye wonder.' [1977]

Angus MacAlister

Like many part-time fishermen, Angus MacAlister was a man of many parts. His mother, Catherine McSporran, was a native of Gigha, and Angus was born on the island, at Keills, while his father, John, was absent during the First World War. After John returned from military service to resume his occupation as gamekeeper to the Duke of Argyll – in which capacity he served for 51 years, latterly as head keeper in Kintyre – Angus was taken to the mainland, only returning to Gigha in 1953, when he married an islander, Charlotte McPherson, who was housekeeper and cheese-maker to Johnny McSporran in the Home Farm.

Angus's first employment, when he left school at 13, was with the Duke. He was chief carter for eight years, at £1 a week, a job which he left when refused extra wages or additional holidays to compensate him for his gruelling labours. During the Estate sheep-clippings, there were about 30 farms from which to collect wool-bags. One week, he left home at 6 a m on the Monday and 'never seen a bed tae the next Sunday mornin at three o' clock'. He was at Strone Farm, Southend, loading at 11 o' clock one night, and when he passed the Creamery in Campbeltown, the town clock was sounding 7 o' clock in the morning. He 'fed the horses, lay doon on a puckle straw for a while an went aweh for Stramollach'. Angus having given the Duke's factor a month's notice, the Estate took him to court, but, with the assistance of a 'poor man's lawyer' – a Council roads foreman, named Kelly, who lacked formal qualifications and charged no fee – he was awarded ten shillings.

Thereafter, Angus took various jobs – ploughman and farm-worker, drainer, fencer and bracken-cutter – and even returned to the employment of the Duke, in the mid-1930s, when his father found himself unable to replace a gamekeeper who had been transferred from Auchenhoan. Angus moved in there and assumed a variety of roles – trapper, ghillie, occasional shepherd and harvest-worker – while surreptitiously doubling as Robert Wylie's crewman at salmon-fishing (p 12). That was his first experience of commercial fishing, but, when he settled on Gigha, fishing became his main occupation. At first, he worked at creels alone in a 14 ft punt; then, as his sons John and Archie left school and joined him, he invested in a series of increasingly bigger boats, culminating in the *Mari-Dor*. [Angus MacAlister, 2003]

Still physically active at the age of 85, and able to take a small boat out to line-fishing, Angus is also a raconteur of compelling power, clearly gifted with an eye for detail and an ear for dialogue.

References and Notes
1. A Martin, 'The Mull of Kintyre hand-line fishery', *Northern Studies*, Vol 20, 1983, p 76.
2. George McSporran Jr, noted 2 May 2003.
3. Letter to author, 17 June, 2003.

Seine-Netting

That the term 'seine-net' is haunted by many ghosts, should be admitted at once. The method of herring-fishing which finally resolved its identity as the *ring-net* was frequently referred to in official reports as a *seine-net*, or else, to confuse matters further, a *trawl*. The term 'seine' – pronounced 'seen' in Scotland – tends to encompass any net used to encircle fish, which certainly applies to the method of white-fishing described as 'seine-netting', except that ropes perform the encirclement and not the net, which, when winched to the boat at high speed, simply collects the fish.

The true parent of Scottish seining was, in fact, the Danish seine-net, so named because pioneered by a Danish fisherman in the mid-nineteenth century. It was adopted by Moray Firth fishermen in 1921 and modified from an anchor-based technique to the 'fly-dragging' method in which the boat's engine does the work of the anchor. The origins of seine-netting in the Firth of Clyde are, however, rather obscure. In 1924, a 'few motor craft belonging to the BA [Ballantrae] district and Ireland' were reported seine-netting in the Clyde and in Luce Bay,[1] but whether this was seine-netting on the new model or 'flounder-seining' – described as a 'modified form of trawling'[2] – remains uncertain. Certainly, a fleet of Swedish anchor-seiners came to Campbeltown to fish hake in successive summers of the 1920s (p 79), but the first local seine-netter appears to have been John McMillan's *Roxana*, launched in 1927, followed by James Robertson's *Pioneer,* which also arrived in Campbeltown in that year.

The real development of seine-netting lay in the immediate post-war period, when road transport opened up markets. By that time, both Campbeltown and Ayr attracted sizeable fleets of East Coast seiners each year, particularly in winter, and local fishermen began to invest in boats built fractionally below 40 ft to permit of their working legally inside the three-mile fishing limit. In Campbeltown, three trim dual-purpose 'forty-footers', designed for both seine-netting and ring-netting, were built for local fishermen in 1949 and 1950 – the *Sea Nymph* (Ian Mitchell and James McLean), the *Janet Lang* (Neil, Duncan and John Lang) and the *Jessie* (James Wareham) – while others brought in suitable second-hand boats from the East Coast and elsewhere.

In 1950, for the first time in Scotland, the seine-net fleet outfished the trawl fleet: 1,604,490 hundredweights against 1,469,793 hundredweights. That trend continued, and many of the top-earning Scottish seiners were built in steel at Campbeltown Shipyard, which opened in 1968, built its last fishing-boat in 1996 and closed in 1997.[3]

Roxana

Neil Short remembers John McMillan's *Roxana* coming new to Campbeltown from Miller, St Monans, in 1927, at about the same time as the *Crimson Arrow*, built for his father and Robert Robertson at the same yard. The *Crimson Arrow* was almost 42 ft long, while the *Roxana* was just under 40 ft, but 'a bittie beamier' and 'built specifically for seine-net fishing'. She replaced a small clinker skiff, the *Mary*, which McMillan sold to his brother-in-law, Duncan Lang, for line-fishing. The *Roxana* came with a diesel engine, but this was replaced with a Kelvin petrol-paraffin engine.

She fished mostly in 'home waters', around Auchenhoan; but, by Neil's evaluation, she was too far in advance of market conditions. At that time, there were effectively only the local shops to supply. The earliest that white fish could be landed in Campbeltown would be the evening of the day they were caught, which meant that, lacking road transportation, they couldn't be shipped out by steamer until the following morning and wouldn't arrive at the Glasgow market until the afternoon – in other words, they were already over a day old and without the benefit, at that time, of ice. 'It was the War, really, when the market took off in Campbeltown.' The *Roxana* returned to Campbeltown (in 1959) as Andrew Brown's *Kia-Ora*. [Neil Short, 1998, 2003]

In classical lore, Roxana was a Persian taken prisoner by Alexander the Great. He later married her, but after his death in 323 BC, she 'behaved with great cruelty' and was put to death.[4]

Unfortunately, there is no record of what motivated John McMillan in his bold experiment. He died in 1936, aged 78, so was already an old man when he ordered the *Roxana*. His son James went to St Monans to collect the boat and liked the place so much that when he married Agnes

Carmichael, a Dalintober fisherman's daughter, in January 1929, it was to St Monans they went on honeymoon. James was later forced ashore from the boat by recurrent asthma attacks and took employment with his brother Neil ('N L'),[5] a clothier who in May 1928 took over ownership of the *Roxana*. When sold to Girvan in 1930, she was renamed *Kia-Ora*.

Pioneer

The *Pioneer*, in Neil Short's recollection, 'did some seine-netting in the late 1930s, but using only a twin-barrelled ring-net winch and no coiler'. A 42-footer, she was built in Arbroath in 1889 and acquired in 1927, as *Pioneer* AH 19, by James Robertson, who also at first skippered her. He registered her CN 226.[6] She worked at ring-netting as well as at seine-netting and appears to have been tied up during the Second World War owing to crew shortage, though Lawrence Robertson – James's grandson – remembered her fishing in about 1948. By the late 1950s, however, she had become a hulk tied against the New Quay.

When Lawrence was 13 years old, he said to his father: 'Am A getting oot wi ye the night?' – 'Aye, come on then, come aweh doon. A don't think we'll be gan oot, mind ye. A don't laik the look o that cerry.' This was the 'carry', or cloud-motion. When they boarded the *Pioneer*, there was an old man with a pipe in his mouth, sitting at the tiller and looking up at the sky. This was Jock Brodie, and he remarked to Lawrence's father: 'A don't think there'll be emdy move the night, Andra.' – 'A wis jeest sehin that tae the young fella,' Andrew replied. 'A wis gonny take him oot wi us the night.' –'Ye'll need tae wait for another night, son,' the old man said. Lawrence also remembered looking down 'the wee hatch' and seeing two or three men sitting below 'wi thir wee *tinnies* – cups – o tea'. The fleet didn't go to sea that night and, as Lawrence remarked, 'That wis me chance lost tae go oot wi the *Pioneer*'. [Lawrence Robertson, 2003]

The Second World War

During the Second World War, the Campbeltown fishing fleet was depleted by the requisitioning of boats for Admiralty service; but seine-netting as well as ring-netting was carried on by those men – the elderly and the young – who were exempt from military service.

As a boy, Denis Meenan was at seine-netting with his uncle, Jock Meenan, in the *Gratitude*. Fishing operations were frequently disrupted by Naval activity. Crews would 'go oot for a tow before the destroyers came roon the Island'; then they'd have another, and a submarine would surface, its conning-tower festooned with seine-net rope. 'Then ye'd be up in front o the commandin officer – another row!'

Owing to wartime food scarcity, 'ye could sell anythin – any wee fish at aa'. Most of the seining was done in the Lodan and further south at the Brig – the bridge at the Second Waters – hauling with a McBain ring-net winch and coiling the ropes by hand. Gloves were unknown at that time, and, with the grittiness of the ropes, the men's hands were swollen 'lik bloody balloons'. [Denis Meenan, 1998]

In Neil Short's recollection, seine-netting 'was really started in Campbeltown during the war by visiting East Coast boats'. Some local ring-netters occasionally worked the method during the cod season, February and March, using only ring-net winches. In the absence of restrictions during the war, the seine-net could be 'fished anywhere inside the limit with any size of boat', and towards the end of the war the *Bengullion*, *Falcon* and *Enterprise* had winches and coilers installed forward, but after a few years these were removed and the crews concentrated again on ring-netting. [Neil Short, 1999]

Seining was initially a winter occupation, to which crews went when the herring season ended in the Clyde, but in the post-war period some skippers – such as Charlie 'Duke' Durnin in the *Bluebird*, Davie 'Stabby' Robertson in the *Annie*, and Andrew 'Bomber' Brown in the *Mairi Elspeth* – 'got into the habit… and jeest steyed at it'. Cecil Finn, who was seining on the *Stella Maris*, as a boy of 17 years, in the winter of 1953, recalled: 'In the moarnin oot tae the west'ard there, it wis quite common tae see fifty an sixty boats jeest in the area, aa seine-netting.' These included local boats, forced to the seine-net by an absence of herring, and East Coast boats that came every year, some of them to escape winter conditions in the Minches. [Cecil Finn, 2003]

Early seining at Tarbert and Ardrishaig

That seine-netting from Tarbert began during the Second World War is apparent from records kept by the late Donald McDougall, skipper of the *Fionnaghal*. In a thick notebook, titled 'Record of Herring Fishing from May 1939 to May 1954', he notes, on 19 September, 1942: 'Ordered seine net winch & coiler.'[7]

According to oral tradition, the first seine-netters to work from Tarbert came from the East Coast during the Second World War, to pursue their winter fishing operations in calmer waters. The most regular of these visitors were the *Glad Tidings*[8], *Lassie*, *Gleaner* and *Heron*. Tarbert fishermen adopted seine-netting seriously in the post-war period, initially in small second-hand boats, such as Duncan McDougall's *Charlotte Anne*,

Douglas McNeill's *Ranger* and Angus 'Molly' Johnson's *Psyche*. Investment in purpose-built 40-footers began in the 1950s.

Willie Lovie, who settled in Ardrishaig from Whitehills in Banffshire, took a 'lot o money oot the Showls' with 40- and 50-box tows which he would land at Ardrishaig as 'roonders' (round, or ungutted, white fish) for the womenfolk to gut while he returned to the fishing ground for more. His son Francis later acquired the *Catriona* from Neil McAllister and renamed her the *Harmony* after his father's old Fifie, which Francis had latterly worked as a 'prawn'-trawler. [Robert Ross, 2003]

'Easties'

Lawrence Robertson's real education in seine-netting began when, as a 15-year-old, he and his elder brother, John, joined the crew of the *Gleaner* of Peterhead, working for two elderly brothers, Charlie and Jimmy Strachan. The Strachans fished from Tarbert, and Jimmy, who was skipper, shared with his wife Grace a rented flat opposite the quay. The Robertson brothers would go up to the flat in the evening for a wash and – if needed – a shave, particularly if they intended going 'tae the pictures', and 'ould Jimmy wid be there every night wi the pipe'.

Charlie, who was the boat's engineer, lived aboard and 'never seen daylight fae ye went oot in the moarnin tae ye came in at night'. When he had started the engine and the ropes had been cast off, he would disappear into the forecastle and from time to time pass mugs of tea and cakes up through the skylight to John and Lawrence as they lifted the ropes from the coilers.

From November until April the Strachans fished around Loch Fyne, along with several other Peterhead seiners, also based in Tarbert. Then they would return home to clean and paint the boat and to rest, returning for the summer hake-fishing at 'the Inch'.

The Robertson brothers habitually took the mid-day Sunday bus from Campbeltown to Tarbert and returned home by the 9 p m bus on a Friday. Having arrived in Tarbert, they would generally seek out the Tarbert boys, who, if they weren't in the Ca'dora Café drinking tea or spooning ice-cream, could generally be found at the back of the Castle gambling with cards. These illicit card schools were popular in Campbeltown, too, but were usually held aboard East Coast boats, and it was not uncommon for a cabin to be so crowded with punters staking 'serious money' until daybreak, that later arrivals could not be accommodated.

In Campbeltown, too, some of the 'Easties' stayed ashore, either in lodgings, with local families, or in rented flats with their wives. The older skippers tended to prefer 'digs' and would return year after year to lodge with the same families until they became almost a part of these families and were 'looked upon as fethers'. The generality of East Coast crews comprised a father, usually the skipper, and perhaps a couple of sons – the elder of whom might rent accommodation in town – augmented by an additional deckhand.

The 'Easties' generally left harbour a couple of hours earlier than the local crews and would have hauled in the dark to a *winky* (flashing light) and be taking two 'lifts' of fish aboard by the time the locals arrived on the fishing grounds. On occasion, as Lawrence Robertson remarked, 'there wirna a birth for us tae shot'. The locals didn't realise at that time that, when working fish 'wi the roe in them', the early morning haul was the big one of the day, which virtually 'guaranteed' a couple of lifts of fish. Come three o' clock on a winter's afternoon, the fish would have 'lifted off' the ground. 'Them men knew that; ye see, they had experienced that on the East Coast.'

By four o' clock, the Easties would be back in Campbeltown with perhaps 40 or 50 boxes of fish on the quay, and by the time the locals returned, at seven or seven-thirty, the Easties would have already moored their boats opposite the Royal Hotel and gone ashore for a wash and a shave and bed.

Although the East Coasters generally had better boats and winches and were technically more advanced than their Campbeltown counterparts, some of them, when they first came to the Clyde, couldn't compete with the locals, the reason being that their nets lacked the height in the head-rope to take whitings and haddies. Four Aberdeenshire crews who came to Campbeltown in the 1950s experienced just that problem, and ordered, from the local net-factory, Joseph Gundry & Co, Vinge nets of the type used by the local seine-net fishermen. These crews, after fishing for three months without much success, went home for New Year. When they returned to Campbeltown, the new nets were ready for them and they soon began to improve their catch-rate. [Lawrence Robertson, 2003]

Gigha

In about 1950, a big fleet of boats, from Campbeltown and Ayrshire, went to seine-net at Gigha, working as far north as the Lightship and westward half-way to 'the Churn', an island off Islay. Cecil Finn thought Archie Graham's *Margaret Rose* was the first boat seining there. Later, he saw 30 boats moored one night at Gigha Pier. Landing into West Loch Tarbert, an average catch for two days' fishing would consist of about

20 boxes of witches, five boxes of skate, 10 boxes of various other fish, and about 20 boxes of large whole 'prawns', for which a market was just beginning. At first, the prawns were 'stoker' – a perquisite for the crew – but became, before long, more valuable than the fish. [Cecil Finn, 2003]

Lochinver

In about 1953, when fishing was slack on the Clyde, several Carradale boats set off for the Minch with seine-nets to try the Heisgeir. 'They went intae Mallaig,' Cecil Finn recalled, 'an the hake wis the height o the bloody quay in Mallaig. They cou'na gie them aweh, an they ended up in Lochinver... A mean, there wir heaps of fish, but ye jeest cou'na sell them.' [Cecil Finn, 2003]

Cecil's brother-in-law, Neil McDougall, was still a schoolboy when his father ended up in Lochinver with the *Acacia*. The *Elma* and *Elizabeth Campbell* were there also. Neil can recall sitting at home and a big vehicle, like a hearse, drawing up outside with ten or a dozen men in it. This was Matha McDougall unexpectedly returned from Lochinver in a hired car, which he had driven all the way. 'An, oh dear, when he'd come home, when ma mother wid be sayin this an that: "Jeest gie me peace. Let me sit." From Lochinver tae here's a damn good run!' His father told him they were catching as much fish as they could gut, but that there was no money for them. [Neil McDougall, 2003]

The herring slump

Archie Paterson of Carradale started seine-netting at about the same time with the *Harvest Queen*, which he part-owned with his brother Dugald and Donald McNicol. Herring, he said, were 'non-existent', and his neighbour at ring-netting, Johnny Campbell, had already gone over to seine-netting with the *Elizabeth Campbell*. Johnny was 'well used' to the method, having been its pioneer in Carradale. 'A think maybe that that had an influence on us – he wis makin some money.'

Johnny Campbell was 'so well acquaint' that he fished inshore 'among the haddies'. There was better money for haddies, at times 2s 6d a stone, against 1s 9d for whitings. Archie fished offshore – 'an hour sou-sou-east from the Light' (Davaar Lighthouse) – which took him down off Sanda. The winch malfunctioned and coils of rope wore out as fast as the boat's shares could afford to replace them, but the crew made wages.

The best week Archie and his crew had at the beginning was £30 a man and £7 10s 'stoker' (p 46) for the fish-roes. 'Ye can imagine the amount o fish that were gutted, an, of course, it wis old men we had an they werena very good at guttin, they werena very quick.' Many other ringers converted to seine-netting, but it was a costly move, involving the purchase of a specialised winch and a full set of gear, and Archie believes that, for many boats, it was 'the straw that broke the camel's back'.

He was among those fishermen, whose boats had been purchased under the Herring Industry Board grant and loan scheme, summoned to a meeting of Board representatives in the Royal Hotel, Campbeltown, to discuss the problems of repayment. He admitted that he was quaking before the meeting; but the boat-owners were told that they could repay loans at £5 a week, which news gave Archie a 'wee lift'. Hitherto, he conceded, he had been rather naive about finance, but he was able to hold on to the *Harvest Queen* by ensuring that the boat's shares unfailingly went to the boat and not to himself or either of the other shareholders. He 'doubled the fiver an made it ten' and was able to complete his repayments to the Herring Industry Board. Some other boat-owners, less scrupulous or less fortunate, lost their boats when the HIB repossessed them in the late 1950s. [Archie Paterson, 2003]

Florian

Built in 1951 by Tyrell of Arklow, in the Irish Republic, she was a fraction under 40 feet and was bought into Campbeltown as *Culzean* BA 172 by John Short Sr., Neil Short and John M Short. She was registered *Florian* CN 2 on 18 June, 1954 and sold to Mallaig in 1957.[9]

Most of John Short Senior's working life was spent in Loch Fyne Skiffs, and, as he neared the end of his sea years, the notion of again working a small boat took hold of him. One night at herring-fishing, after the evening 'brash' of work had slackened, the Shorts' *King Bird* went alongside a Dunure ringer, the Andersons' *Marie*, to pass the time. In addition to their ring-net winch, the Andersons had a seine-net winch fitted and told John that they'd be changing to that method after New Year and that the signs were good.

John must have mentioned his notion for a smaller boat, because the Ayrshiremen then told him about a forty-footer lying idle in Dunure harbour. She had been built as the *Culzean* for a seine-netting partnership which had subsequently dissolved. John's interest was instantly aroused, and, as his son Neil recalled, 'Aw, dear, that's all A heard aboot efter that, wis this boat'.

John finally bought her and brought her to Campbeltown. She was renamed the *Florian* – an amalgam of the Gaelic for his own forename, and the forename of his wife, Flora McLellan – and the *King Bird* was sold to Tommy Ralston and his son, also Tommy.

The *Culzean*, when Neil saw her, did not appeal at all to him. 'When she wis comin at ye head-on, she looked all right – she had quite a nice-lookin bow – but she dinna carry her beam at all; she wis all the wrong way about, too thick aft.' More than that, he suspected that she had been 'built on the cheap', and that suspicion was confirmed when, under subsequent ownership, one of her planks was stove in and the carpenter who repaired her discovered that the planking was not pitch-pine, but merely 'white wood'.

Neil would rather have had a 40-footer built to the Shorts' own specifications or simply held on to the bigger *King Bird*, which had been well maintained. The decision, however, had been taken, and to seine-netting they went in the *Florian* with a crew of five: John Short Sr., Neil himself, John Jr., Dugald Blair Jr. and old Jock Brodie, who, with his brother Malcolm 'Packsy', had worked the Port Righ-built skiff, the *Isabella*, before the War.

In the *Florian*'s first week at seine-netting, Neil's cousin, Duncan Lang, from the *Janet Lang*, accompanied her crew to 'show them the ropes' and was replaced on his own boat by one of the *Florian*'s crew. Thereafter, they were on their own and fished well in the first few weeks, with 'divides' of up to £30 a man. As Neil remarked: 'Ye could call it beginners' luck.'

In the deep water of the Kilbrannan Sound they worked seven coils of rope a side and 'very occasionally' eight; in shallower water, such as off Auchenhoan Head, six coils sufficed. 'Most days ye wir doin well if ye had a dozen or fifteen boxes,' Neil recalled. The most plentiful catch in the Sound was whitings, but at times the market for them 'wisna great'; but 'a spot o haddies', for which better prices obtained, would occasionally appear. Flatfish were relatively scarce and the crew was 'lucky', in a day's work of six or seven hauls, to gather a box of 'mixed flats'.

White fish were scarce in summer, so when James 'Noon' Macdonald in the *Rhu-na-Gal* approached the Shorts and suggested switching over to herring-fishing and 'going neebors to him', they accepted. Though the boat was small, her winch was dual-purpose and could be turned 'beam-on' to haul a ring-net, and the Shorts had kept their herring gear. From June to October or November, for three years in succession, the *Florian* neighboured the *Rhu-na-Gal* at ring-netting. Since Neil had no liking for seine-netting, this was a welcome diversion which also generated a wage until the white fish were 'coming on thicker'. [Neil Short, 2003]

Bluebird

A 48-foot Fifie, she was built in 1917 at Sandhaven, Aberdeenshire, and, as the Grimsby-registered *Horning*, was bought in 1926 by Charles Durnin of Campbeltown, who changed her name to *Bluebird*. He fished her, with his brothers James and John – later shareholders – at ring-net, long lines and finally seine-net until she was sold, in 1956, to Frank McDonald of Dunmore East in the Republic of Ireland.[10]

John was a skilled footballer and played for the noted local club, Academicals, before the First World War. In 1914 he signed for Plymouth Argyle, moving c. 1920 to Swansea, which side he captained before returning to Campbeltown and amateur football as a member of the successful mid-1920s Pupils side which also included an Italian internationalist, Gioni Moscardini.[11]

While Lawrence Robertson was still a schoolboy, he seined for six weeks – the duration of a summer holiday – with the *Bluebird*, and his enduring memory of the three old Durnin brothers was their carefree spirit. By then, they were approaching retirement and satisfied if they landed five or six boxes of whitings and haddies to Donnie Gilchrist or James Thomson, the local fishmongers. [Lawrence Robertson, 2003]

Charlotte Ann

When Duncan 'Tar' McDougall of Tarbert bought the *Charlotte Ann*, his uncle, Dunky McDougall, observed that there were 13 letters in her name and that her registration numbers, TT 49, came to 13 when added. Thirteen was, of course, considered an unlucky number, and it was no surprise that Dunky had spotted the inauspicious combinations, for he was full of *freets*, or superstitions. [Robert Ross, 2003]

Marks

After Duncan McDougall had equipped the *Charlotte Anne* for seine-netting, he got a Campbeltown fisherman, John Robertson, to transfer from the *Gleaner* to 'teach him the ropes'. On John's fishing skills, Robert Ross was emphatic: 'The man that used tae amaze me wis that John "Knuckler". John could take all these shots withoot a sounder, cause he wis great wi marks. He had a great heid on him.' [2003] Some skippers kept written records of their seine-net hauls. Ronnie Johnson of Tarbert dictated the information to his wife, Margaret, and she wrote it in a special notebook. The following extract pertains to a haul at Catacol Bay, on the west side of Arran: 'Start abreast paling on Categol side of Church Point. Keep Loch Ranza land just opening and closing. Shot up till arch of bridge is almost all open. Fast* with telegraph pole on Kiosk, and pole mid-way up hill, on the straight edge of the field above.'[12]

* *A seabed obstruction, to be avoided.*

Names

Like ring-netting, seine-netting both utilised existing place-names and generated new ones. Examples can be found throughout this work, but a few may be added. 'The Sinkers', off the Iron Rock Ledges, on the south-west coast of Arran, was named from the profusion of wartime dummy mines, or 'sinkers', which snagged nets and bedevilled fishing operations in the early 1950s. 'The Grips' off Davaar Island described the 'fasteners' there which would 'grip' gear. 'Three Lumps o' Billy's' were hillocks beyond Dun a' Theine, Macharioch, that supplied a north-south bearing when seining off Ru Stafnish. 'Johnny [Ma]clean's Hill', on the north side of Campbeltown Loch, was the mark for the Plane, a sunken aircraft, when viewed in a certain configuration with Davaar Island. [Cecil Finn, 2003] A complete record of seine-net marks used by Campbeltown fishermen alone would fill a small chapter.

References and Notes
1. *Fishery Board for Scotland Annual Report*, p 36.
2. *Ibid.*, 1920, p 25.
3. A Martin, 'The Campbeltown Fishing Industry', *The Campbeltown Book*, Campbeltown 2003, pp 62-63.
4. F A Wright, *A Classical Dictionary*, London 1948, p 551.
5. Duncan L McMillan, Campbeltown, pers comm, 15 Jan 2004.
6. Register of Fishing Boats, National Archives of Scotland, Edinburgh, AF22/29.
7. Notebooks in possession of Mr Peter McDougall, Tarbert.
8. A 40-footer previously owned in Campbeltown by the Blair family and registered CN 202 when brought, in 1922, from Avoch as INS 162. Robert Ross recalled her rounded stem 'for sailin over the drifts in the Inverness Firth'.
9. Register of Fishing Boats, National Archives of Scotland, Edinburgh, AF22/29.
10. *Ibid.*
11. Alex McKinven, Campbeltown, letter to author, 21 March 2003.
12. Margaret Johnson, letter to author, 23 Sept, 2003.

Crustaceans

The common lobster *Homarus gammarus* (Gaelic *giomach*) is naturally dark blue in the shell, but turns bright red when boiled. It is formidably armed with a pair of claws, the smaller having saw-like inner edges for fragmenting prey or carrion and the larger having merely a few blunt knobs on the edges. Either claw can inflict injury, and it is the practice of fishermen to immobilise them by binding each with a strong rubber-band as soon as the creature is taken (in earlier times, cutting of the claw 'tendon' was a standard practice). This measure also prevents the lobsters injuring or killing one another while confined in the floating *keep-boxes* in which they are stored alive until sufficient in number to be collected and sent to market. In the wild, given time, a lobster is generally able to regenerate a severed claw or leg. Lobsters inhabit rough seabottom – both coastal and deep water – and find protection in rock crannies. Given the chance, they can be long-lived: 20 years is not unusual, by which time they can exceed three-and-a-half feet in length and 11 pounds in weight,[1] mere tiddlers compared with a specimen of the American lobster *Homarus americanus* which weighed 35 lbs, of which the claws accounted for 23 lbs.[2]

Lobster

Commercial lobster-fishing in Scotland began around the mid-eighteenth century on the East Coast. It was initiated by English merchants, who provided fishermen with boats and gear, to be paid off in instalments, and who collected catches in smacks for shipment to the London market. These smacks contained a chamber in which sea-water could circulate through holes in the hull, thus preserving alive the consignment, or a part of it.[3] Getting lobsters and crabs to market alive has always been problematic, but markets demand the live product. The remoteness of the Scottish West Coast explains the relatively late development of commercial lobster-fishing there and the absence, owing to prohibitive freight charges, of any appreciable commercial fishery for crab until the late twentieth century.

Commercial lobster-fishing probably began around the mid-nineteenth century in Kintyre. An early glimpse of that fishery appears in Edward Bradley's *Glencreggan*, a fascinating account of his stay in Kintyre in 1859, published two years later under the pseudonym 'Cuthbert Bede'.

Around Muasdale he noticed the 'abundant evidence' of lobster- and crab-fishing, namely 'pots' and 'traps' scattered on the beaches or piled in boats. His 'pot' plainly refers to the circular design, woven from wicker and with an entry-hole on the top, while his 'trap' is just as plainly the construct of netting stretched over bent hazel rods, which ultimately found favour with West Coast fishermen and which is generally known as a 'creel'.

'Rows of these traps and pots, baited with fragments of fish, are lowered at night in likely places along the rocks, and raised in the morning,' he remarks. 'Lobsters form a chief portion of the income of the Muasdale fishermen, who catch them in large quantities, and send them off to Tarbert or Campbelton, from whence the steamers will convey them... A shilling was the standard price for a lobster at Muasdale – size making no difference.'[4]

Muasdale he described as '... a fishing village, down by the shore, on the level between the sea and the cliffs, and like Barr and all other Cantire villages, in having one street of outwardly-whitewashed and inwardly-dirty cottages, one storey high and thatched with heather – with two superior houses for the inn and the shop...'[5]

Making creels

A creel is quite simply a trap, comprising a rectangular weighted wooden base with rods bent over it to form the 'bows'. Once covered with netting, a hole is cut on each side to receive the 'eye', which is a fine-meshed passageway easier of access than of exit. Once roped and baited, the creel is ready to begin its work.

At Muasdale, the bows were predominantly of hazel. Fifty or sixty rods would be cut at a time from some glen where hazel grew. 'Black willow' was also suitable, but there was seldom enough of it. [Neil Thomson, 1978]

Robert Wylie's 'favourite spot' for cutting hazel was at the foot of Balnabraid Glen, south of his home at New Orleans, the wood being close to the Second Waters, where he could beach his boat. Archie Graham latterly accompanied him to the wood and reckoned that each of them would carry about three-quarters of a hundredweight of rods and make 'several journeys' between glen and boat, selecting the rods which were straightest and of a circumference – about three-quarters of an inch – that corresponded to the holes drilled in the creel-base to receive them.

Rods were steamed in a pipe until pliable, then bent over wooden 'moulds' or 'jigs' to form the desired shape, tied at the base and the excess length trimmed off. Archie admired the 'nice flatness' that Robert achieved on the tops of his pots, a case of creating 'optimum space' by avoiding peaking. The whole process of pot-making was based on uniformity of measurement, and each component – rods, base, slats and net-covering – fitted exactly. [Archie Graham, 2003]

On Gigha, when hazel was difficult to bend unaided, the rods, or *rongais*, would be lowered on a length of string into the steam-pipe. When removed, that string was used to tie the ends of the rod after bending. Willie McSporran has cut hazel on the island – at Bruach an Taighe Bhàin, near Druimyeonmore steading – but the bulk of the rods were cut on the mainland by the fishermen themselves or by acquaintances who lived close to a 'good hazel burn' and would send them a bundle. Rods could be kept supple, until required, by steeping them in Tobar Thearlaich (Charlie's Well) or the ditch connected with it, on the shore opposite Gigalum. [Willie McSporran, 2003]

Machrihanish creel-fishermen had various spots where they cut hazel. Davie McVicar went to High Tirfergus and James McMillan had several locations in Southend, one of which was Glenamucklach. After the rods had been steamed, they would be bent over a knee and jammed into a wooden fish-box, which was 20 inches wide at that time. The shape was thus both formed and retained until the rods were needed for creel-making, when, as bows, they would be selected in threes of corresponding height to ensure that the 'top strap' was level. Creels at that time were made in two base-sizes, 30 inches by 20 inches and 26 inches by 18 inches. [Davie McVicar, 2003]

The use of hazel rods was phased out when imported cane appeared on the market. It was sold by the hundredweight and Archie Graham would buy about half-a-ton at a time. It too would be steamed to render it pliable. [2003] At Machrihanish, in the absence of a steamer, cane would be steeped in a water-filled bath and thus bent without its splitting. When cane appeared on the market, a conservative element among fishermen predicted: 'It'll naw fish like hazel.' Steel pots were similarly condemned in advance of trial. [Davie McVicar, 2003]

Robert Wylie wove his own netting to cover creels, but when Archie Graham went to lobster-fishing he bought netting, which was synthetic and neither required to be preserved by drying nor constantly repaired. [2003] An uncle of Willie McSporran's, Alasdair Graham, could knit a cover from start to finish in twenty minutes. When knitting with tarry twine, fishermen would smear their hands and forearms with margarine to 'save them from the tar'. Some Gigha fishermen believed that a black-twined creel-cover 'always fished better' than a cover made in any other colour. [Willie McSporran, 2003]

Wooden creels had to be ballasted. The traditional weight was a stone, and Neil Thomson in Muasdale used nothing else throughout his lifetime, but Robert Wylie preferred concrete, as did Archie Graham. The mix would be poured into a wooden mould about a foot square and two inches deep on the base of the pot, reinforced by wire and with sheets of newspaper acting as a 'barrier' on the base. One day, Archie had a quantity of pots lying outside his net-store at Peninver ready for ballasting. A visitor, noticing the peculiar feature, enquired: 'What have you got the newspaper in there for?' – 'Well,' Archie replied, 'the lobsters like to read something when they're in the pot.' Steel-framed pots, when introduced in the mid-1960s, required no ballast and would 'stand more abuse'. [Archie Graham, 2003] At Machrihanish, both flat stones and concrete were in use. Once, when James McMillan had creel-bases laid out for concreting, a visitor informed him that the fishermen in his locality of Canada used house bricks as ballast, but first steeped them in tubs of paraffin so that, when sunk, the oil oozing from them acted as an attraction to lobsters. James lost no time in experimenting with the paraffin-steeped bricks, but they made 'not a bit o difference'. [Davie McVicar, 2003]

Bait

Virtually anything fishy or fleshy could be used as lobster-bait – as Neil Thomson put it, 'Anything bar a man!' – but fishermen had individual preferences. Archie Graham favoured mackerel, which was firmer than herring, of a suitable girth for quick insertion into the bait-string, and as 'keen' as any other bait owing to its oiliness. When mackerel shoals appeared off the coast, he'd go out and jig (p 116) for them when alerted to their presence by the appearance of diving 'solans', or gannets. After the mackerel season ended, he'd buy saithe or any white fish he could get on Campbeltown Quay. Bait was best salted, salt being a deterrent to crabs, but not to lobsters. If crabs had occupied a pot, lobsters wouldn't be so keen to go in. Robert Wylie salted dogfish and his bait-barrel stank with an ammonia-like odour which repelled Archie. He objected to rotten bait, anyway, having once, when delving gloveless in a bait-bin containing whitings, received a jag in the hand. Streamers of poison ran up his arm and a painful whitlow developed. [Archie Graham, 2003]

It was the practice among Gigha fishermen when velvet swimming crabs, known as 'jessacks' (from Gaelic *deiseag*), were taken in creels, to 'knock them out and put them in the sling along with the bait', in the belief that these red-eyed crabs attracted lobsters. [Eoghann Henderson, 1978] On Gigha, the usual bait was saithe and mackerel, which the fishermen themselves would try to supply, using *darrows* (p 116) by day and rods come evening. Saithe would first be salted in a barrel for two or three days. 'If they were too fresh, all the small crab an that would eat it out, but when it was a few days in salt it was tougher an it would stand longer in the creel.' [Duncan MacNeill, 1978]

Archie Graham's bait was held between a taut doubled string attached to top and bottom of the pot, but other fishermen preferred to contain the bait in a bag of netting or in a simple wooden box. Neil Thomson always used the bait-box, as did his father before him. He believed his creels fished longer, because the bait, being inaccessible, lasted longer; but after three days, it would 'get terrible high' and need to be replaced. [1978] Some of the Gigha fishermen also used bait-boxes, one advantage of which was that, while on passage to the lobster grounds, one set could be baited and ready to replace the set already fishing. As Willie McSporran reasoned: 'It was quicker and it was cleaner and the bait lasted longer where there were *partain* (small crabs); and the lobsters still got the smell of the bait, which was enough for them to go in.' Salted 'peuchkie' (saithe) was common bait on Gigha, but if a lythe, say, was taken home to be eaten, the head might be kept. Being tougher to chew than flesh and longer-lasting, particularly if crabs had infested the creel, a fish-head made fine bait. [Willie McSporran, 2003] Davie McVicar has observed that creel-fishermen are now 'screamin for fresh bait', because salted bait, being a deterrent to crabs, has lost its value since markets developed for the small common and velvet swimming-crabs (p 41). [2003]

When Teddy Lafferty was employed with the Ministry of Public Building and Works, the NATO Jetty in Campbeltown was one of his work-places. Some of his workmates there in the 1960s – Willie Kelly, Bobby Kelly, Peter McDougall and Donald Martin – had four or five creels which they'd drop off the end of the jetty for lobsters. When lacking conventional bait, they would shove a sheet of rolled-up tinfoil into the bait-string, and it worked! [Teddy Lafferty, 2003]

A court case

A court case, reported in the *Campbeltown Courier* of 15 July, 1905, affords an insight into bait-fishing at Southend. Richard Gillon (p 13), Dunaverty, and Gilbert Stewart, Machribeg Cottage, were charged with a breach of the Salmon Fisheries (Scotland) Act, 1844, Section 1, by 'having, on 19th June, wilfully fished for salmon, sea trout, or other fish of the salmon kind in the sea and within a mile of low water mark... next to Carskey water foot, by means of a boat and net'. Their acquittal was undoubtedly aided by the evidence of Daniel Dempsey of Sanda, who was 'called for the defence'.

Dempsey said that he was 57 years old and had been longer engaged at fishing than any other man in Southend, having started when about seven. Asked if he ever fished with a net for lobster bait, he replied emphatically: 'Twenty times, a hundred times!' He had two nets, the heavier of which was used 'when there are four in the boat', and the lighter one when two in the boat. His description of the method – '... they came round in a circle' – identifies it as a *plash-* or *screenge-net*, which was certainly also a favoured method of poaching salmon and sea-trout. He had seen Gillon's net and it was 'a bit of a common herring net'. It was, he said, 'an absolute necessity for a lobster fisherman to fish with the net for bait, which was very difficult to get at times', and, when asked what kind of bait was fished for, he replied: 'Saithe, eels, flounders or anything that will come into it.'

'There is not,' Dempsey said, 'a bay from the Mull to Glenehervie but I have hauled a net in.' He had also fished for bait with a rod, but the net was 'by far the best method when the weather was suitable'. Since Gillon and Stewart had been apprehended fishing at night, Dempsey was asked if night was the best time to fish. 'It is no use any other time; it must be after sunset,' he replied. 'There was no suspicion in being out at two in the morning.' He himself had fished the Carskey shore 'a thousand times' without hindrance and had seen 'the full of a boat of saithe got at the place where Gillon and Stewart were fishing'.

Fishing

Neil Thomson always worked with single creels, the main float (*ceann àrcan*, 'head cork') on the end of the hauling-rope consisting of three corks through a piece of wood and four or five individual corks spaced below it. When testing unfamiliar bottom, a creel could be pulled astern to see if it would lift *wreck*, or seaweed, or a lead-line dropped overboard. It was a saying, in Gaelic, that, 'If ye don't get the wreck, ye don't get the boy (lobster).' [1978] Some Gigha fishermen would trail an iron bolt on the end of a line to test for stones and seaweed. If it was 'catching', then that would signify promising ground. [Donald MacDonald, 1978]

Out from the lime-kiln in the Galdrans, there is a spot of ground from which could be taken 'the loveliest speckly-blue lobsters' and, near the Mull Light, lobsters had a reddish tinge, which became more pronounced as they dried out. That reddish coloration, also observed closer to home at Sgeir Mhór, was attributed to the presence of rusting shipwrecks. [Willie Colville, David McVicar, 2003] Archie MacAlister of Gigha, on separate occasions in 2003, took two lobsters, each of which had matching 'crusher' claws, the 'scissor' claw being absent. [2003]

One day in the Sound of Sanda, as Archie Graham was hauling a creel, he saw a big lobster on, but not in, the creel. It dropped off. Robert Wylie, who was with him, suggested sinking another creel there as a marker, but with the eyes opened wide, the better to admit the lobster. That was done, and the following day, as Archie hauled the creel, he remarked to Robert: 'We'll be canny – he might be there today.' The lobster was there, but once again fell off on his way up. He was captured – trying to enter the creel 'claws first' – at the third attempt and weighed eight or nine pounds.

On another occasion in the Sound of Sanda, Archie for some reason had to haul a fleet of creels immediately after shooting it and there was a lobster in one of the creels 'as quick as that – within minutes'. He captured two lobsters, one in the Sound of Sanda and the other off MacRingan's Point, having seen them, through clear water, walking on the seabed. Each time, he lowered a landing-net and tipped the lobster into it with the boat-hook. Each weighed about eight pounds. [Archie Graham, 2003]

Fishing grounds

The Gighamen fished lobsters round Gigha and Cara and in the Sound of Gigha, before they 'made an attack on them' in West Loch Tarbert. Lobsters were late in spawning there, and an old Gigha fisherman said to Neil, in Gaelic: 'There's no use going up till you'll see the corn changing in there.' [Neil Thomson, 1977]

Davie McVicar considered the coast between Machrihanish and the Mull 'excellent', but remarked that when fishing with the traditional wooden creels, 'Ye could get a blow in late June an that wid clean ye', whereas modern gear is more durable and can be left out until October. Nonetheless, the old men's saying, 'For every [creel] ye've got in the watter, ye'll haev wan in the shed', still held true: a creel-fisherman has to be able to replace lost gear. He regrets the passing of the 'patient' style of fishing practised by the older men. James McMillan and Dunky McGown would move their gear off a good spot of lobster ground before it became 'blank' and also leave 'the bits closest tae hame for the back en', the handier to retrieve gear should the weather break. These policies, which were respected by other creel-fishermen, are no longer sustainable, and Davie attributes much of the blame to velvet-crab fishing which targets ground indiscriminately. He considers the actions of fishermen who keep immature lobsters to be a 'worse crime' than that committed by trawl-fishermen who unintentionally destroy fish, because the creel-fisherman has the choice of returning unmarketable stuff alive to the sea, whereas the immature or 'over-quota' fish a trawlerman catches are already dead. The cynical breaching of conservation measures is an issue on which he feels passionately. [Davie McVicar, 2003]

Archie Graham would stop salmon-fishing about the third week in August, when 'jellyfish became so thick the nets didn't fish so well', and turn his attention to lobster-fishing, at which he remained until December and occasionally beyond. The accessible and sheltered east coast of Kintyre, being easily fished and its stock of lobsters 'skint', or virtually cleaned out, his main fishing grounds were around Sanda and north of the Mull of Kintyre. His old mentor, Robert Wylie, suggested to him once that he put a foredeck on his boat and sleep aboard her, the easier to resume fishing on the following day, but Archie didn't care for the idea, preferring to return home nightly. He would say to his wife, Margaret, 'I've got enough fuel, if the weather worsens, to get to the West Loch'; but he always managed home, albeit with difficulty on occasion.

Initially, Archie confined his efforts to close inshore, but Robert told him that, when he had fished from Sanda, one of the families there had set creels 'out a bit' and evidently fished well. Using his experience as a herring-fisherman, Archie 'armed' himself with a feeling-wire – used for locating fish and testing the nature of the seabed – and was able to feel the bottom. Much of what he felt was 'barren rock', but he concentrated his fishing effort on the areas of deep water where tangles – which offered protection to lobsters – could be felt. There were problems, however, in the deeper water – the tide ran harder and the hauling of the creels from depths of nine or ten fathoms, rather than the usual two or three, was exhausting. Instead of working single creels, he worked fleets of up to a dozen strung together and also invested in a small winch. Fifty or 60 lobsters daily from 40 creels in the Sound of Sanda was not an exceptional catch and up to five lobsters could be taken from a single creel. 'Sometimes you got as much out of one train that would keep you happy that day.' Once he had established where the richest lobster grounds were and memorised the marks on the land, the feeling-wire could be dispensed with, and when he got his 22ft *Harvester*, although she was fitted with an echo-sounder, he did not discover much new ground except for deep water pinnacles off Sanda. [Archie Graham, 2003]

Territoriality

When Archie Graham began lobster-fishing, he was obliged to respect the implicit rights of the resident Sanda and Southend fishermen and would bypass their preserves. Lobster-fishermen, he said, were 'inclined to be territorial', but added: 'Necessity knows no law'. [2003] When Willie McSporran of Gigha fished lobsters with Archie MacAlister in the *Rob McB*, from Machrihanish north to Kilberry, they wouldn't venture 'inside', where local part-timers had their creels; but, in winter, when the locals had finished for the season, Archie and Willie would 'come in and give it a sweep', finding that 'there was always a scatter left'. They had adopted the 'soft eye', or entry, in preference to the traditional eye which admitted lobsters through a solid ring formed of hazel or fencing-wire, and found that, 'Wi the soft eye, the granny o the ones that ye wir catchin before wis able tae get intae the creels'. [Willie McSporran, 2003]

Billy Wareham and a crewman were once menaced with a shotgun off the Arran coast when they shot creels on ground which the aggressor plainly believed existed for his exclusive use. Having been advised of the man's tenuous grip on reality – he threatened to 'fill them full of holes' – Billy decided to clear out. Some local creelmen employed more subtle methods of keeping strangers off favoured grounds, such as sinking stones on the end of buoyed ropes to create an impression of a concentration of creels already in place. The ground was thus 'rested' and the trickster could come and shoot his creels whenever he wanted.

The surreptitious pilfering from creels was another problem which affected lobster-fishermen. On one location at the south end of Arran, Billy Wareham consistently lost lobsters to local opportunists who lifted creels on Sundays when he was not at sea. A Campbeltown crew, who were at that game themselves, once hauled a creel and found a bottle containing an uncomplimentary message inside it! As Billy reasoned, however, sometimes suspicions of pilfering were unfounded. 'If there's naw much in the creels, it's aafu easy tae accuse somebody else, especially when ye're new tae creels.' An experienced fisherman is able to detect when a creel has been tampered with, though lobsters can be removed without trace through an eye. [Billy Wareham, 2003]

The insertion of razor-blades into the strands of creel-ropes was allegedly resorted to as a vicious deterrent. Some fishermen would tie a slip-knot on the rope and if, when hauling, they felt the knot release itself, they were satisfied that the creel had not been interfered with; but, as Davie McVicar pointed out, that device was not infallible because a knot might come undone in strong tide. Opportunistic yachtsmen had the reputation of lifting the odd creel in the hope of finding a free meal inside it. [Davie McVicar, 2003]

Immediately after spawning, when lobsters were 'desperate tae get a shell on [and] really on the move', creels could be lifted at two-hourly intervals. Thereafter, however, they got 'more fussy', and in spring, with cold weather, would be slow to enter a creel. Peter Blackstock at Bellochantuy would say to Neil Thomson in spring: 'Ach, A'm no goin down tomorrow... A'll leave them for a couple o days – two days is no too long for them at this time o year for tae go in.' [Neil Thomson, 1977]

Neil's biggest catch

The biggest catch of lobsters Neil Thomson ever took in a day's fishing was evidently 110 from about 70 creels 'looked twice'. Willie Watson well remembers that day because he was out, as a boy of 15 years, helping Neil and his wife May in the biggest of the Thomsons' boats, an unnamed white-painted 22-footer. Willie's job was to haul the creels, which Neil emptied and re-baited, while May operated the engine and steered. Ordinarily, Willie managed out only in the evenings, but that particular day – in August, 1958 – was a Church Fast Day, therefore a holiday. Willie, however, opted not to attend the religious service – which was strictly observed on North Muasdale Farm, of which his father Lachie was tenant – and instead went out fishing. He wasn't the only one who dodged the obligation – while at sea, he watched a family 'rucking hay' because 'the weather was so bad'.

Neil's usual bait was herring, which came lightly salted and stinking in barrels from Tarbert, but if fish were unobtainable it was the practice to go ferreting for rabbits, though rabbit flesh tended to attract masses of crabs. There was no market at that time even for 'croobans', and these would be kept for household use. Spurdogs (p 110) were often abundant on the stretch of coast – from Cleit to Barr Burn – where Neil's creels were set, and for amusement some of them would be treated to a 'dunt' (knock) on the head against the boat's rail 'jeest tae see them in action'. When returned stunned to the water, the fish would swim in circles on their backs for a time, then flip over and dive out of sight.

Despite coming from a farming background, Willie 'loved the sea', an attraction generally attributed to his great-grandfather David Watson's having owned and skippered cod-boats. [Willie Watson, 2003]

Markets

Between the wars, fishermen talked in dozens of lobsters when discussing a day's take. 'Ye wid get them anywhere,' Neil Thomson said; but, against that, markets seldom favoured fishermen. 'Ye wid hardly get anythin for them, sendin sixty pound weight boxes down to London for under a pound o money.' Sometimes a note would come with the money, explaining the low return. One such comment lodged in Neil's memory:

'Giants and cripples are of practically no value.' A 'cripple' was a lobster which had lost one or both nippers. Lobsters which arrived dead were also counted as worthless. At that time there was no market in Glasgow, and lobsters had to be sent to Billingsgate, so it was little wonder that a part of the catch arrived dead.

The lobsters, packed in sawdust, would be put on the morning mailvan at Muasdale. If the driver couldn't take them, they'd be returned to the water and kept for another day. If he could take them, they were loaded on to a steamer at Tarbert and shipped to Gourock, whence they were carried by train to Central Station, Glasgow, and transferred to a London-bound train. When Neil started lobster-fishing just after the First World War, catches 'wirna so bad', but thereafter 'they went down, they wir terrible for a while', before picking up again and becoming plentiful. [Neil Thomson, 1977]

Malcolm MacNeill and his logbooks

The main boat in Malcolm MacNeill of Gigha's family was the 31 ft *Janet*, a small Loch Fyne Skiff. She was bought from Tarbert in 1909 by Malcolm's father, Duncan – who skippered her until Malcolm himself took over – and in December, 1920, she had an 8-10 hp Kelvin engine installed.[6] Malcolm's daughter, Betty, remembers her father's absences from home while lobster-fishing around Knapdale and Kilberry, or 'up country', as he put it (in an earlier period, he sailed to herring drift-net fisheries in the Minches). There was usually a crew of four – all MacNeills – lobster-fishing on the *Janet*: Malcolm, his father, brother Duncan and a cousin, Dougie. Malcolm described himself and Dougie as 'the two stravaigers'. When working 'up country', they couldn't content themselves aboard the boat, so, with crabs as gifts, they would set off to visit local families and 'hear what was going on round about'. Malcolm's brother Duncan preferred to stay aboard the *Janet*: 'You'd think the boat was going to run away on him!'

Malcolm's wife, Mary MacColl, belonged to Tayvallich, and it was there that she took Betty to be born. Malcolm died in 1957, aged 63 years, of heart failure. Mary was 92 years old when she died in 1995. They raised a family of nine children, of whom three – Betty, Malcolm Jr and Kenny – remain in the family house at Keills. Betty remembers her father as one who 'loved writing', and who maintained his diary both at home and at sea.

Very few skippers kept logbooks, but such as survive are, by virtue of their rarity, of singular historical value. Those I have examined are certainly not literary productions, but they contain dated records of the duration of fishing seasons, details of grounds fished and of quantities caught, and accounts of income and expenditure, along with noteworthy incidentals. From the logbooks of Malcolm MacNeill may be gained some appreciation of the day-to-day life of a typical self-employed small boat fisherman.

It appears that his customary grounds were Loch Stornoway, 'Sgeir an Neich', Eilean Mór, Eilean Dubh, Loch Caolisport, Keills Bay, Loch na Keal, Loch Craignish, East Tarbert Jura, Crinan, and Salen Mór, the first six locations being most frequently mentioned. Catches naturally fluctuated from season to season, depending on weather and other variables. The total number of lobsters caught in 1916, for example, was 1316; in 1932, it was 3971. The duration of seasons also varied from year to year. In 1918, he left for Loch Caolisport on 1 July and finished fishing on 19 November. The 1924 season began on 24 June and ended on 20 November. Two years later, in 1926, the season both started and finished earlier: 26 May – 6 November.

An account for 1929 details his markets. The bulk of his catch was usually despatched in batches of 50-plus and 60-plus to several named merchants – Coverty, Seasalter and Bennett – with smaller numbers sold locally, at from 2s 6d to 5s each, to such customers as the proprietors of Ellary and Stonefield estates. Malcolm also had a regular, unnamed customer in Stratford to whom he supplied boiled lobsters by post. On 27 May, 1931, for instance, he despatched four lobsters at 2s 6d each, charging 2s for 'cooking of same' and 1s 3d for postage.

His notebooks contain occasional entries that enlarge on the normal bare particulars of date, location and catch. On 24 July 1923, 'Minister's Induction' was noted. On 2 August, he was 'At home at Aunt's death'. He 'only hauled 28 creels', for 14 lobsters, on 16 October, 1929. No explanation was given, but during the succeeding four days he was 'very ill with flu' and wasn't at sea. In 1930, he was 'at Tayvallich sale with folk' on 11 June and didn't lift any creels; on 23 July, with a catch of 26 lobsters from 'Sgeir an Neich', he 'went home for Guild sale'. On 7 June, 1932, he noted: 'Left for Jura had to come Loch na Keil with engine trouble.' On the following day, the report was, 'Creels not shot'; but he was back at work on the day after that. There was more engine trouble. On 11 July: 'At home, cylinder holed.' On the 16th: 'Half of creels ashore to dry.' On 22 August, he 'Did not leave home – at J McGougans funeral.' In 1933, on 25 July, he had another funeral – 'Uncle Johns.' On 10 October, the weather was 'stormy' – a recurrent complaint – and he hauled only a few creels. At the very start of the 1935 lobster-fishing season, on 10 May, he reported a 'rope in propeller' and on the following day he 'went home to get bracket put right'. On 6 August, he sold six creels at 7s each. At Eilean Mór, on 13 September, he had to leave 12 creels unchecked owing to their ropes being 'below with tide' and therefore irretrievable. On the 20th, after a westerly gale kept him in harbour the previous day, he noted '6 creels missing'. Into October, a gale started at 9 p m on the 18th. He came in with 12 lobsters that day, but on the following day recorded: 'not out fearful gale.' On 3 August, 1937, among his catch of lobsters he noted '1 dead'. In 1938, 'salt herring' for bait cost him 3s on 14 June and on 12 July he noted '11 in 12 creels'. On Sunday, 3 September, 1939, he remarked: 'War Declared.'

All his expenses, no matter how trifling, are meticulously logged: various engine parts, petrol and lubricating oil, cutch (for tanning nets and ropes), rope, tarred twine, fish-hooks, nails and tacks, wicks and candles, 'Life Buoy' soap, tar, varnish and boiled linseed oil for the boat's maintenance, postage stamps, telegrams, postcards, labels, pier dues, basic provisions such as biscuits, bread, tea, sugar, milk, butter, salt, eggs and cheese, with a very occasional extravagance, as 'Jar App & Rasp Jelly' purchased in 1934 from Neil Orr, shopkeeper on Gigha.[7]

The *Jessie*

Although Billy Wareham has seined, trawled and dredged in a succession of boats for the greater part of his working life, creel-fishing has always been an interest of his and remains so in his retirement. He hand-hauls a hundred creels in and around Campbeltown Loch for velvet and shore crabs, lobsters of any size now being rare. His interest in creel-fishing was stimulated in the mid-1950s when the family boat, the *Jessie* – a 40 ft seiner-ringer – went lobster-fishing, encouraged by the success of a small fleet of Campbeltown-based East Coast creel-boats, the *Betina* and *Summer Rose* among them. These boats began operations at the Brown Head, and, as the season progressed, shifted south to Sanda and then north around the Mull to Gigha, where the *Jessie* joined them. As Billy remarked: 'Ye wir aye looking for doors tae open.' The Jessie's crew consisted entirely of Warehams: the brothers Jock (skipper), Hamish and Billy, and an older relative, Willie. They shot their creels off Machrihanish Bay and south towards the Mull, looking for 'peaks' and 'hard ground' on the echo-sounder and generally fishing further offshore than the small local boats. They had to, anyway, on account of the *Jessie*'s length and draught. One of the East Coast skippers was setting creels in 15 to 20 fathoms of water, at which depths he specialised. Jock and his crew, though novices, fished well enough, but prices were poor. One of the lobsters they caught in Machrihanish Bay weighed 14lbs. The first creels they made in the family net-store on the New Quay fell apart when hauled because the nails driven into the bases hadn't been bent over. Thereafter, bases with bows already attached were bought and required only to be ballasted, netted and roped. Later in the summer, when the hake fishery started in home waters, creel-fishing was abandoned and the *Jessie* never returned to the job. [Billy Wareham, 2003]

A big lobster

One of the yarns Sandy MacFarlane of Tarbert (p 98) told concerned a big lobster he caught on the West Shore. Having removed it from the creel, he put it down in the punt and carried on with his work. 'A laid ma pipe doon on the beam an A turned roon, an the next thing, ye know, that labster wis smockin ma pipe!' [Robert Ross, 2003] It may have been Sandy's creels that someone was admiring and was prompted to remark on: 'Bonny creels.' – 'Aye,' was the reply, 'bonny creels – they're queuin up tae get intae them.' [Peter McDougall, 2003]

Other creatures taken

Lobster-creels are far from being selective in the creatures they trap, yet, compared with most modern fishing methods, incidences of accidental and unnecessary destruction are infrequent. Most time-served lobster-fishermen have taken dead otters out of creels occasionally. Malcolm MacNeill of Gigha, in his fishing notebooks, records an 'otter in creel' on 11 June, 1936; four days later, the receipt of 10s for its skin is noted. Drowned *scarts* (cormorants or shags) are also found in creels.

If a creel is allowed to lie unchecked for too long, an octopus *Eledone cirrhosa* might invade it and devour the imprisoned lobsters, leaving only shells. To accomplish this, the octopus 'inserts its beak in some chink in the middle of the under part, injects a paralysing fluid, and then eats the lobster by sucking out its contents'.[8] Davie McVicar has seen the remains of two lobsters in one of his creels and the culprit 'sittin bloated'. Billy Wareham has seen as many as three octopuses in one creel at the mouth of Campbeltown Loch; they generally keep clear of one another when trapped. Billy invariably liberates them, despite their predations on his velvet crabs – 'naethin but empty shells' – reasoning generously that they too have to get a living. When creel-caught squid – *gibearnach* – were thrown back into the sea, they'd 'spout out ink', which Duncan MacNeill of Gigha was told – and doubted – could cause blindness if taken in the eyes. [1978]

Starfish of all descriptions are attracted by bait and, once inside a creel, can, if large enough, kill and eat lobster and crab. Along certain coasts, the crawfish *Palinurus elephas* (p 45) is infrequently taken. Small crabs of all kinds will enter creels. The velvet swimming-crab *Portunus puber* and 'green' or shore crab *Carcinus maenas* have ceased to constitute a nuisance and – since the mid-1980s – attained commercial value, and Davie McVicar predicts that a market will open for hermit crabs, which protect their soft abdomen by occupying empty winkle and whelk shells. These whelks or *buckies*, as they are locally known, also invade lobster-creels. Since the early 1990s, they have been fished commercially, for Far Eastern markets, using rudimentary plastic pots; but, with the largest class of *buckie* becoming increasingly scarce, indications are that the local fishery has entered a decline. Once, at the mouth of West Loch Tarbert, Billy Wareham took a scallop *Pecten maximus* from a creel, and in Machrihanish Bay Davie McVicar lifts 'clabbydoos' *Modiolus modiolus* (p 76), caught up on creel-ropes.

On some coasts, squat lobsters may be taken occasionally in lobster-creels, but are more common in 'prawn'-creels and trawls. All species are edible and the tails marketable. The two main species encountered are *Galathea strigosa*, some three inches long and greenish-brown in colour, and the larger *G squamifera*, which is bright red and patterned with blue dots and lines, 'the most handsomely coloured of our crustaceans', in the estimation of eminent marine biologist, C M Yonge.[9] Squat lobsters are essentially crawlers rather than swimmers, and Davie McVicar credits them with 'great climbing abilities', having often observed them moving around on the rock faces of the Leac Bhuidhe tidal holes.

The largest of the sea-urchins, the spine-covered pinky-blue *Echinus esculentus*, is generally found on creels or in the eyes, rather than inside the creel itself. Its reproductive organs, voluminous in summer, have been esteemed as a food around the Mediterranean since classical times.[10] Most of its local names derive from its ovoid form. In south Kintyre, it is a *sea-mar's egg* or *mar's egg*, 'mar' being a corruption of Scots *maa*, 'gull'. In Tarbert, it is a *ron's egg*, a hybrid name, *ròn* being Gaelic for 'seal', while around Muasdale, the full Gaelic form, *ugh ròin*, survived with Neil Thomson [1978]. On Gigha, as also on Islay, the urchin was called *coinean mara* – 'sea-rabbit' – or *ugh ròin*, as on mainland Kintyre.

Many species of fish are lured into creels, including lythe *Pollachius pollachius*, saithe *Pollachius virens*, Ballan wrasse *Labrus bergylta*, bearded rocklings *Gaidropsarus vulgarus*, *Ciliata mustela* etc., ling *Molva molva*, bass *Dincentrachus labrax* and 'rock cod', a small red-tinged variety of *Gadus morhua*, which Willie Watson of Muasdale considered 'lovely to eat'. The gurnard was reckoned by many lobster-fishermen to be a superlative bait (p 104). Those caught in creels around Gigha were generally seven or eight inches long and would make three baitings when cut up. 'Ye were pretty sure o gettin a lobster always when ye had that in the creel for bait,' Duncan MacNeill observed. [1978]. On Gigha and along the adjacent mainland, the gurnard was known as *carrachan a' chinn mhóir*, which roughly translates as 'the fellow with the big head'. Billy Wareham reckoned the conger eel *Conger conger* to be the most destructive visitor to a creel, being capable, if 'powerful enough', of bursting through the netting: 'Ye'll see the hole an the slime aa roon it.' Dogfish – both the spurdog and lesser-spotted (p 112) – were encountered. The latter will 'pretty well fill a creel' if full-grown. Billy saw specimens three feet long – 'big brutes o things' – in creels off Machrihanish. Davie McVicar has taken small tope *Galeorhinus galeus* from creels.

On 26 September, 2003, from a creel off Glenacardoch, on the west coast of Kintyre, Archie MacAlister took a species of the generally tropical or sub-tropical file fish (*Monacanthidae* family), so rarely encountered in British waters that it does not feature in standard textbooks. It was his second, the first having been lifted in a clam-dredge off Gigha in the 1990s. [Archie MacAlister, 2003]

John McKerral's most unusual 'catch' was a bottle of whisky which he brought up in a creel off Crossaig in the summer of 1972, but there was no mystery attached to his good fortune. He had loaned a few creels to a married couple who had expressed an interest in trying for a lobster or two while on holiday, and the bottle was their gesture of thanks before they returned home. [John McKerral, 2003]

Rearing lobsters

For 14 years, Davie McVicar devoted himself to an unusual hobby: lobster-rearing. His experiments were at first directed towards practical questions, chief of which concerned the relative merits of different baits, but as time passed he began to see the lobster as a more complex creature than he'd initially supposed it to be. Even after 14 years of studying them, he could admit: 'It amazes me – ye'll never know enough aboot them.'

During the first five or six years of his experiments, his captive lobsters all died; but thereafter he successfully reared seven to maturity and released them back into the sea. He obtained baby lobsters by baiting 'prawn'-creels – designed for catching *Nephrops norvegicus* – which he first 'closed off' using an extra sheet of netting, or 'blinder'. In the early years, he kept the lobsters in a workshop, but thereafter they lived with him and his family, occupying a 3 ft-long tank in the living-room at Bayview,

Machrihanish. The sea-water in the tank was never renewed, but kept topped up with fresh. As he said: 'The waater evaporates, the saalt steys.' He always tried to keep the salinity level in the tank constant, and to that end employed a hydrometer. As a merchant seaman, he was regularly away from home, but during his absences the current lobster would be tended by his wife, Helen.

Over the years Davie has accumulated a fund of fascinating insights into lobster behaviour, though he'd be the first to admit that the behaviour patterns of captives might not always correspond to those of creatures in their natural environment. He experimented with many baits, timing the responses of lobsters to each type. The food would be placed at the opposite end of the tank from where the lobster was lying and Davie would note how long the lobster took to smell and seize the bait. The most effective bait, he concluded, was a piece of fish – such as haddock or whiting – which was just slightly 'on the turn'. 'Sixteen seconds an he wid be at that.'

He also discovered that a lobster will kill and eat all species of live fish – eels, saithe, codling, etc. – deposited in the tank with it, except the 'ling', or bearded rockling. He first noticed the rockling's immunity from attack when snare-fishing the pools at Leac Bhuidhe. All fish would 'scatter' at the appearance of a lobster. 'The hole will clear. Ye'll see them aa backin aweh. Ye know he's there. Although ye canna see him, they're seein him.' Yet, a rockling could pass through the pool fearlessly. Davie suggested tentatively that the rockling could be 'a kind of pilot fish' to the lobster, a theory strengthened by his repeated observation that, when hauling a fleet of creels, 'if ye get a ling in wan creel, yer man'll be in the next creel'. As he admits, however, proving such a relationship is the problem.

Another trait of the lobsters' that he noticed concerned sea-anemones. He was able to ease anemones off the rocks at low water and transfer them to the tank to act as 'live filters'. When feeding a lobster, however, he had to be careful not to let the food 'swirl' towards any of the sea-anemones, because if one got its tentacles on food, the lobster would immediately launch a headlong attack on its rival.

A lobster's appetite would intensify, Davie observed, after it had cast its shell, which it did twice a year, generally growing about a quarter-of-an-inch after the year's first cast and a fraction less after the second. When casting, a lobster would invariably lie facing north, having first cleared a spot in the tank and selected a particular stone against which it would lay its head. Several lobsters turned a shade of 'duck-egg blue' after shell-casting. Davie had a display of successive cast-shells – perfect even to the eye-sockets – arranged on a board, but it was removed from his house and not returned. As C M Yonge explained in *The Sea Shore*[11]: 'Such moulting is the lot of all crustaceans; it is the price paid for the protection furnished by an external skeleton which is too stout to stretch as the animal grows.'

Davie found lobsters very clean. Using the front pair of pincered legs, beneath the claws, a lobster would regularly 'bulldoze' the area outside its home – a section of field drain-pipe or plastic roan-pipe – and would also 'rearrange' its entire environment, shifting stones and other objects on the tank-floor. The lobsters buried food, responded inquisitively to music and to noise generally, and reacted to any long-haired human visitor by half-emerging from the tank with, Davie reckoned, a degree of aggression.

When returning an adult lobster to the sea, Davie would put it in a plastic bag containing 'his ain watter' – i.e. water from the tank – take it to Uisead, transfer it into another bag containing sea-water, leave it in that bag for a time and finally deposit it in a rock-hole, where 'he wid jeest take his bearings, then off'.

Davie's lobsters attracted interest in the village. School children would come to the door asking to be shown the current captive, and his late mother-in-law, Mary MacPhee, took her turn at looking after the lobsters and would unselfconsciously talk to them. His years of experimentation came to an end when it was noticed that the sideboard on which the tank was kept had begun both to sag with the weight and to warp with the water-evaporation. 'We'll need tae get rid o this,' his wife Helen decided. Yet, when the last lobster was liberated, she was as upset as Davie himself. [Davie McVicar, 2003]

A fright

The operation of a small boat close inshore among rocks and tide is not without its dangers. Archie Graham's most alarming experience was actually self-inflicted. He had become acquaint with an Orcadian lightkeeper at the Mull of Kintyre who built his own clinker dinghies and fished a few creels below the lighthouse. This keeper remarked to him one day: 'Archie, A never see ye goin through that sound on the Machrihanish side. Archie Cameron always goes through there.' Archie Cameron was a Southend fisherman and the sound referred to was the channel between an offshore rock and the cliffs north of the Mull. One day, when tide was raging outside the rock, Archie decided to try the channel. He was 'racing up' with the tide, but when he entered the narrows he discovered that there was also a powerful current running in the opposite direction and it caught the bow and began sweeping his boat straight for the rock face. To avoid 'knocking her stem out' he had to put the boat astern, whereupon she drove away for the rock. In the end, she passed through the channel stern-first and out of control. Some time afterwards he met Archie Cameron and said to him: 'Archie, that sound on the other side of the Mull Light...' Before he could complete his question, Archie Cameron broke in: 'Archie, ye never attempt that with the tide.' [Archie Graham, 2003]

A capsize

The dangers of inshore navigation were surely greater when fishing boats were powered solely by sail and oar. In the *Campbeltown Courier* of 14 May, 1881, there appeared a report of the capsize of a lobster boat belonging to the Pans (Machrihanish, p 62). Three Gilchrist brothers* were returning from 'the Moil' when, about a quarter of a mile from home, their boat capsized and they were 'thrown into the water'. Their course had been through 'the sound known as Skerevore, where there are a good many sunken rocks', and the boat was 'caught by a heavy groundswell'. Fortunately for them, their 'perilous position' was seen from the shore and Robert Sillars, village blacksmith, and two masons, Dugald Fraser and Robert Murray, launched a boat and went to the rescue. Having taken the three fishermen off the upturned boat's keel, the rescuers took the boat in tow and brought her and her crew to land.

Probably Peter, Daniel and Archibald, all fishermen recorded in separate households at Pans in the 1881 Census.

Crawfish

For most local lobster-fishermen, the crawfish or crayfish *Palinurus elephas* is but an occasional occupant of a creel. Around Gigha, however, it has occurred in such numbers as to constitute a modest commercial resource. Though of a size with the lobster and sharing the lobster's habitat, its shell is brown- or rust-coloured and spiky, its powerful

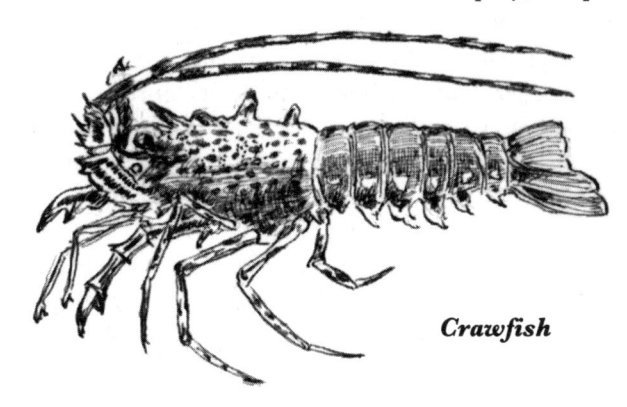

Crawfish

antennae may exceed its body-length, and, at a glance, it appears to be clawless. In France it is 'esteemed a greater delicacy than the lobster'.[12]

In Gaelic it is *giomach-cuain*, or ocean lobster, which name Willie McSporran attributes to its migratory tendencies. He has heard older men talk of rowing out to sea in late evening to fish with rod and fly and hearing the crawfish surface; some of these men, indeed, managed to 'scoop an odd crayfish aboard wi the oar'. Gigha creel-fishermen could sometimes land two or three marketable crawfish in a day, but they were harder to disable than lobsters – though multiple rubber-banding would later solve that problem – and 'creakin buggars' as they shuffled around the boat. [Willie McSporran, 2003] Certain shelved reefs around Gigha were particularly rich in crawfish, as divers found to their satisfaction. Archie MacAlister has seen three dozen crawfish – plucked by the feelers from their crevices and dropped into canvas bags – taken in a couple of dives. Since the 1980s, some Gigha fishermen have engaged periodically in tangle-netting for crawfish. Archie, in his *Ceol na Mara*, has worked half-a-dozen of these nets – 300 ft long and 3 ft deep – on the west side of the Island. Catches are never spectacular – two or three per net, perhaps – but at up to £20 a kilo for individuals weighing 2 or 3 kilos, the crawfish can be a lucrative sideline to creeling. [Archie MacAlister, 2003] Crawfish – lobsters too – occasionally come up in trawls. On a day in autumn c. 1998, Robert Gillies, prawn-trawling off Gigha in the *Morning Dawn*, took two good-sized crawfish for which he received £90. [2003]

In July, 1885, 'an extremely large and beautiful specimen of the crawfish' was caught on the Askomil shore of Campbeltown Loch by a local fisherman, Peter McCallum. Disappointingly, there is no mention of how the creature was captured, but it measured 'about three feet from tip to tail, 18 inches of this length being taken up by the feelers alone'.[13]

'Prawns'

The Norway lobster *Nephrops norvegicus* – a hard-shelled, pink-coloured crustacean with long slender claws – lives in extensive colonies occupying mud-tunnels in deep offshore waters. Its burrowing habit has been instrumental in its conservation, for in strong tides and bright sunlight it proves elusive, and despite intensive local exploitation for more than 40 years, stocks continue to support a fishery, albeit one increasingly dependent on 'lice', or immature individuals.

'Prawns', as they are colloquially known, were, when caught in seine-nets, a nuisance to be shovelled back overboard without a thought, but in the late 1950s a market developed. At first, prawns were 'stokered' –

Prawn

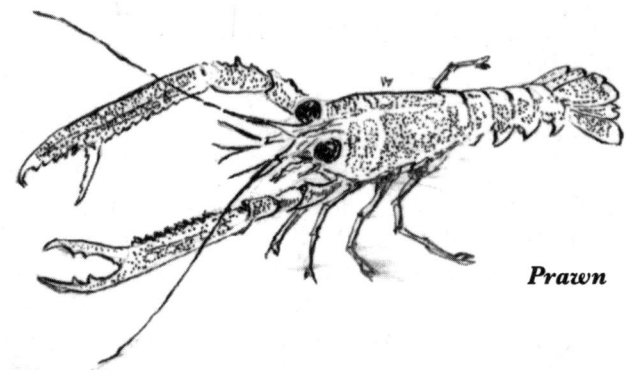

i.e. sold on the side and the entire proceeds split among the crew – but when it was realised that the prawns were earning more for the crew as 'stoker' than the main fish catch, a dedicated trawl fishery began (p 22).

When, in the mid-1950s, John McKerral started fishing as a boy with the brothers Neil, John and Duncan Lang in the *Janet Lang* of Campbeltown, big prawns, taken in the seine-net, were kept and landed whole. Donnie Gilchrist, a local fish-merchant, paid £1 a box, which was 'stoker' for the crew. At that time, five shillings was the nightly payment, but the custom declined after the taxman declared an interest in it. [John McKerral, 2003]

Initially, seine-net winches and ropes served the fishermen, but the more efficient trawl-winches – which wound steel towing wires on to a drum – were soon adopted, and steel doors or 'boards' – for spreading the mouth of the net – replaced the wooden originals. These improvements took place in the early 1960s, by which time many skippers had turned to prawn-trawling as their main occupation. For other skippers, prawning was a monotonous and ultimately degrading seasonal necessity and remained secondary to herring-fishing; but by the late 1960s, with the total failure of ring-netting, prawns had become the mainstay of the fleets, though mid-water trawling for herring and hake (p 83) offered greater scope for the 'purists'.

Nonetheless, the prawn fishery advanced from a routine clean-bottom operation using land-marks, to one based on precision-towing with Decca Navigator and track-plotter, which, conjoined with robust, purpose-designed gear, progressively opened up new grounds, previously too destructive for trawling over.[14]

The expansion of the prawn fishery in Scotland was rapid. Landings increased from 2,994 hundredweights, valued at £5,539, in 1950, to 192,493 hundredweights, valued at £5,010,564, in 1973.[15] Catches are generally processed in factories, becoming 'scampi', but good-sized prawns, like lobsters, may be marketed whole, and specialised creels are in limited local use as an alternative to trawling, which is notoriously destructive of immature and unmarketable fish.

Compared with ring-netting – and even seine-netting – in which the hunter's instincts were freed to take him where he pleased and his technical skills were honed to perfecton, an air of tedium and drudgery hangs about the legacy of prawn-trawling. The skipper in his wheelhouse, chatting interminably to other skippers by radio and perhaps chain-smoking to ease the relentless boredom, and the crew on deck, gathered around a heaped board, screwing the heads off tens of thousands of small crustaceans, hour upon hour upon hour, are the average fisherman's abiding memories of the job.

A notable Tarbert ring-net skipper, forced for the first time to prawn-trawling, was reputed to have shovelled a catch overboard while on passage back to port. When his crew reappeared, after a cup of tea, they found him hosing down the empty deck. 'I winna tail them masel, so A'm no' gonny ask you tae tail them,' he explained. 'We'll go in an clean*.'

*Spring-clean the boat.

Crabs

The edible crab *Cancer pagurus* is in Kintyre generally known as a 'crooban' – Gaelic *crùban* – or 'red crab', from its shell-coloration. It is the largest of all the native crabs and some attain awesome dimensions. In July, 1879, one Major Saunders, fishing with baited hook in Campbeltown harbour from his yacht *Mayflower*, caught a 'monster' which measured 14 inches by 7 inches and weighed 8¾ lbs. It was despatched by steamer to Rothesay Aquarium and arrived there 'alive and well'.[16] In September, 1891, a fisherman caught one weighing 6 lbs 7ozs at the head of Campbeltown Old Quay.[17]

In September, 1895, Malcolm Newlands and his crew in the *Seline Packet* netted, in the Lodan, a watering-can containing two crabs, the larger weighing 5 lbs 2 ozs. 'This crab seemingly had taken up its abode in the can when young and remained there till it had grown so large that it was made a prisoner, the narrow mouth of the article hindering egress.

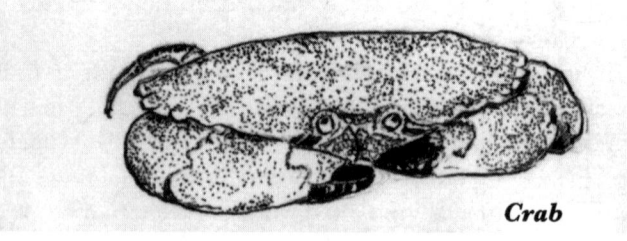

Crab

It had obviously been able to obtain sustenance without quitting its adopted home. The can had to be broken before the captive could be released, and when this was done a smaller animal of the same species was found underneath the monster crab, being very soft in substance, and evidently having derived nutrition from its imprisoned relative.'[18]

When George McSporran was growing up in Campbeltown, he and his brother John spent part of their school holidays in Southend. His father, George Sr, a master mariner and native of Southend, would lodge the family with Flory Niven, and George recalled crab-hunting along the Keil shore at ebb tide. These July outings would take them from the Islaymen's Port westward to the Graveyard Rock. His father knew the rock-holes where croobans could be found and would roll up his sleeve, put his arm into a hole, announce, 'Here's one here', and pull it out. 'How he did it, I just don't know,' George remarked. Neither he nor his brother had the courage to try it. His father would faithfully clean out the holes, removing stones and sand. George recalled seeing up to a dozen crabs – some of them eight inches across the back – 'hanging up in Flory Niven's', their nippers tied with string. Some were eaten and others used as line-bait. [George McSporran, 2003]

The practice was known elsewhere. James McNeill, in *Meanders in South Kintyre*, refers to Bogha a' Chrùbain – Crab Rock – at Port nam Marbh, Machrihanish. That rock has an underwater cleft, locally known as a 'cruban feg', in which 'can always be found a crab or two if one knows the spot and has the nerve to try the game'. McNeill tells of a local fisherman's taking a visitor out one Saturday afternoon to let him try his hand at cod-fishing, and, having no time to haul a creel for bait, rowing over to Bogha a' Chrùbain.

'Slipping his oars, he let the boat glide quietly alongside and jumped on to the rock. Lying on the rock with shirt sleeve rolled up to the shoulder, he groped with his hand in the feg. Almost instantly he withdrew it holding a fine-sized crab by the large claw. With a sweeping movement he tossed it into the boat and proceeded to repeat the act a little further along the feg. Success in this operation needs skill and experience, for if the crab is disturbed by fumbling or hesitation, he places his feet on the floor and presses his back so firmly against the roof of this feg that it is impossible to dislodge him.'[19]

When an old woman, gathering *maorach* (shellfish) at Muasdale, pulled a crab from its crevice in the offshore rock subsequently named Creag an Airgiod (Silver Rock), 'held tenaciously in the crab's claw was a coin of the realm – one shilling sterling. The crustacean, it was commonly accepted, hailed all the way from Aberdeen'.[20]

The word 'crooban' was well-known to children in South Kintyre. A game with the hands to amuse children, whose probing fingers got nipped, was accompanied by the rhyme: 'Put yer finger in the crooban's hole./ The crooban's no in./ He's roon at the back door/ Lookin for a pin.'[21] 'The Crooban' was a game involving the participants' letting the upper half of their bodies fall backwards on to the support of their hands, so that they could move slowly about, crab-like, with bodies arched and faces turned upward.[22]

References and Notes
1. S Buczacki, *Fauna Britannica*, London 2002, p 50.
2. J Crompton, *The Living Sea*, London 1957, p190.
3. A Martin, *Fishing and Whaling*, Edinburgh 1995, pp 49-50.
4. *Glencreggan*, Vol II, 1861, pp 172-74.
5. *Ibid.*, p 194.
6. Registers of Fishing Boats, National Archives of Scotland, Edinburgh, AF22.
7. In possession of Ms Betty MacNeill, Gigha.
8. J Crompton, *op. cit*, p 196.
9. C M Yonge *The Sea Shore*, London, 1961 edition, p 91.
10. C M Yonge, *ibid.*, p 166.
11. *Ibid.*, p 88.
12. A Hardy, *Fish and Fisheries*, London 1959, p 144.
13. *CC*, 18 July 1885.
14. Largely adapted from A Martin, 'The Campbeltown Fishing Industry', *The Campbeltown Book*, Campbeltown 2003, p 72.
15. Martin, *Fishing and Whaling, op. cit.*, p 52.
16. *CC*, 26 July 1879.
17. *Ibid.*, 3 Oct 1891.
18. *AH*, 23 Sept 1895.
19. J McNeill, *Meanders in South Kintyre*, 2nd edition, Campbeltown 1996, p 21.
20. Rev D J MacDonald, 'Antiquities of Killean and Kilchenzie, Part III,' *CC*, 29 Oct 1932.
21. Malcolm Docherty, Drumlemble, 1996.
22. Jean Paterson, Carradale, 1978.

Saithe and Lythe

The saithe or coalfish *Pollachius virens* is a member of the cod family. Its back is dark, but with a definite greenish sheen which fades rapidly after death. Although it has rarely been a valuable commercial species locally, its past importance as an abundant and easily caught food is incalculable. Anybody at all could go to the rocks and catch saithe, not just for immediate consumption, but as winter provision when cured and dried. Saithe also provided liver-oil, extracted by slow-heating. Fish-oil had many uses, but mainly as fuel for the *cruisie*, a metal dish with a wick formed from skinned and plaited rushes, which was in universal use among coast-dwellers and islanders until the mid-nineteenth century. In the late eighteenth century, saithe-oil was 'often sold at 16d per Scotch pint' in Craignish, the mainland promontory opposite the north end of Jura. A solitary fisher could take '9 or 10 score' in a morning or evening, 'the only time of day when it will take the fly'.[1]

Saithe

During the Second World War, with its food shortages, the ordinarily commercially worthless saithe became so valuable that Campbeltown fishermen renamed it 'goldfish'.[2] Being classed as white fish, its 'controlled price' was actually fixed higher than that of herring, as a 1943 entry in Skipper Donald McDougall of Tarbert's fishing notebook (p 80) shows: 'Jan 19th 86 bts (baskets) herring @ 24/6 [a basket]; 88 bts saith @ 32/6; 29 bts saith @ 30/-.'[3] On 4 January of that same year, off Port Righ, Donald McAnsh of Torrisdale (p 128) caught 611 baskets of saithe, which fetched, per basket, 32s for 316 and 25s 3d for 295.[4]

Ronnie Brownie was only born in the year these diary entries were written, but he heard of the big money Carradale fishermen made in the wartime years and was familiar with the status of the 'gleshan'. 'They wirna waantin tae fish them. There wis a kinna stigma. Ye're better wi herrin – they're cleaner.' [2003] Most families involved in full-time fishing despised saithe. I recall a family anecdote concerning a sister of my great-grandfather, John Martin. Her engagement was being discussed unfavourably by her sisters in Dalintober. Not only was she marrying a fisherman over in Campbeltown, but his background was poor. 'Christ,' one of the sisters remarked, 'the *gleshan* bones are stickin oot his erse!' The flesh of the large saithe, or *stanelock*, however, was considered excellent for mixing with mashed potato to form fish-cakes; and, at ring-netting, a simple and tasty meal could be produced by boiling a *stanelock*, picking off the cold flesh and frying it in a pan with butter and pepper. [Robert Gillies, 2003]

A rich seam of culture has accrued on the billionfold bones of the humble saithe. The bones of saithe, indeed, are predominant among fish-bones found in the Mesolithic middens which hunter-gatherers left behind on the island of Oronsay more than 6000 years ago.[5] A sure pointer to the unbroken value of saithe in the diet of the 'common people' is the number of names attached to the fish, in its various stages of development, around the entire Scottish coast. In Kintyre, Lochfyneside and Gigha the legacy is understandably almost entirely Gaelic.

The smallest stage is *cudainn*, anglicised as 'cuddin' or 'cuddie'. *Ceiteanach* (pronounced 'cayjanach' and deriving from *Céitean*, 'May'*) and *glasan* (the 'gleshan' of South Kintyre, and deriving from *glas*, 'grey') are the next stages up, though their relative sizes tend to be a subject of disagreement. *Piocach* – pronounced 'pyoochky' and sometimes 'pyoochty' – is a half-grown saithe, more or less. The largest of all is the *stanelock*, which is Scots borrowed into Gaelic. When, in the early 1970s, Kintyre fishermen joined with Ayrshire fishermen in a lucrative, but short-lived, mid-water pair-trawl fishery on saithe, an Ayrshire word for saithe, *podlie*, caught on locally and remains prevalent.

A fish which has reached its first May, having been spawned the previous spring.

In Neil Thomson's early years, saithe were preserved, but generally only by poorer families. Around October, these fish would be well-steeped in brine then tied in pairs by the tails and hung over a wire to dry at the back of the houses. Saithe could be caught in bulk by the use of a small net set around the fish by boat and then dragged ashore, much as sea-trout were taken by splash-net (p 119). This activity was known as *scrìobadh*, 'scraping'. [Neil Thomson, 1977, 1978] In South Kintyre the net was known as a *screenge*, which is Scots: to scour the seabed. Archibald D Cameron remembered 'some o the old fishermen' going round Southend village with a cart selling *gleshans* caught with a net drawn ashore. [1977] Working a 'trawl net' – the earlier form of the ring-net – off Carradale pier in February 1880, Alexander Ritchie of Sanda and his crew on the *Isabella** on successive days caught 50, 30 and 30 boxes of 'glassons', which sold for 6s per box and were sent to Glasgow by the Campbeltown steamer.[6] On 16 September, 1887, she arrived in Campbeltown with 'a cargo of Sanda saithe, and being of fine quality and a favourite fish with many in the town, they were rapidly disposed of'.[7] At Bellochantuy, on the west coast of Kintyre, in September, 1886, 20 cartloads of saithe were caught by drift-net and sold at '4d per bushel'.[8]

Known as the 'Sanda lugger', she was wrecked on 26 January, 1888, after breaking her moorings in Sanda Bay.

1. The rock fishing promontory of Leac Bhuidhe, with the tidal bathing pool visible in the outermost large rock. Photograph by George McSporran, May 2003.

2. Robert Wylie, oilskins over his arm, landing at the Fisherman's Cottage, New Orleans, after a day's fishing in October 1972, the year before he died. Courtesy of Archie Graham, Peninver.

3. Southend fisherman, Dick Gillon, in the final years of his long life, c. 1960. Courtesy of Mrs Betty Gillon, Southend.

4. Seine-net skipper, John 'Knuckler' Robertson, on Campbeltown Quay shortly before his death in 2002. Photograph by Lachie Paterson.

5. Swedish seine-net boats moored at the New Quay, Campbeltown, c. 1925. Author's collection.

6. The *Gleaner* of Peterhead, acquired by Cecil Finn, John Robertson and Jamie McKinven of Campbeltown and later sold to Ronnie Johnson, Eoghann Smith and Willie Dickson of Tarbert. Coils of rope, seine-net winch and flagged dhan are visible. Courtesy of Cecil Finn, Campbeltown.

7. Colin Campbell (left) with his uncle, Jock Campbell, seine-netting on the *Silver Quest* of Carradale, c. 1958, Carradale Bay. Photograph by George Lang.

8. Captain George McSporran casting with bamboo rod from the Gardener's Rock, Southend, c. 1935. Courtesy of George McSporran Jr.

9. Looking west from the Duan towards Salt Pans village. An illustration by James Stewart, from William Smith's *Views of Campbelton and Neighbourhood*, 1835.

10. A Gigha fishing crew, c. 1925. L–R Dougie, Malcolm, Donnie and Duncan MacNeill. Dougie and Donnie were brothers as were Malcolm and Duncan and all were cousins. Courtesy of Ms Betty MacNeill, Gigha.

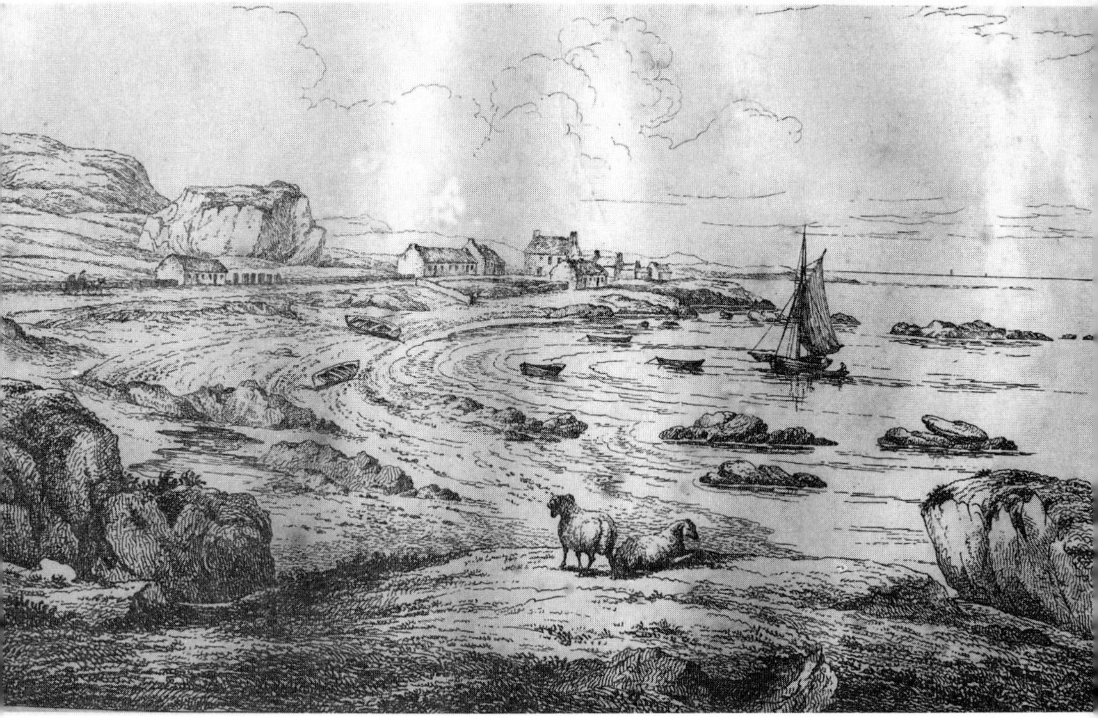

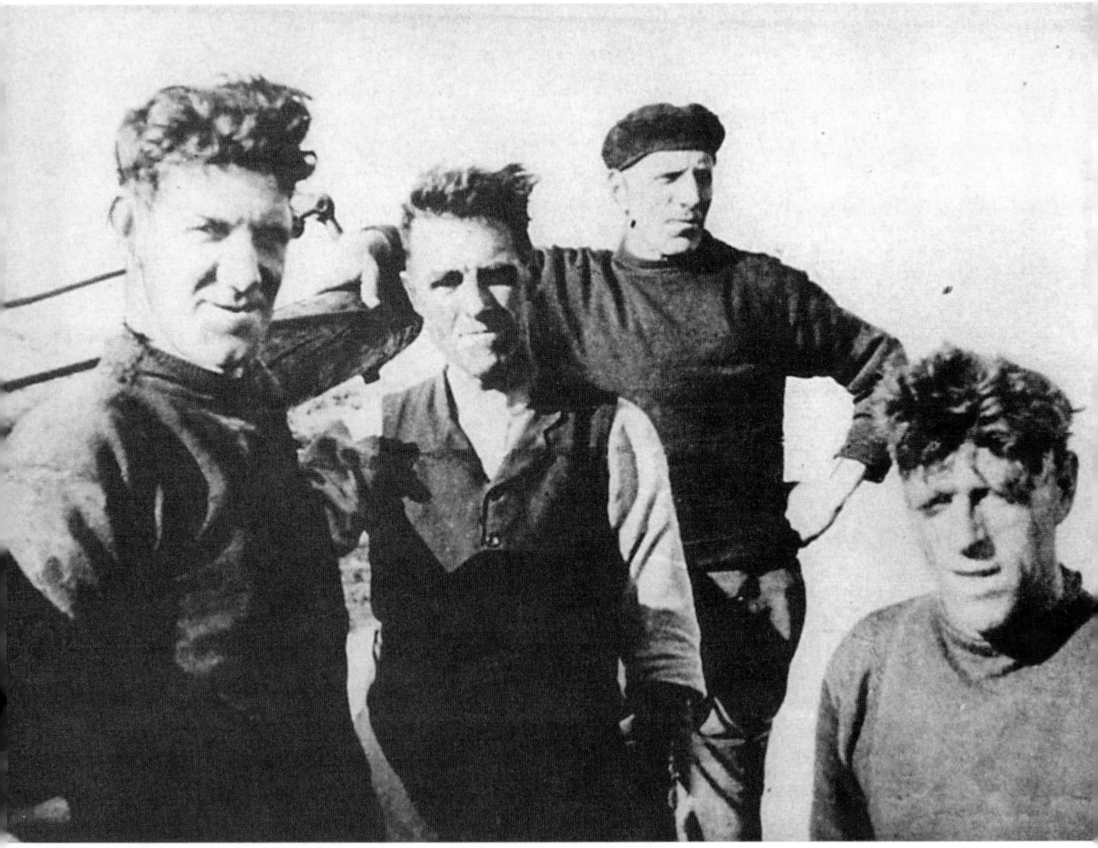

11. Skipper Willie McBride (1866–1937) of Pirnmill, Arran, on the foredeck of his skiff the *Ella* in Lochranza harbour, c. 1922. Courtesy of Mrs Margaret McBride Harvison, Pirnmill.

12. The end of a giant – the tail and middle portions of a basking shark, taken in the *Silver Spray*'s prawn-trawl, around Christmas, c. 1970. It is being towed into Tarbert for disposal. Courtesy of Peter McDougall, Tarbert.

13. Campbeltown fisherman, William 'Oakie' Gilchrist, with sturgeon, c. 1920. Courtesy of Jenny Black, Campbeltown.

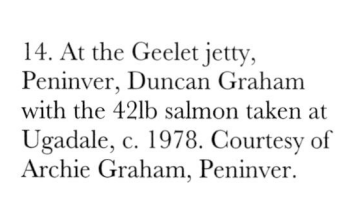

14. At the Geelet jetty, Peninver, Duncan Graham with the 42lb salmon taken at Ugadale, c. 1978. Courtesy of Archie Graham, Peninver.

15. At the crofthouse, Silvercraigs, c. 1925, Duncan Campbell (second left) with daughter Maggie seated on his left. Courtesy of Mary MacBrayne, Campbeltown.

16. Donald MacVicar at Low Kames, Lochfyneside, 9 November 1983. Photograph by the author.

Lìon-scrìobaidh

Donald MacDonald of Gigha was born in 1891 at Port nan Cudainnean, which translates as 'port of the young saithe'. He remembered using the *lìon-scrìobaidh*, or 'scrape-net', on several occasions in his youth. His father got the net, which was 'getting done at the time', from Achamore House. The only success they had with it was one Hallowe'en night in the bay – which was 'good for keeping fish in' – at the Mill on the west side. Donald and an older man held the end of the net at the rock from which it was shot from the boat and paid out in a semi-circle, then joined the two other men in hauling the net after the boat had landed. Hundreds of saithe were taken in that haul. Donald at the time was working on a farm at the north end of the island and, the following day, brought a horse and cart from the farm and loaded up with the fish, which were taken to Port nan Cudainnean to be gutted, salted and dried. [Donald MacDonald, 1978]

Bag-net

When Archie Carmichael was growing up in Tarbert, there was a woman from Stornoway, a Miss Nicolson, who caught 'pyoochkies' for salting and drying, using a bag-net consisting of an iron barrel-hoop with netting laced on to it and a rope attached. Her fishing spot – the rocks at the 'Ootside Pier', or Concrete – was well chosen, being where fish-curers disposed of herring guts by means of a chute into the water. Having laid the net on the sea bottom, she would scatter some bait, wait until the fish were swarming, then raise the net, taking perhaps 40 or 50 fish at a time. A 'good-livin'' woman, she stayed in isolation in a small house behind the Columba Hotel. [Archie Carmichael, 2003]

That bag-net was no doubt known in Gaelic to its practitioner as a *tàbh*. Duncan MacInnes of Eriskay described the typical *tàbh* as consisting of 'a round hoop with staves down the side, covered in a small mesh net', the net containing a stone to sink it and with a long handle attached for raising and lowering it. Limpets would be knocked off the rocks with a sharp stone, pulverised in a *pollag* – rock hole (p 57) – using a round stone called a *molag*, and thrown into the net to attract tiny saithe. Duncan has seen 'as much as four buckets of cuddies caught in one haul'. As a schoolboy in Bunavullin, he saw old John Johnston making just such a net. The cuddies, when eaten fresh, would be boiled or coated in oatmeal and fried. [Duncan MacInnes, 2003]

Rod-fishing

Tarbert folk fished for saithe with rods from small boats or from the quay, where there was 'so much herring going over the side' from boats discharging. These saithe – many of them sizeable 'half-stanelocks' – would be boiled and eaten with potatoes, bread and tea. 'That wis a great thing in the winter.' [Archie Carmichael, 2003]

Demand at Inveraray

During Bob Smith's time as curator of Auchindrain Museum (1977–86), with rod and fixed line from the rocks he caught and dried many saithe and lythe both for display and for occasional personal consumption. The rod would be 7 to 10 ft of hazel, or a rowan sapling of similar length, and the best lure was simply strands of wool gathered from fences or brambles and whipped to a bare hook. If he used bait, it was always mussel. That rig caught lythe and saithe up to two pounds in weight, but if that class of fish was absent, he might resort to modern gear – shop-bought rod, fixed-spool reel and metal lure – casting some 80 yards out into deeper water for bigger fish. The late Johnny Dewar, fishmonger (and much else) in Inveraray, had some elderly customers who longed for saithe, fresh or dried, but Johnny couldn't supply until Bob told him that he was catching them. 'As the quantities involved were small, neither John nor myself bothered about money.' [Bob Smith, 2003]

By boat from Muasdale

The only son of Neil Thomson's who was interested in the sea was Hector, and his companion on fishing trips was a farmer's son, Willie Watson. In August and September evenings they'd go out together to fish for *gleshans*. Hector was an excellent oarsman, so he rowed while Willie sat on a board at the stern holding three fishing-rods, one jammed under each leg and one in his hands. Sometimes there would be fish on the three lines simultaneously, and 'fanklin', or tangling, would result. Lures used were white or red flies. The main fishing ground was located by lining up the Mull of Oa, Islay, with South Muasdale Farm, with Glenacardoch Point an additional landmark. If there were no *gleshans* in that area, they might go north to Sgeir Mhór and try for fish 'tight to the reef'. Since they were just boys, a strict limit was imposed on the length of these fishing-trips. They shipped rods and rowed for shore when MacBrayne's bus would pass through Muasdale at 8 p m, and if the evening was misty, they would listen for the same bus. Catches could range from nothing to 120 fish, and whatever they caught would be tied in strings of a dozen and given away to villagers. [Willie Watson, 2003]

By boat from Gigha

In Donald MacDonald's youth 'over on the west' of Gigha, his family kept a goose, from the feathers of which his father would make the flies for saithe-fishing. A big gull feather could also be used for making the 'white fly' used in rod-fishing, and Donald MacDonald has seen a long line laid out ashore, with some baits still attached, for the purpose of catching a gull. [1978] The feather would be 'tapped', or tied, on to the hook, which was attached to about a foot length of gut, and the gut itself attached to a light line. Rods – perhaps young fir-trees, 'as soople as could be' – would be cut in a wood. In summertime, rod-fishers would row out from land at eight or nine o' clock in the evening and not return until perhaps three o' clock in the morning. [Willie McSporran, 2003] White dog's fur, bound to the hook by sheep wool, was used as a lure on Skye. [Donald Macleod, 2003]

Lythe

The pollack *Pollachius pollachius*, invariably *lythe* in Scots, is largely a fish of rocky coasts and kelp-covered offshore reefs. Although the saithe in its youth shares the habitat of the pollack, in maturity it generally migrates offshore and exposes itself to the predations of commercial fishermen. The pollack, however, is infrequently taken in a trawl or seine-net and its breeding stock is likely to be much healthier.

Lythe

In more recent times, when lythe-fishing at sea, a rubber eel towed at speed with the weight attached to the line 6 ft or more from the lure, was the preferred method. Indeed, Willie McSporran, when towing an eel at 'full throttle' off the *Aska* shipwreck, was almost hauled over the stern when a big lythe seized the bait. Fish of 3 or 4 lbs weight he considered a 'decent size for eating', but he has seen lythe up to 11 lbs taken, and one night, in the bar of the Gigha Hotel, Hughie Wotherspoon appeared with a very large fish he had caught 'up by Dearg Sgeir'. Hughie, who was Willie's best man when he married, was about 5 ft 6 ins tall, and was holding the fish at shoulder height, yet 'its tail was on the ground'. The lythe in Gaelic is *liùgh*, and a young one is *liùghag*. If the small red-tinged lythe were abundant and taking, one of the older men would invariably remark, in Gaelic: 'Oh, *liùghag* – we'll get buggar all.' They were usually right – a prevalence of these small fish was a sign of scarcity. 'Ye wid never get many other fish if ye started gettin them.' [Willie McSporran, 2003]

Lythe were fished using rubber eels in the shoal waters around Sgeir an Trì, a reef off Muasdale. Willie Watson would accompany Neil Thomson and his wife May in the biggest of their boats. They always went when the wind was offshore – when onshore, or westerly, the fish wouldn't 'take' the same – which caused them some anxiety, because the outboard motor was very temperamental. Some of the lythe caught there were very big, ten-pounders being not unknown. As Willie remarked: 'When ye caught it, ye knew it.' The fish were sliced into steaks and fried with butter or else made into cakes. [Willie Watson, 2003]

Rock fishing

Rock fishing for saithe and lythe was carried on to a great extent on Gigha, where no one lived any great distance from the sea. The Rev William Fraser, minister on the island in the late eighteenth century, evidently had a keen interest in fishing, for he entered into great detail on fishing matters when writing his *Statistical Account*; nor did he neglect the humble rock fishers.

Fish taken from the rocks he identified as lythe, mackerel, saithe and 'rock-fish' or 'sea-perch'*. The equipment was a 'stout' rod, 'hair line' – presumably twisted from horsehair – and hooks. For fishing the 'cuddie', a small bent pin and smaller rods and shorter lines sufficed. Hooks were 'mounted' with a goose or gull's feather or a strip of white leather, though at certain times of the year the cuddie could be taken with parboiled winkle-meats. 'Each person fishes for himself on the rocks, only the whole party join in pounding the bait, and casting it into the sea, in order to collect a greater number of the fish.'[9]

**This cannot, however, be the sea-perch* Sebastes marinus, *which is a deep water species. 'Rock fish', I suspect, is an anglicisation of* creagag, *which might make the fish in question a ballan wrasse.*

When rock fishing, boiled potatoes would be broken up and thrown into the sea as *pronnan*[10] to 'gather' the fish. [Donald MacDonald, 1978] As Willie McSporran put it: 'If ye were goin rock fishin an ye wir boilin potatoes, ye would need tae put on an extra one for the fish.' In the 'back end' – October and November – the *piocaich* would be served regularly with fragments of boiled potato or old bread for some six weeks to habituate them to coming in for food, after which they would be fished by casting out beyond the seaweed with a long rod used in a 'sweeping' motion. The rocky point, on which the Gigha ferry-slip is now built, was the customary fishing rock of Archie Milloy, who fed fish there. Great fishings were taken from the rocks in winter. The *piocaich* were cured, tied by the tails in pairs with sheep's wool and hung on lines and fences outside the houses until they were 'as hard as the table'. Then they would be stored in old flour-bags as winter food.

At many of Willie's habitual fishing spots, he noticed holes – perhaps 8 inches across by 4 inches deep – formed in the solid rock. In these hollows, he understood, limpets would be pulverised for bait or – perhaps more likely – as ground-bait to draw in fish, for William Fraser refers to the communal task of 'pounding the bait, and casting it into the sea...' (p 56). Willie heard no Gaelic name for these bait-holes, nor did he ever observe any in use, but he has seen one at Port Righ, one at the foot of the dyke at Kinerarach, one at Tris and 'umpteen' at Grob. [Willie McSporran, 2003]

Similar rock-hollows for pounding limpet or mussel baits were in common use in the Orkneys and Shetlands. One Shetland account, dating to 1885, points out that these cup-holes are frequently found in groups of three, two small and one large, and that the pounding was done – usually by boys – in the smaller holes, the larger hole being the store for the *soe*, or ground-bait.[11]

Betty MacNeill of Gigha carried more than sixty *piocaich* home after an evening's fishing one 'good year'. This was from Leim, a popular rock fishing location. On another occasion, she went there to fish with companions and found the place already crowded with other young fishers. About half-an-hour after she arrived, 'Other two heads appeared over just south of Leim, and who was this but the teacher, Minnie McGeachy, and Mary McNiven, also after the fish. I heard them laughin, higher up, when they saw half o the school was down!' When Betty would return home with a string of fish, her father would say to her: 'Well, ye've got them now – clean them!' The fish were fried or used in a fish-soup called 'savas' (Gaelic *samhs*), which she relished and considered 'very nutritious'. [Betty MacNeill, 2003]

References and Notes
1. *Old Statistical Account*, Vol 7, pp 438-39.
2. A Martin, *Herring Fishermen of Kintyre and Ayrshire*, Colonsay 2002, p 46.
3. In possession of Mr Peter McDougall, Tarbert.
4. Diary of Angus McBride, in possession of Mrs Margaret McBride Harvison, Pirnmill.

5. G and A Ritchie, *Scotland: Archaeology and Early History*, London 1989, p 15.
6. *CC*, 7 Feb 1880.
7. *Ibid.*, 17 Sept 1887.
8. *AH*, 25 Sept 1886.
9. *Old Statistical Account of Gigha and Cara*, Vol 8, p 42.
10. From Gaelic *pronn*, 'to break up', a generic term for all fragments 'but usually boiled potatoes thrown and frequently spat great distances by some old *bodaich*... In Tiree, Coll and Ardnamurchan, *sonn* was the term for this bait to gather fish'. Iain Henderson, letter, 25 Nov 2003.
11. A Fenton, 'Craig-Fishing in the Northern Isles of Scotland', *Scottish Studies*, Vol 17, pp 74-75.

Cod

The cod *Gadus morhua* was for generations the object of intensive winter fisheries on its spawning congregations both within the Clyde and to the west of Kintyre. The traditional method of catching cod, and also ling and other large species, was by 'big line' (*eagach*, or 'deep', in the Gaelic of west Kintyre and Gigha), technical particulars of which, relative to Campbeltown and Tarbert, can be sourced in my *The Ring-Net Fishermen*. The emphasis here is on the cod fisheries of Gigha and the smaller Kintyre fishing communities at Southend, Machrihanish and Muasdale, though Donald MacDonald remembered Tarbert fishermen arriving early in the morning and shooting their lines to the west of Gigha, then coming ashore at Port nan Cudainnean, where his mother would make them tea. [1978]

Cod

In the Scots of South Kintyre, the cod is just that, and in Gaelic it is *trosg*; but there were many descriptive names for the fish, some of them possibly peculiar to their localities. In Campbeltown Scots a spent cod was both a *drowd* and a *glibe*, which in Tarbert was *glipe*, possibly from Gaelic *clibean*, 'anything flabby'.[1] In Kintyre generally, the small rock cod was *bodach ruadh*, Gaelic for 'red old man'. In Muasdale, at any rate, the young of the cod which grew to become the commercially-fished deep water *trosg*, was *bodach glas*, or 'grey old man'. On Gigha, a cod about 2 ft long was simply a *bodach*, or 'old man', and in Tarbert – the 'old man' yet again – a 'half-sized' cod was *geàrr bhodach*, *geàrr* being 'short'. A spent cod in Muasdale was *cailleach bhàn*, the white old woman, probably a reference to its unhealthy pallor.

The Mull of Kintyre

Captain Hugh McShannon was born in 1901 in Southend. His father, Jamie McShannon, trapped rabbits in winter and fished during the rest of the year with either Archie Cameron or Dick Gillon. The lobster-fishing at the Mull of Kintyre began in early spring, and the hand-line fishing for cod and saithe in June or July. The first signs of the arrival of cod and saithe would be the appearance of gannets feeding on the herring shoals that rounded the Mull on their migration from the Atlantic into Clyde waters. Word would be received from the shepherd at Glemanuill or from the lighthouse-keepers at the Mull, who could, from the rocks below the lighthouse, bring up herring in a perforated draw-bucket at slack water.

As a boy, Hugh went to the Mull cod-fishery with Archie Cameron or Dick Gillon. The Southend boats – Irish-built 'Greencastle skiffs' in Hugh's time, but square-sterned vessels at an earlier period – would leave Dunaverty with ebb tide and arrive off the Mull before slack water. Owing to the strength of tide, fishing effort was limited to the period before slack water, to slack water itself and for a while afterwards. 'Ye'd be lucky if ye got an hour-and-a-half.'

When flood began, the lines 'wouldn't go to the bottom tae get a cod' and the boat herself would be swept off the fishing ground. Hugh's job was to 'handle her back in again wi the oars'. He was too young, anyway, to haul up a full-grown cod, and if he did catch one, 'it had tae be gaffed by some o the men an taken aboard'. The hand-lines were baited with a strip taken from the belly of a cod or *stanelock*. That 'cleeban' (Gaelic *clibean*, 'a dangling end') – about six inches long and tough enough to last several fishings – would be secured by passing the hook through it several times.*

The natural spectacle under the Mull cliffs was awesome. Hugh remembered 'the sunlight, an the rocks along the shore glitterin... The swirl o the tide passin round the rocks there and the roar it caused and the screamin o the burds... When ye got below them, they really blotted out the sun, ye thought... some o them divin not very far off the boat, a few feet away from ye...' The fishermen said that if one of these 'big heavy gannets' had landed on the boat, it would have gone through her.

A part of the catch was sold fresh – Dick Gillon had a wheelbarrow and would take fish through the village – but the bulk of it was cured and dried in the sun. Archie Cameron hung the fish to dry, but Dick, who lived in the Lifeboat House at Dunaverty, had an 'ideal place'. He would spread the fish on the concrete surfaces on and around the slip. The Southend grocer, William Reid, bought salt cod both from the local fishermen – belonging to the village and to Sanda – and from the Islaymen who also fished the Mull. There was a 'big demand in the countryside for them' and households generally bought half-a-dozen or more. Most families would eat fish at least once a week, 'salt fish day' as it was called. [Hugh McShannon, 1982]

**The line itself consisted of a 2 ft-long snood, attached at one end to the main line, and to the other end of which was attached the hook, the whole weighted with a long lead sinker.*

Islaymen

Fishermen from the twin villages of Portnahaven and Port Wemyss on the Rinns of Islay evidently began to come to the Mull fishery about 1900 owing to the failure of the local saithe fishery. The bulk of their catch was taken back to Islay to be sold later at the Lammas Fair in Ballycastle, Ireland, a major event in their calendar. They would remain in Ireland for a week or more, buying up commodities, such as household goods, which were unavailable or expensive on Islay.[2]

The villagers at Southend saw nothing of the Islaymen except when they'd land salt fish at Dunaverty slip. At the opposite end of Dunaverty Bay, west of Garadh Dubh, there is a rocky inlet called the Islaymen's Port. Hugh McShannon was told that the Islay fishermen used to land there. He could remember only one boat coming from Islay. [1982]

Alistair Beattie, of shepherding stock and himself a shepherd, well remembered the Islay fishermen, for their huts were on the shore below the cottage at Glemanuill, which was occupied by his mother's siblings, Ronald McAllister – an unmarried shepherd – and sister Phemie. Alistair went to Glemanuill during his summer holidays from school and would be sent down to the huts in the evening with a batch of freshly-baked scones and a can of buttermilk for the fishermen; but their basic diet was the fish they caught. 'Man, ye know, when they wid come in wi thir boat fae the fishin they wid jeest boil a fish in a pot an when it wis ready they jeest teemed the whole lot oot on tae the rock, a kinna clean flat bit o rock, ye know. The water, of coorse, wid aa run off an they jeest got round that an got at it wi thir fingers. Right ould hardy men they wir.'

The huts (visible to this day) were small structures built up with stones and turf and roofed with spars and thatch. They were entirely unfurnished and the fishermen's bedding was a layer of dry, withered bracken spread on the floor. The Islaymen's boats would be hauled above high watermark every evening, and Alistair would 'gie them a hand'. These old men had scarcely a word of English, but that was no handicap to them at Glemanuill, because Ronald and Phemie McAllister both had 'plenty o Gaelic'. If the Islaymen had occasion to go up to the cottage for 'anythin extra' or Phemie went down to the shore, as she sometimes did, 'they'd get at the Gaelic right aweh'. [Alistair Beattie, 1977]

Archibald D Cameron, who was born at South Carrine Farm, Southend, in 1894, remembered, as a schoolboy, going with his father to the Islaymen's huts to buy the salt fish that were dried on the rocks. The Islaymen 'weren't very keen on sellin locally' because 'they could get more for them over in Ireland'. Nonetheless, one of them, whose name was MacMillan, would sell Archibald's father cod for a shilling each; *stanelock* were cheaper. He remembered three boats, 'not more'. [Archibald D Cameron, 1977]

The end of the fishery

In 1915, when the Islaymen came to occupy the huts at Glemanuill, 'the police put them away' (under the wartime Defence of the Realm Act, prohibiting lights along the coast). The local fishermen continued fishing and did quite well, but the following season was a total failure. 'The fish didn't come at all. There wir nothin to be seen. Not a vestige of a burd or a fish tae be seen on the Mull o Kintyre. A lot o the locals spoke about it at the time and couldn't understand it an said: "Well, they put away the Islaymen an they also put away the fish." An that wis the final of it; they wir never seen again.' [Hugh McShannon, 1982]

'Rock Cod'

The 'rock cod', or *bodach ruadh*, rarely exceeded 5 lbs in weight. Neil Thomson's father told him that, when 'the old rock cod was in its heyday', there were 'boats galore' – 12 to 14 ft long and kept for line-fishing – hauled up along the shore. 'My father told me aboot the rock cod an how they went away. They dinna go away – I think they wir fished out.' [Neil Thomson, 1977] The coloration of these cod appears to be 'conditioned by environment… a red or dark brown colouring when the non-migrating fish is immature and living among inshore rocks and weedbeds'.[3] This accords with the belief of Machrihanish fisherman, James McMillan, that the red 'Pan cod' was a 'groundkeeper', in other words it kept to its own ground. [Davie McVicar, 2003]

'Pan Cod'

The cod – both 'red' and 'grey' – caught off Machrihanish were popularly known as 'Pan Cod', from the old names of the village, Salt Pans, Mary Pans or simply Pans, commemorating a sea-salt evaporation industry carried on there in the seventeenth and eighteenth centuries. These cod were fished with creel-caught *buckie* or crab bait, from skiffs anchored over the fishing banks. When the skiffs returned to Pans, they'd be met by Archie MacLean from Campbeltown – himself known as 'Pan Cod' – with his spring-cart and pony. 'When each boat's catch had been weighed, the fish were loaded into the cart. The catches might run from 8 to 12 stones per boat and he paid 1s 6d per stone. "Pan Cod" then set off for Town, ringing his bell and calling "Pan Cod". The fish were soon sold, as they were prime quality – red or grey – caught in the open sea.' Two Pans crews sailed annually to the Island of Mull to fish cod, living in turf huts on the shore until they had 'a sufficient load of prime cured fish' to bring home for sale.[4] In February, 1875, 'a cart load of excellent Pan cod' failed to secure a 'fair price' in Campbeltown and was returned to 'the Pans' to be salted.[5]

Cuthbert Bede, in 1859, declared Pan cod 'the best and finest upon the coast' and remarked that the '... old system of hand-line fishing has for many years been abandoned for the more remunerative long-line system', using 1000 to 1500 hooks, one set of lines being replaced, after eight or ten hours, with an alternate set. 'The village,' he wrote, 'can boast of its little quay, school-house, and inn; and with the exception of a few farm-houses, and gentlemen's seats, all the cottages are inhabited by fishermen.'[6]

The main nineteenth century fishing families at Pans were McMillan (Dugald and sons), Gilchrist (p 45) and Rae. The Raes came from Aberdeenshire to Pans in the early part of the century. They fished and kept the inn there, but their horizons were wider. A consortium of brothers – Robert, John, William and George – invested heavily in luggers for the drift-net fisheries in Irish and northern waters, and the family also held salmon-fishing rights at Carradale, Ugadale, Kildalloig and Dunaverty as well as at Machrihanish.[7] Nineteenth century fishing boats at Machrihanish included the Raes' *Annie*, *Helen*, *Nellie* and *Beauty*, Daniel Gilchrist's *Bee* and the McMillans' *Onyx* and *Garrion*.[8]

Dugald Macintyre, gamekeeper and author (p 7), fished the reefs, in 9 to 15 fathoms of water, where the Pans fishermen had formerly sought the rock cod, which 'ran from about 4lb upward' and were 'of the most lovely golden colour'. Shooting tenants who were served the cod described them as 'the best eating fish of the sea', an estimation with which Macintyre concurred: 'The cod were like, but better than, lobster to eat. No wonder, for if you opened the stomach of one you found full-sized edible crabs in it, quite whole, and we used those to increase our supply of bait.'[9]

The name 'Pan cod' has assumed a new significance in the twenty-first century. At Uisead, Machrihanish, in a joint venture involving a commercial company, Machrihanish Marine Farms Ltd, and the Department of Aquaculture, Stirling University – which in 1992 established a marine environmental research unit in and around the old lifeboat station – cod are hatched and reared for 'farming' in cages elsewhere. It is the first purpose-built hatchery of its kind in Britain and the object is to raise 'up to two million cod juveniles per year' to augment depleted natural resources of the species.[10]

Muasdale

Muasdale fishermen also sailed to Mull for the cod-fishing. Long-lining for cod had ended by Neil Thomson's time (he was born in 1904), but he remembered 'the bones o two old boats' lying on the shore. Each had a *den*, or small forecastle, containing a tiny stove, called a *bogie*, and a stove-pipe going up through the deck, but no provision for sleeping. He recalled, however, a derelict smack which did have bunks. The smack was known in Gaelic as a *trosgair*, from *trosg*, 'cod', but was also used for lobster-fishing.

The salting and drying of cod was carried on 'upstream from the village'. The vats for curing were beyond the old bridge, and there were rocks on which the fish could be spread to dry. 'The womenfolk were puttin them out an turnin them an keepin them covered if it rained.' [Neil Thomson, 1977]

Loch Fyne

The main catch of Tarbert hand-line fishers was codling, which included 'rock cod'. These tended to be 'wormier' than deep-water cod, and the advice, when sitting down to a meal of them, was: 'Put the light oot an ye'll no see the worms.' Cockles were considered the best bait and could be dug in the harbour, or at the head of Dubh Chaol-linn, and carried to sea in a bucket. Exceptionally, there was one man in Tarbert, Gorrie McCaffer, who made his living at hand-lines and of whom it was remarked: 'Gorrie fed his femily wi two hooks – other men cou'na feed thir families wi a thousand.' During the summer, he ran holidaymakers to and from the slip at the White Shore in his motor-boat, the *Alison*. He was a native of Islay and his son, Willie 'Gorrie', became a noted ring-net skipper. [Robert Ross, 2003]

One of the spots frequented by Tarbert hand-line fishers was a sunken rock north of Garval Point. It was known as Roc a' Chaisteil, 'The Castle Rock', because the landmark for it was Tarbert Castle opened on the point. 'Put doon yer line an ye wir right on the top o it, seven or eight fathom. Ye know, they wir gettin fish aboot it, cod an haddies an whitins.' [Hugh MacFarlane, 1977]

Around 1955, Alasdair Macleod – manager of Achnaba Farm, near Lochgilphead, and a native of Skye – lifted a $41^{1}/_{2}$ lb cod from a deep hole off the perch on Otter Spit. The fish – 'all head' – was foul-hooked using a formidable home-made 'jigger' comprising four bare great-line hooks, each attached to the stainless steel blade of a table knife, a solid block of lead for weight, and the whole device held together with bolts and brass snare-wire, twisted for strength, and suspended on doubled hanks of heavy-duty fishing twine. [Donald Macleod, 2003]

Gigha

The long line fishing at Gigha evidently lapsed about 1768 and was not revived until 1788, when the laird, John MacNeill, had a boat fitted out 'by way of trial'. Her crew fished about six miles north of the island, on a bank the north-east end of which was said to have been frequented, from the beginning of February until the end of March, by 'fine grey cod', weighing from 6 to 16 lbs; from March until May, the south-west end was frequented by 'fine red cod'.

In the following year, 1789, two boats were employed line-fishing, again with 'little success'; thereafter, from five to eight boats were fitted out annually, each crewed by four men and having four additional men employed ashore salting and drying the fish. The lines used in cod-fishing were 700 fathoms long, having from 400 to 500 'large white tinned hooks' baited with *buckies* (whelks). From June until January, some 60 Gigha fishermen were also employed at the Irish and Minch herring fisheries.[11]

Line-bait

The dependence of the Gigha line-fishermen on buckie bait is attested as far back as the late eighteenth century in the *Old Statistical Account* of Gigha and Cara[12]. At the start of the fishery a dog would be killed and singed, and its rotting flesh cut into small pieces and placed in the creels. 'The flesh of the dog, in its putrid state, is said to attract the wilk, which crawls up round the sides of the basket, and getting in at the top, cannot get out again, owing to the shape of it… ' After the first day's fishing, the island dogs were spared further grief, and the creels – woven from hazel wands and sunk with stones – were baited with the heads and entrails of cod and with line-caught skate and dogfish.

In the early twentieth century, the Gigha big line fishermen worked two fleets of 25 buckie creels. The banks where the buckies were fished – *banca nan cnomhagan*, in Gaelic – were in the deepest water out in the Sound of Gigha, closer to the island than to the mainland. These creels were 'seen to every day'. [Eoghann Henderson, 1981]

Muasdale line-fishermen worked two sets of a dozen buckie-creels, which were left out permanently for the duration of the fishing season. The northern set was shot off Sgeir an Trì, where rock met with mud – 'the buckie wis better there, the edge o the rock an the edge o the mud' – and the southern set off Bellochantuy. Whether they hauled the northern or the southern set depended on the favourability of the wind. These wicker creels – circular with a hole in the top for entry – were woven by the fishermen themselves and baited with a cod-head. [Neil Thomson, 1977]

Damage by steam-trawlers

In the final years of the nineteenth century, local line-fishing operations began to be disrupted by the activities of steam-trawlers. The first report of trouble appears in 1895, when two beam-trawler skippers were charged at Campbeltown Sheriff Court with illegal fishing.

John Wotherspoon, of the *Bella* of Gigha, told the court that on Saturday, 30 March, he shot his lines – 900 hooks, with 15 ft between each hook – about half-a-mile off the south-west coast of Gigha and streamed them west. When he went out on Monday morning to haul his lines, he found them damaged. There were seven trawlers working in the Sound, all of them within the three-mile limit, he said. He went across to the two that were closest inshore and followed the *Adriatic* of Hull, hailing her skipper and asking him if he knew he was within the limit; 'but as a pretty fresh breeze was blowing we failed to hear the answer'. When examined by Archibald D Wylie, representing Edward Turner, master of the *Adriatic*, John Wotherspoon denied that he used 'bad language towards the crews of the trawlers', but admitted that he objected to 'English trawlers coming to these waters' and said that, if he could, he would 'keep them out there altogether'. The case against Turner failed on grounds of insufficient evidence, and a like charge against the master of a Fleetwood trawler was consequently abandoned.[13]

These raiders were seldom convicted, but in April, 1906, Richard Bettess, master of the steam-trawler *Wyre* of Fleetwood, pleaded guilty to trawling within the three-mile limit off the Gigha coast on 27 March, and was fined £50. He was caught by the fishery cruiser *Vigilant*, but 'decamped' while she put into Gigha to obtain evidence. On his arrival at Fleetwood, however, Bettess was served with a citation.[14]

The nuisance continued unabated, and in 1924 the Government was petitioned to provide assistance. Malcolm MacNeill (p 37), then of Ardminish, wrote complaining of the 'complete failure' of the line-fishing, that season and the previous season, 'which the fishermen maintain is attributable to the continual depredations of steam trawlers over the fishing grounds, and also the great destruction wrought upon their gear by these predators'. MacNeill claimed that 'the fishermen and their dependents are now almost face to face with starvation', and sought the exclusion of steam-trawlers from the area north of 'a line drawn from the Mull of Kintyre to the Mull of Oa in Islay' during the line-fishing season, from 1 February until end of May.[15]

The fishery officer in Campbeltown, George McGee, considered 'the allegation of distress bordering on starvation… an exaggeration', and testified to having seen 'no signs of such distress or lack of nourishment while on the island'. None of the Gigha crews was entirely dependent on line-fishing – some worked at lobsters full-time, others part-time, and one crew usually fished herring all summer – McGee reported. He did sympathise with the fishermen's grievance over the destruction of lines by illegal trawling, and supported the call for 'more attention to the policing of these waters', while pointing out that 'a good deal of the damage complained of is admitted to have been caused by trawlers working quite legally outside territorial waters, and as the lines were unattended, the trawlers cannot be held responsible for this'. In 1924, five Gigha boats were engaged in cod-fishing and landed 500 cwts (25 tons) valued at £500.[16] These statistics presumably refer only to salt fish and are therefore incomplete.

The fishermen had a ready market for fresh fish, which, of course, gave an immediate return and obviated further labour. One of the notebooks kept by Malcolm MacNeill details, under '1929 – Fresh Cod Sold', some 141 transactions between 7 March and 27 April. Most of these concern individual cod sold locally for a few shillings each, but boxes of cod – both gutted and ungutted – were despatched frequently by the Islay steamer to J Campbell in Bowmore and Hugh Cameron, Port Ellen, and realised anything from £1 1s to £2 6s 8d at a time.[17]

In the final years of the Gigha cod fishery, the curing and drying of fish completely ceased. In 1939, three boats fished in March and April and took 310 hundredweights which sold 'locally in fresh state' at £1 per hundredweight. In 1940, two boats landed 97 hundredweights which were again sold fresh at £1 per hundredweight.[18]

The main Gigha cod banks lay to the west and south-west of the island and were mostly named after bearings and marks – Carn Mór (Big Hill), Cnoc a Baile Ùr (Ballure Hill), Taigh Sgoil (School House), Stang mu Dheas (South Ditch) – but there were also banks to the north. A catch would be gutted aboard the boat on the way back from the cod banks. After the cod-boat had been moored, the fish would be taken ashore in a small boat to the *clamp*, which was the foundation of stones on which the cured fish were stacked. The *clamp* with which Eoghann Henderson was most familiar was situated below Gigalum Cottages, at Eilean Port a' Chaolais.

The head and upper half of the backbone would be removed and the fish split to the tail, leaving the skin intact. After the fish had been cleaned on the rocks, using sea-water and a little heather brush called a *rubair* – 'something like an old-fashioned pot-scrubber' – they would be put into pickle in a *togaid* (hogshead). When judged to be 'properly cured', they would be transferred to another barrel 'to drip', then placed on the square-built clamp, which was always 'covered from the weather' with a tarpaulin or sail.

At the end of the fishing season, all the fish were removed from the clamp and spread on the rocks to dry. Great care was taken to watch over the fish. If heavy rain came, they would be hastily collected and piled on the clamp and covered. The drying process was confined to daytime; when evening came, the fish would again be gathered into the clamp. When properly dried, the cod were weighed out in half-hundredweight and quarter-hundredweight bales and tied with twine. Some fish would be sold locally and some shipped to mainland Kintyre. 'They even went as far away as Ayr to get it sold, with their own boats.' Individual crews had their own particular customers. After the fish had been sold, expenses would be deducted and the remaining money shared among the crew. [Eoghann Henderson, 1981, 1982]

Malcolm MacNeill's logbooks

In 1916, Malcolm MacNeill put out his lines on 23 February and hauled 10 cod on the following day. His lowest daily catch was six fish, on 28 February and 1 March, and his highest catch, 99 cod, was taken on 21 March. On 5 May – the end of his season – he hauled 30 cod and took his lines ashore. In the following year, 1917, he set his lines on 12 February and finished on 27 April with 21 cod. His lowest catch that season was three fish, on 19 February, and his highest 103 on 24 March. His cod-fishing log for 1931 is particularly detailed as to the marks of grounds fished. He mentions 'Bhealach a Gharrain', 'Cnoc a Captain',

'Old Bank', 'Cairn Mhor', 'Edge of Wood', 'Balure Hill' and 'Balure House'.

A list of customers for cured cod in 1931 runs to more than 90 names, some on the island itself, but most of them farmers on the adjacent Kintyre mainland, though some outliers appear, for example 'A McConnachie, Blasthill', Southend. Beyond Kintyre, customers are named in Islay, Jura, Tayvallich, Dunadd, Ardfern and Balvicar. The usual quantity ordered was either a half- or a quarter-hundredweight, which cost £1 7s 6d and 13s 9d respectively. A few island customers took only a stone of fish – the smallest quantity sold – while a Kilmichael Glassary farmer, Neil MacNeill, Dunamuck, purchased a hundredweight, to which he later added two stone.

Although Malcolm MacNeill's main market was salted cod – in 1921, an estimated three-fifths of Gigha cod were 'cured dried by the crews'[19] – he nonetheless sold what fish he could fresh. In 1917, 39 boxes of cod were despatched to a Tarbert fish-dealer, D Connell, at £1 a box, in addition to many sales of smaller quantities locally, in Islay and on mainland Kintyre. The crew of the MacBrayne paddle-steamer, *Pioneer*, which ran between West Loch Tarbert and Islay and called at Gigha, accounted for some 40 transactions that year, with specific individuals – mate, pilot, steward, fireman, cook and clerk – mentioned. A total of £143 14s 1d was realised in that year from fresh sales. Sales of fresh cod in 1924 included boats other than the *Pioneer*, namely 'crew of Minna' (a fishery cruiser) who paid Malcolm 4s and a 'Puffer', to which went one fish costing 1s 8d.

Archie MacNeill was born in 1906 at Muasdale. When he went to school he had 'no English', only Gaelic. He was a farmworker before becoming a bus-driver, which employment brought him into seasonal contact with Gigha salt cod. The cod – weighed out in hundredweights and half-hundredweights and the unwrapped bundles tied with tarry twine – were landed at Tayinloan for loading on to the bus. Some bundles would be delivered en route to Campbeltown – left at farm road-ends for collection – and the remainder deposited in the 'yard', or depot, whence farmers from Southend and other rural parts would come and collect their orders. [Archie MacNeill, 1977]

Bonanza at the Bennan

One morning, in the mid-1950s, towards the end of February, two of the small Campbeltown-based East Coast seiners – one of them the *Trustful* – went across to the Bennan, on the south end of Arran, and returned to Campbeltown with boatloads of big spawny cod. Since the crews consisted of elderly men, the fish-salesman in Campbeltown, Robert McPherson, rounded up two or three local men to assist with the gutting and landing of the fish – some 100 boxes per boat – an effort which wasn't completed until 9 or 10 p m.

On the following morning, the Robertsons' *Felicity* followed the Easties to the Bennan grounds and, on arriving there, found the *Trustful* lying with a netful of cod, 'huge fish floatin belly-up in the watter'. There was a black spot showing on the echo-sounder and Lawrence said to his brother, 'There a nice spot there, John – shot aweh', but John's answer was: 'Naw, ye'll naw come here – it's aa *heckle* (jagged rock).' An INS-registered seiner, however, appeared and shot his ropes around the spot and netted 200 boxes of cod. The 'wee totie' seiners 'that hardly made a penny aa winter wi us', were filled three days' in succession and their crews, satisfied, went home to the East Coast on the Thursday. [Lawrence Robertson, 2003]

Peter McDougall's biggest shot for a day's seining amounted to 105 boxes of gutted codling from Skipness Bay in the *Nancy Glen*, c. 1967. There were clam-boats working in the bay that day, 'smashing up' beds of queen scallops on the sea bottom, and the codling gathered to feed on the remains. 'Ye winna believe the destruction the dredges must've done on the bottom,' Peter remarked. The price received for the codling was low, however – 1s 6d a stone, or 9s for a 6-stone box of fish. [Peter McDougall, 2003]

References and Notes
1. L McInnes, *Dialect of South Kintyre*, Campbeltown 1934, p 11.
2. A Martin, 'The Mull of Kintyre hand-line fishery', *Northern Studies*, Vol 20, 1983, p 75.
3. M Pritchard, *Fresh and Saltwater Fish*, Glasgow 1986, p 138.
4. J McNeill, *Meanders in South Kintyre*, 2nd edition, Campbeltown 1997, pp 20-21.
5. *CC*, 20 Feb 1875.
6. *Glencreggan*, Vol I, 1861, p 213.
7. A Martin, 'The Campbeltown Fishing Industry', *The Campbeltown Book*, Campbeltown 2003, p 79.
8. Registers of Fishing Boats, formerly at Campbeltown Fishery Office.
9. *Wild Life of the Highlands*, London, revised edition 1950, p 105.
10. *The Herald*, 5 April 2003; *Campbeltown Courier*, 6 June 2003.
11. *Old Statistical Account for Gigha and Cara*, Vol 8, pp 40-42.
12. *Ibid.*, pp 41-2.
13. *CC*, 29 June 1895.
14. *Ibid.*, 28 April 1906.
15. Letter to Rt Hon Sir William Sutherland, MP, 17 April, 1924, Letters Book, Dec 1923 – March 1926, p 59, Campbeltown Fishery Office.
16. *Ibid.*, Letters Book, Dec 1923 – March 1926, p 63-64.

17. Notebooks in possession of Ms Betty MacNeill, Gigha.
18. Campbeltown Fishery Officer's Reports etc., March 1926 to Dec 1940.
19. *CC*, 30 July 1921.

Haddock and Whiting

It is frequently remarked that, for quality of eating, the East Coast haddock surpasses the West Coast haddock and that the West Coast whiting surpasses that of the East Coast. However, in the impartial estimation of Bob Smith, an East Coast man with a fishing background, the haddies he caught off St Catherine's in Loch Fyne were 'every bit as flavoursome' as those he caught off North Berwick.[1]

Both species belong to the cod family *Gadidae*, but are easily separated. The whiting *Merlangius merlangus* takes its name from the lightness of its skin. The haddock *Melanogrammus aeglefinus* is dark-backed and has, on each flank, just above the pectoral fin, a black blotch resembling a thumb-print. These marks, which are widely accorded Biblical origins, are locally known as 'Saint Peter's thumbprints', from the notion that it was the fish from which Saint Peter took tribute money. A medium-sized haddie is known in Campbeltown as a *dannie*.

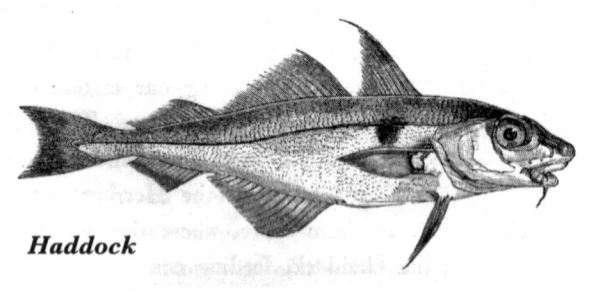

Haddock

Queuing at Pirnmill

The idea of boats queuing at a certain haul and their crews taking it in turn to shoot there for recurrent bags of fish might seem improbable, but the practice was known in the peak years of seine-netting and occurred at ring-netting too.

When Lawrence Robertson was crewing on the *Gleaner* of Campbeltown in the 1950s, he saw 14 seiners lying lashed alongside one another at Pirnmill, Arran, waiting their turn to shoot in a 'wee *trink*' known as the 'South Shot at the Mull'.[2] The waters of Kilbrannan Sound, as the boats steamed north by Carradale Bay with day breaking, were seen to be alive with 'appearances', the natural signs that often guided fishermen to success. The land was practically obscured by a white mass of 'pickers' – gulls in their thousands, swooping to the surface to pick on 'rid shrimp' – and the sea itself was boiling with 'cuddies', the density of which caused a 'black-out' on the echo-meter.

The *Gleaner* had already shot elsewhere in darkness for six or seven boxes of flats, codling and small haddies, and, consequently, was twelfth in the queue. The *trink* was a very tight and tricky haul, requiring an exact shooting procedure, and as soon as one crew had picked up its *dhan* and started to winch in the ropes, the next in line would shoot away its *dhan* some 30 or 40 yards astern and begin streaming out the ropes. The *Green Pastures* of Portknockie netted about 100 boxes of haddies; the Buckie seiner, *Scotia*, got about the same, and both steamed away for market. Those crews still waiting became increasingly 'edgy', and someone on the *Gleaner* suggested: 'Will we naw go up tae shot the North Mull?' – 'Them fish,' John Robertson reasoned, 'is lyin in that wan wee trink. There naw a fish clear o it. Jeest be patient.' But it was galling to see, as Lawrence himself put it, boats leaving 'coal-loaded, an us bein locals that knew the tow, we cou'na get intae it, cou'na breck the rules'.

Some of the crews were patient enough, going aboard other boats to exchange books. One of the Campbeltown skippers, however, did break the rules and shot out of turn. This impetuous decision caused an uproar among the remaining crews, but the offender paid no heed and carried on shooting until the next boat in line, the *Sincerity* of Fraserburgh, suddenly pursued him and forced him to heave back. The *Sincerity*'s crew then shot and hauled, and when her net came to the surface, the crew 'lifted it aboard wi thir han'.

The *Gleaner*'s crew had shot by this time, and the sight of that empty cod-end put them in a foul mood; but, if the Fraserburgh crew – newcomers to the Clyde – had judged the operation wrongly, the local crew got it right and lifted 80 boxes of haddies. The boat was 'completely full' and her crew hauled the net forward and piled it on top of the ropes on the fore side of the wheelhouse. They gutted all the way back to Campbeltown and landed 80-odd boxes of fish. 'The *Green Pastures* wis landin at the quay; the *Scotia* wis landin at the quay. That wis incredible. That wis in wan deh. The grun wis that hard, ye had only the *trink*, an ye had'ae be in that wee bit [which] must've jeest been fillin in wi fish, jeest as ye wir catchin them.' [Lawrence Robertson, 2003]

Greatest bulk

The greatest bulk of fish Robert Ross took in one seine-net haul was 100 boxes of haddies at Pirnmill, c. 1958. There were six boats queuing that day and his *Dalriada* was fourth or fifth in line. It was a haul, however, that he 'hanna got', but he watched how the skippers ahead of him shot and got an idea of the marks. When his turn came, in the excitement of the moment he began shooting his ropes to port, following the example of the other boats; but his gear was arranged for a 'starboard-hand shot', and when he realised his mistake he called to the crew: 'Christ, it's a port shot we're takin – we're makin a right arse o this.' They had to unshackle and 'reverse' the net, shooting the ropes – six coil a side – all the while. An East Coast seiner had shot ahead of him and her winch was in top gear, finishing the haul. The *Dalriada* was 'sailin down by him', with four coil to come and her winch just starting in top gear. 'That man's a braw bag o fish,' Robert remarked to his crew as they watched the other boat's net break the surface. The assessment, however, was mistaken, for the crew lifted only four or five boxes of fish aboard. 'A know what we'll get this time's fuck all!' Robert predicted, but he was wrong again, for the net 'bounced' to the surface with 100 boxes of haddies – 'all clean' – in it. That one tow grossed £196, which gave the crew £20-odd a man for their work. A boat's expenses at that time scarcely amounted to £20, with fuel costing just 1s per gallon. [Robert Ross, 2003]

Cecil Finn recalled that day at Pirnmill. There were about eight boats queuing to shoot on the haddies. 'It's a very very narrow bit o ground. They must've been as thick as the grass, because there wir no spread. Ye cou'na spread yer gear. There wir no room. Wi spread gear ye can gether up fish, but there wis no room. It wis jeest a case o gettin yer net aweh in among the fish.' Robbie McKellar was there with his new forty-footer, the *Golden Chance,* and Robert Ross arrived from the north with his *Dalriada,* there being few fish 'up the way'. Robert asked what was happening and was told that the *Felicity,* with about 30 boxes of fish aboard, was about to shift. Since Robert wasn't yet acquaint with the haul, the Campbeltown crew offered to 'run up the first rope' to get him started. So, Robert shot away astern of the *Felicity,* which then headed north and left Robert to it. Shortly afterwards, one of the Campbeltown crew remarked: 'I think Ross turned the other wey there.' When about two miles distant, some one noticed the *Dalriada* lying motionless. 'Oh, hell, there's somethin wrang wi that man. We'd better go aweh doon an gie him a han.' All that was 'wrong' was that Robert had struck a massive spot of haddies, which were spilling overboard as successive lifts were boated. 'He wis takin them in wan side an they wir gan oot the other.' Cecil estimated the catch at 90 boxes. He saw 600 boxes of haddies taken from that one tight haul at Pirnmill in a single day's fishing. [Cecil Finn, 2003]

'Don't bother comin for Willie'

Before ice became readily available for the preservation of fish, summer catches at times fetched uneconomic prices on the market. In August, for three years in succession, a 'good spot o haddies came on inside Otter Spit'. Robert Ross took the *Dalriada* to the north side of the Spit one Monday morning and, working there alone, fished 60 boxes for two or three tows. The catch fetched 4s 6d a stone and his docket came to £110 for the day's work. Duncan 'Tar' McDougall wasn't at sea at that time, but, hearing of Robert's success, took the *Charlotte Anne* off the beach and hauled his ropes aboard. There was just himself and Malcolm 'Tamar' Johnson, so he enlisted an uncle, Willie McDougall, and Davie MacFarlane to make up a crew and headed for Otter on the Tuesday morning. Both he and Robert had 60 boxes of haddies for the day, but when they brought their catch into Tarbert they 'never got an offer'. There was nothing to do but load the fish on to Jimmy Prentice's lorry and send them to the Glasgow market. When the 'line' arrived from Glasgow the following morning, Robert discovered that his 360-stone shot of haddies had realised the sum of £16. Neither he nor Duncan, who had fared no better, put to sea again that week. When Duncan's Uncle Willie went aboard the boat that morning and heard the news, he remarked to 'Tamar': 'Mawlcolm, the next time ye're looking for a man, don't bother comin for Willie.' [Robert Ross, 2003]

Latest catch

The latest catch of spawning haddies Robert Ross ever took was in the first week of April, c. 1961, in the *Dalriada*, after the cod had 'taken off' in the Kyles. He fished 50 or 60 boxes of haddies from the deep hole off Glacknabay on the Bute shore of the West Kyle. He and his crew steamed back to Tarbert in the afternoon, to catch the first market, and he recalled seeing, parked on the quay, two MacBrayne buses packed with passengers returning to Glasgow from their Easter holiday. [Robert Ross, 2001]

A lucky break

One Christmas, c. 1959, Cecil Finn decided, since he had been 'doin pretty well' up till then, that he would spend some time with his children.

He told his crew to take the boat out if they wanted to; they decided not to, but 'filled ice anyway'. Coming out of church after mass, he saw a sight which pained him: a concentration of boats lying in the Loch, their crews 'knee-bended guttin haddies... ninety-box shots'. Next morning, having missed out on the previous day's fishing, he went to sea ahead of the fleet and was 'first on the shot'. The haul, however, yielded merely five boxes of haddies where the fish had earlier been taken in abundance. When the fleet came out and started shooting round about, Cecil shifted ground – as the haddies had done – to 'the back of the Grips', about a mile-and-a-half off Davaar, and got 30 boxes, 20 boxes and then a 'scatter' to finish off his day. He got about 10s a stone when he landed his 60 boxes that night and reckoned that he grossed more for the day than the other boats did for two days' fishing, because the glut of the previous night had put the price down to half-a-crown a stone. [Cecil Finn, 2003]

Golden haddies

Lawrence Robertson was seining off Furnace, Loch Fyne, in 1950, on the *Gleaner* of Peterhead, when he saw his 'golden' – or albino – haddie gleaming amid a lift of fish on the deck. It was about a foot long and 'beautiful, pure gold,' he recalled. It was given to the fishery officer at Tarbert, who forwarded it to the Marine Research Laboratory at Aberdeen. He never saw another. [2003]

The first 'golden haddie' Cecil Finn saw was in Tarbert, but he didn't remember who caught it. The yarn at the time was that if a golden haddie was seen, it signified 'thick' shoals. Decades passed before he saw another. His son Tommy got one while pelagic trawling in the Kilbrannan Sound and passed it on to the fishery officer in Campbeltown. Cecil described the fish as 'full and healthy' and complete with Saint Peter's thumb-print. [2003]

The *Campbeltown Courier* reported two 'golden haddock' caught in 1954: the first by the *Jessie* of Campbeltown off Otterard and the second by the Peterhead-registered *Our Lassie* off Skipness. Both were sent to the Marine Research Laboratory in Aberdeen.[3]

Spotted haddies

In February or March, it was 'quite common' for a Campbeltown seine-net skipper, Robbie McKellar, to drop his *dhan* off Craigard House, on the north shore of Campbeltown Loch, and shoot his ropes eastward past the Showl Meith, a bank close to the mouth of the loch. Cecil Finn himself saw Robbie take 40 boxes of small haddies out of that haul. These fish were so distinctive – all had 'nice wee black spots' on them – that Cecil was of the opinion that they formed an 'indigenous' stock; but a day's work would effectively 'clean up' the spot for that year. [Cecil Finn, 2003]

Beakie Whitings

Whitings caught in Campbeltown Loch, in the area of the Beakie*, were also distinctively black-speckled, on a brownish-coloured skin, unlike the whitings taken elsewhere, which were a 'clean blondie colour' with 'a light line doon the middle'. The Beakie was a popular spot for hand-line fishing and on some days two or three small boats could be seen anchored in a line there. 'Ye could tell the Beakie fish,' James Macdonald stated. 'It wis a definite thing. Ye could tell: "Oh, ye've been at the Beakie."' There was a seine-net haul from there out to Donal Stott's Broo, on the west side of the Isle Slip, and back, but very few whitings would be netted, the bulk of the catch being flatfish 'the size o yer palm'. [James Macdonald, 2003]

The stone-built beacon, now unlit, on the crook of the tidal Doirlinn.

Seining for whitings

Whiting-fishing, in the late 1950s, centred on the grounds off Blackwater, Arran, the Otterard Buoy, north of Campbeltown Loch, and the 'Half o Sanna', out in the middle of Kilbrannan Sound, with half of Sanda Island open on mainland Kintyre. It was commonplace at that time to be back in Campbeltown by one or two o' clock in a November afternoon with 40 or 50 boxes of gutted whitings, perhaps 10 of selected large and the rest medium and small. These fish fetched from 1s 9d to 2s 3d a stone, which, with an added subsidy of about 8d a stone, allowed for 'a bob or two to be made'. [Cecil Finn, 2003]

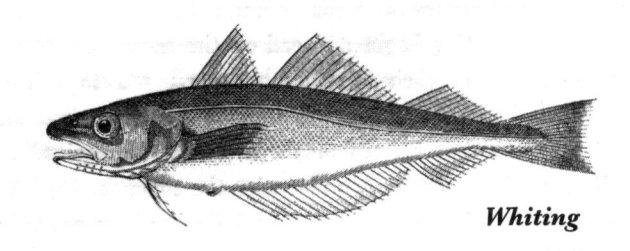

Whiting

Hand-lining

Hand-lining for whitings and haddies was a common recreational fishery until the 1960s, and small rowing-boats, crewed largely by old men and boys, would set out from communities all along the coast. Around Carradale, 'punts' would be launched from Port na Cùile, Port Righ, Waterfoot and Torrisdale and rowed towards such fishing spots as Whitestone Bank and Clabbadoo Bank. These banks were precisely located using marks on the land, and on the sea too, for the Cruban Buoy was an invaluable positional aid. The Clabbadoo Bank, off Tor Mór, was named from the presence there of horse mussels,[4] which, John McConnachie heard, would 'take a bit out of' the old cotton ring-nets if they clamped on to the meshes. Punts often returned from a fishing trip 'loaded' with whitings. 'Ye winna get wan the day,' John McConnachie remarked. [Ronnie Brownie, John McConnachie, 2003] The sandy sweep of Carradale Bay itself was rich in white fish. Donald McIntosh told of a man who would row south to the Bay with two companions to fish for whitings. With hand-lines, two of the men could catch 10 or 12 dozen whitings between them, but the third man 'never got wan fish… He cou'na feel them at his bait'. [Donald McIntosh, 1974]

In 'Campbeltown Fifty Years Ago', a series of memoirs published in 1912, Donald McLean looked back at the fishing industry of his boyhood. Among the hand-line fishermen were two 'outstanding men', the McKillops of Dalintober, who regularly fished the Lodan and 'seemed to know to an inch where to cast anchor and get a good haul'. McLean and his youthful fellow-fishers 'often got as near to them as we could with decency go, and were favoured with a share… '

McLean most often accompanied 'a well-known worthy by name Malcolm McLady,[5] who was lame but a born sailor-man'. Their most popular fishing spots were 'Kilkerran burn, Otterard, the red buoy, the black rock [and] the loaden'. Malcolm would 'come round to our back windows between 3 and 4 a m to pull the string that was attached to my big toe, whilst in bed, to get me up to go on a fishing expedition'.[6]

In 1936 and '37, when Angus MacAlister was at Auchenhoan in the Duke of Argyll's employ (p 15), he was accustomed to going line-fishing with another Estate employee, Johnny Russell, gamekeeper and rabbit-trapper, who had bought a new-built open boat for £8. On the shore below the Boathouse at Kildalloig, they laid rails to carry a winch-hauled 'bogie', or carriage, for launching and beaching the boat. The hand-lines were made from an umbrella-spoke, with a hook at each end and a dangling 'sinker' in the middle. The finest bait was lugworms, dug at the Doirlinn. The marks for that whiting bank – 'swept clean' many years ago, as Angus's friend, Skipper Robert Gillies from Campbeltown, informed him – was High Crossibeg Farm lined up with Sanda Light, and the boat – which had no engine – was allowed to drift during fishing operations. The fill of a quarter-cran basket of whitings was not uncommon. One 'back end', after a 'devil o a haal', nobody wanted the whitings, so Angus took them home and salted them in a large crock. 'All ye had'ae do in the winter wis tae gie them a waash an steep them for a night an they wir dead fresh agane. Wan o them made a good meal.' [Angus MacAlister, 2003]

As a teenager in the early 1960s, George McSporran went out hand-lining with a retired farmer, John Russell, who lived at Glenramskill and kept a 12ft clinker rowing-boat on the beach there. John had marks for fishing spots west of the Beakie, off Davaar Island and down in the Lodan, and Doirlinn cockles were used for bait. The bulk of the catch, which was mostly whitings, was used to bait John's lobster-creels. Robbie McArthur and his son Campbell also kept a boat for line-fishing. She was a sizeable ship's lifeboat and the McArthurs were sometimes joined by others, among them Dan Girvan and Jimmy Hall. [George McSporran, 2003]

Donald Macleod's cross-bearings for a Loch Fyne haddock bank were – the point of Glas Eilean on a red-painted boathouse in the middle of Achnaba Bay and the Otter perch on a nick in a hill above Stronachullin. Bait was cockle or – if time to dig it – lugworm. A bright afternoon with the tide in mid-flood gave the best conditions for trying for haddock, which seldom took in the evening or in heavy rain. [Donald Macleod, 2004]

Bill Harvison, whose mother Margaret was a McBride of Pirnmill, holidayed annually on Arran and spent much of his time hand-line fishing. Razor-fish was the preferred bait (p 175). His most memorable fish was a 22-lb cod caught off Pirnmill when he was about 16 years old. Once, when he and a companion were fishing in quite deep water about a mile south of Erines Bank and 'absolutely filling the boat', several seine-netters noticed their success and came around them; but the verdict, after echo-sounding observations, was: 'We can't fish here – the ground's too rough!' If fish were scarce, the rocks off Imachar would be visited as a 'last resort'. A couple of dozen rock cod could be caught there, but these were 'not such fun to catch'. Hand-lining off Pirnmill year after year from the 1950s on, Bill observed a gradual decline in white fish stocks, culminating in a sudden plummet in the 1970s, from which the stocks have never recovered. Most of the once-abundant species, haddock included, are now virtually unknown. [Bill Harvison, 2003]

References and Notes
1. Letter to author, 31 August 2003.
2. A *trink* is a deep trench, or 'gut', in the seabed. The term seems to have entered the vocabulary of Kintyre fishermen with the advent of seine-netting, and was most likely adopted from visiting East Coast fishermen. 'Mull' represents 'mill', the shortened form of Pirnmill.
3. 11 March and 3 April.
4 *Modiolus modiolus*, for which there is still a small commercial demand. 'Horse', used thus, invariably denotes largeness or coarseness, as in 'horse mackerel', 'horse mushroom', etc. 'Clabbadoo' or 'clabbydoo' derives from Gaelic *clab dubh* (black mouth).
5. This name must surely represent McLardy/McLarty. There was a Malcolm McLarty, aged 40, in Campbeltown in 1854.
6. *AH*, 16 Nov 1912.

Hake

The hake *Merluccius merluccius* is streamlined, silvery in appearance and has a capacious mouth with needle-sharp teeth. Unlike the bulk of commercial white fish species which are winter-spawners, the hake spawns in summer and therefore eluded the traditional winter long-lining effort. Also, since the hake is essentially a deepwater species, it likewise escaped the attentions of the subsistence line-fishers. In truth, then, the hake was a little-known species of uncertain commercial value until well into the twentieth century when local markets began to develop and some fishermen, notably from Tarbert, began long-lining in deep water. Seine-net and later mid-water trawl crews also exploited the hake shoals.

Drift-netting for herring on the east side of Arran, c. 1916, a Maidens, Ayrshire, fisherman, Turner McCrindle, recalled 'shootin at daylight an getting that many hake in the nets we threw them over the side. There wir no market in Ayr for them'. [1976] The Clyde hake stock attracted the attention of visitors, however, long before the resident fishermen, whose real focus was herring-fishing, took notice of the lucrative resource off their own coasts. Fleetwood trawlers made early incursions into the Clyde to plunder the virgin stocks and a fleet of Swedish hake-seiners based itself in Campbeltown in the 1920s.

Hake

Swedes

Neil Short was a boy when the Swedish anchor-seiners came in the 1920s. He recalled a fleet of 'ten or a dozen big lumps o boats' which lay in Campbeltown most week-ends. They were white-painted and registered 'GG', for Gothenburg, though in one year – or possibly two years – another fleet appeared from Sweden, with the registration 'LL' (Lysekil). He recalled the 'fearful noise' the Swedish two-stroke Bolinder engines made, a distinctive 'bump-bump-bump'. The men themselves were 'friendly and very well-behaved', and he recalled going down to the harbour on Sunday evenings and seeing the crews assembled on the boats' decks playing music. Mandolins particularly were in evidence.

He understood that the boats arrived as a fleet and fished the hake together, 'out by the Craig there', each crew taking its turn at running the collective catch to Fleetwood. When the hake 'took off', the Swedes also left. There was no opposition to their presence, because the locals were fundamentally herring-fishermen and conflict of interest did not arise.

Neil was to see one of the Swedish boats again in the 1930s when the Clyde ringers began landing summer herring into Castlebay to obviate the 'long steam intae Mallaig'. The Swedes were buying mackerel for shipping away in barrels, the fish having first been gutted and the bellies packed with salt. [Neil Short, 2003]

Mr Hamish MacKinven, a retired journalist, in a letter to the *Campbeltown Courier* published on 27 February 2004, recalled: 'On Sundays the entire personnel of the little fleet formed a circle at the head of the New Quay and held a religious service. From man to boy all were dressed in old-fashioned black suits like figures out of Hans Christian Anderson. The older men wore black top hats... Sadly, a small group of locals would gather nearby and snigger at these proceedings.'

A month later, Mr Jack Shepherd, Campbeltown, responded with his own memories of the Swedes. His father, Sam, was managing director of Eaglesome's shop, and the cook from one of the Swedish boats used to buy provisions there: 'The cook was a boy of 17 or 18 years old and he had fairly good English. He got all the shopping to do, but the Skipper always came with him and made up the order. We got on very well with them and they came here for about four or five years.

'The final year they were here the fishing was very bad and the engine of one of the boats broke down, so they didn't come back because they had such a bad year. I always remember them coming to my father and asking him to lend them £40, which was a lot of money in those days, to pay for a new piston for the engine. My father gave them the money. Time was going on and going on and then one day it arrived. They were extremely nice people and very trustworthy.'

Danes

In June of 1953, when Cecil Finn was heading south for the Manx herring fishing in the *Stella Maris*, he saw Danish anchor-seiners working east of Sanda. There were two or three of them, and their method was to drop an anchor, marked by a flagged *dhan*, and take successive hauls around that central point. Once they had encompassed all the ground, they would lift the anchor and shift a few miles away and resume operations. He understood that they were based in Whitehaven, where some of them had settled. Further south, the ring-net crews would encounter French hake-trawlers and go alongside and exchange fresh provisions, such as bread and milk, for 'a fry o fish'. [Cecil Finn, 2003]

Donald McDougall's notebooks

Although Donald McDougall of Tarbert's substantial reputation was established as a herring ring-net skipper, and the logbooks he kept reflect that preoccupation, he nonetheless remarked occasionally on other fishing activities. The following extracts are from the records of 1953. In the third week of February, herring-fishing was poor, with only 'odd puckles good quality got', and prospects poorer at the spawning fisheries at the Brown Head, Arran, and Ballantrae Banks, off Ayrshire. 'Most of fleet at clams & lines,' he noted. 'Good fishings with lines of hake at Barmore.' In the last week of February: 'Very few boats out; all at lines & clams; good fishings with lines of hake; some boats doing well. Only us & Jackson at herring fishing. £4 2/- per man.' In the second week of March he fished 'Escart, Cour, Crossaig, Grogport. Slack fishing; odd puckles. Most of strange fleet tied up; only us & Jackson at herring here; rest of fleet at lines; fair fishing of hake. No herring at Brown Heads or Banks. Some herring got at Loden. £7 17/- per man.' In the third week of March, herring-fishing was so slack that the division of the boat's money was 'held over until following week'. Most of the Tarbert fleet was 'tied up or at lines', but hake were 'getting very scarce owing to big fleet at lines'. In the last week of March, his herring-fishing grounds were Kilfinan and Pluck, but it was a 'slack fishing, odd puckles poor herring going for bait & fishmeal', and only he and his brother Archie in the neighbour-boat, *Maireared*, remained at herring. The remainder of the active Tarbert crews were 'at lines but hake very scarce'. On 11 April, he recorded: 'Out Monday night but nothing to be seen. Finished for season; drying nets and doing odd jobs. All the fleet at lines; some days fair fishings; other days very little.' His last reference to hake-lining, in that year, was on 16 May, by which time he had begun fitting out for a resumption of herring-fishing: 'Some fair shots of hake got by liners but bait very hard to get locally.'[1]

Seine-netting

The seine-net fishery on spawning hake always started about 'the turn o the night', or the summer solstice, and lasted well into August. The hake would leave deep water to spawn on muddy seabed, in about 40 fathoms, off the West Shore and up at Maol Dubh and Otter, with the last of them – which, Robert Ross speculated, were 'different fish, that came up from the deep watter at Carradal' – being taken between Claonaig and Catacol Bank. There were plenty of hake in deeper water, but when seining in over 60 fathoms, the ropes were liable to 'mud up'. 'If ye wid get her home, ye wid get two or three boxes,' Robert recalled; but if the net wouldn't 'come' cleanly, the most that could be expected would be 'a box o the big hake, mashed in the wings'.

When that hake fishery was going strong, Robert, in the *Dalriada*, teamed up with two other skippers, Jackie Sinclair in the *Nancy Glen* and Archie Kerr in the *Maisie*, to take turn about at running catches to Ayr on Fridays. The basic routine was, they fished all day Monday – having perhaps thirteen tows – and a part of Tuesday – perhaps eight tows – then each ran to Ayr, discharged his catch and took on ice. They then fished Wednesday and Thursday entire, storing their catches, boxed and iced, in the hold, and finished early on Friday. One crew would then load the catches of the other two and run all the fish to Ayr, returning to Tarbert with a ton of ice for each boat, the supply for Monday and Tuesday of the following week. By that arrangement, as Robert put it, 'ye got two Fridays oot the three home'. The lack of an ice-making plant in Tarbert, at that time, forced them to land at Ayr. [Robert Ross, 2003]

Chat hake

'Chat', or small, hake could be taken all summer on the fishing grounds, but at that time – the late 1950s and early '60s – the price was low, 1s 6d a stone (or 9s a box) and in one year in particular the seine-net fishermen were 'running away clear o them'. Robert Ross went out one Monday and had a tow at Mabel's (Escart) for 25 boxes of the unwanted chats; he cleared out to the back of the peak at Sgolaig and shot again, for 20 boxes 'off the deck'; his next haul was at the back of the Inch, for a dozen or 15 boxes. He landed 50 boxes of gutted chats on the quay at Tarbert and got £23 for the day's effort. [Robert Ross, 2003]

A big spot of hake

Cecil Finn is fairly certain he remembers when that big spot of hake appeared in the Clyde, and reckons it was about 1960. The *Brighter Morn* was on the beach at Campbeltown having her bottom scrubbed. Cecil was working about the boat's deck when he heard Jamie McKinven, who was in the ebb with a scrubbing-brush, call to him: 'Come here an see the sprats or *sile*, Cecil.' – 'Wherr ir they, James?' – 'In this pool here.' It was dead low water at the time. When Cecil looked into the pool, he noticed a curious detail when the tiny silver fish opened their mouths – the insides were blue. He drew out several with a bucket and examined them more closely. They were the size of sand-eels or herring fry, but in addition to the coloration of the inner mouth, each of the fish had rows of tiny sharp teeth. They were hake fry and obviously in such abundance as to constitute a phenomenon.

In the following year, local boats began 'marking' immature and still unmarketable hake. In the year after that, at a depth of 25 to 30 fathoms, 'ye could easy get ten or a dozen boxes jeest by chance if ye wir lookin for whitins or haddock'. One day, when seining operations were hampered locally by breezy weather, Cecil headed up Kilbrannan Sound and shot at Airde Bhain, north of Crossaig, 'lookin for a wheen o haddock an whitin'. Instead, he got 30 boxes of chat hake in the haul, which, however, fetched only 1s 9d a stone when landed. 'When ye shoot that wey an get therty boxes in an isolated patch lik that, ye can nearly seh tae yersilf, there's a lot o fish roon aboot... Ye wirna even lookin for them.' The survivors of that stock grew and were fished year by year until they reached the length of a fish-box, after which they 'scattered or died oot'.

Hake-fishing was a summer job at the seine-net. Cecil reckoned that the 'height' of the fishery, which began early in June, was Glasgow Fair, the last fortnight in July; thereafter, the fishery 'went back'. The summer-spawning hake were fished out at the Puffer – a seabed obstruction, believed to be the wreck of a small coastal trading vessel – an hour's steam from Davaar Island, and with Davaar Lighthouse 'open', or visible; and from there east, but 'higher' – or north – of Ailsa Craig. In the earlier part of the season, fishermen would get the hake on both sand and mud; then the fish would seek the mud for a while and spread out there. 'The fish wir that big,' Cecil recalled, 'ye wid haul for maybe eight fish… That wis the full of a box. Well, if ye got that six times at a pound a stone, ye had a deh's work. But it wis kinna monotonous, right enough.' When that fishery came to an end, after the Glasgow Fair, the fishing effort would shift to Claonaig and the hake season would end there with 'a nice wee bit fishin'. [Cecil Finn, 2003]

Claonaig hake

The hake caught at Claonaig were distinctive. Cecil Finn believed that one could take a box of hake fished there, send it to any market in Britain, mix the fish in with hake caught anywhere else and that any man, 'in the habit o fishin Claonaig', when asked to pick out the Claonaig hake could do so without hesitation. These hake were 'stubby' in the tail and some of them had a 'wee humph', or hump, on the back. He conjectured that the Claonaig hake formed an 'indigenous' stock and agreed with Robert Ross's conclusion that they migrated from the deep water off Carradale to spawn. [Cecil Finn, 2003]

Greatest value

The greatest monetary value Robert Ross ever received from one seine-net tow was £200 for 20 boxes of hake taken at Sgolaig on the West Shore, c. 1962. This was in February, too, not the best season for hake-fishing. His crew on the *Dalriada* at the time was Willie 'Bull' Smith, Malcolm 'Tamar' Johnson and Colin 'Cocoa' Clark. Hake being an exceptionally 'flotty' fish*, the bag of the net 'bounced' when it came up. Willie 'Bull', who preferred herring-fishing above all else and 'hated' the seine-net, remarked to 'Tamar': 'Aye, ye'll need tae see that wance a week at this bloody job.' – 'Ye'll live all yer days,' 'Tamar' replied, 'an ye'll never see that agane, ma boy.' [Robert Ross, 2003]

When hauled rapidly from the seabed, the swim-bladder becomes grossly distended and the fish float belly-up.

Pair- and pelagic trawling

Colin Campbell in the *Silver Fern* of Carradale and Denis Meenan in the *Stella Maris* of Campbeltown, when 'neighbouring' at herring pair-trawling, began towing for hake in the winter of 1975 in deep water at 'the back of Arran' during slack spells in the herring-fishing. Lachie Paterson was crewing with Colin Campbell at the time and the year is fixed in his memory, because, in April, 1975, while the fishermen's blockade of ports was in progress*, the *Silver Fern* had a net-monitor installed. Without that instrument, which electronically relays the net's fishing depth to the wheelhouse, the sinking of the net in order to catch hake on or near the seabed would have been a hazardous exercise.

Around 1978, single-boat pelagic trawling for hake began in the deep waters of the Clyde – Kilbrannan Sound, Loch Fyne, off Ardlamont, etc. – and in the North Channel. That fishery generally began in October and lasted until February. The average tow was of six to eight hours' duration, with the nets 'tripping the bottom', i.e. within a fathom of touching and occasionally actually touching if the bottom was 'clean'. Fifteen to twenty boxes of fish – which could include cod and other species – was considered a 'good tow'. [Lachie Paterson, 1992 and 2003]

Commenced 31 March and lasted four days.

Reference
1. Notebooks in possession of Mr Peter McDougall, Tarbert.

Flatfish

Halibut

The halibut *Hippoglossus hippoglossus* is the largest and most prized of the flatfish, but, being essentially a northern deep-water species, big specimens are rarely taken in local waters. The few records which follow are certainly not complete, but the very newsworthiness of these catches demonstrates the rarity of the fish. May 1868: 'not less than two hundredweight', caught by Thomas Eaglesome, Ugadale, and 'immediately despatched to Greenock'[1]; April 1879: 84 lbs and measuring 5 ft in length, caught by James Rae, Kildalloig, and offered for sale by Mr Blue, fishmonger, Cross Street, Campbeltown[2]; February 1882: 175 lbs, caught by James Wareham, Campbeltown, in the Lodan, bought by Archibald Scott, fish-dealer, and sent to Glasgow fish-market[3]; July 1891:

168 lbs, caught near Carradale by the mate of the SS *Rona*[4]; February 1913: about 108 lbs; landed at Campbeltown and fetched 5d per pound[5]; March 1913: about 4 ft in length and between 2 ft and 3 ft in breadth, it was landed by one of the Gigha cod-liners and 'despatched fresh to Messrs McKinney and Rafferty, fishsalesmen, Glasgow'.[6] Malcolm MacNeill of Gigha must have caught a halibut in March, 1925, for an entry in one of his logbooks (p 37) notes the cost of 'Telegram about halibut' as being 3s 8d, and a subsequent entry, of 1 April, notes the sum of £4 11s 3d against 'Halibut'.

Mightier individuals have been taken in distant-water fisheries. One, caught by the Aberdeen trawler *Ben Gairn* off Iceland, in May, 1962, was the heaviest recorded halibut landed by a Scottish vessel. It exceeded 7 feet in length and weighed 532 lbs, and, by examination of its otoliths, or ear-bones, its age was reckoned at 25 years. The heaviest ever recorded was caught on the Newfoundland Grand Banks on Armistice Day, 1918, and weighed 680 lbs.[7]

George Newlands remembered vividly the day the big halibut was caught. He was crewing on Charlie McKinven's *Puritan* and it was the day of the Ayr Agricultural Show, in April. The steamer *Dalriada* was leaving Campbeltown, heading for Ayr with a load of day-trippers, and passed close by.

George had the first basket of lines that day. The crew got hold of the *dhan* and began hauling, but as the anchor was coming up, George remarked: 'I've merr as the anchor here this moarnin.' – 'A big *dunny*,' Eddie McKay speculated, 'it'll be a big *dunny* ye've on ye.' As it transpired, George's line had hooked not a large skate, but a halibut, which took three men to haul aboard.

When the *Puritan* returned to Campbeltown, the fish was landed at the north side of the quay, where line-caught fish were customarily brought ashore and laid out on a cement slab for the scrutiny of the

Halibut

buyers. The fish-market scales being incapable of coping with the fish, it was taken to the Weigh-house at the head of the quay, where carts with their loads were weighed and logged. It registered 101 lbs and the fishermen received either ninepence or tenpence a pound.

'There ye are. That's what we got for it. We thought that wis grett money. A hundred an wan pun. It took three o them tae gaff it aboard. An we got quite a good fishin that deh, cod an everythin, aye.' [George Newlands, 1975]

Cecil Finn got a halibut weighing about two stones in Machrie Bay one day and landed it in Campbeltown, but it disappeared from the lorry transporting it to Glasgow market. 'He never arrived in Glesca. He loast his way between Campbeltown an Glesca, so we never got peyed for him.' Next time a halibut was taken, the fish was cut into portions and shared among the crew. [Cecil Finn, 2003]

Most of the halibut James Macdonald saw were caught in deep water on the Gigha fishing grounds, 'jeest nice fish for keepin for yersel, twinty-odd pun an that kinna size'. His biggest was caught in the *slunk** off Port na Cùile, north of Carradale harbour, while bobbin-trawling in his steel *Crimson Arrow*, c. 1972. It weighed about 35 lbs, 'aboot the size o a wee table'. An older fisherman, James 'Rockall' McGeachy, had earlier told him of a halibut of legendary dimensions caught in the same area. When finally taken, its mouth was 'full o hooks', the legacy of previous attempts at capture. [James Macdonald, 2003]

* *A deep, muddy trench in the seabed.*

That halibut, which appeared in the deep water off Carradale in the early part of the twentieth century, is still spoken of in the village. When ring-net crews were *redding*, or clearing, their nets in Port na Cùile after a night's fishing, this 'hell of a size of a fish' would appear to feed on discarded herring. Repeated attempts were made to catch it – some fishermen even had the village blacksmith fashion heavy-duty hooks – but, according to local tradition, it never was captured. [John McConnachie, 2003]

Halibut, albeit of a smaller class, continue to be taken. Prawn-trawling around Gigha, the *Morning Dawn* of Campbeltown caught two in 2002 and three in 2003. [Robert Gillies, 2003]

Turbot

The turbot *Scophthalmus maximus*, round in shape and thick in the flesh, is another prime flatfish species which fetches a high price. It was rarely caught in any abundance except at spawning time in spring, when the fish congregated on certain grounds.

Willie McBride of Pirnmill, Arran, once presented a turbot to a king. The king was Edward VII, who was cruising in Clyde waters, c. 1902, in the royal yacht, *Victoria and Albert*. He declined an invitation to board the yacht and meet Edward, but subsequently received a message of thanks from the King's Private Secretary, and signed by the King himself. [Margaret McBride, 2003]

Turbot

As a schoolboy, Cecil Finn would be on the quay at Campbeltown most evenings, watching the boats landing. When 13 or 14 years of age, he saw the East Coast seiners, *Green Pastures* and *Lochie*, landing daily at about 6 p m in the month of April, 'ten an fifteen boxes o turbot, beautiful big turbot, fae the Soon o Sanna'. They were taking these turbot from a bank, a couple of miles south-east of Glenehervie, which local fishermen called the Wee Bank, because it was a 'one shot' spot, having room enough for only one haul, towing 'through', or against, the strong tides that ran there. However, seiners could 'fire away' on it all day, taking a box or two of quality fish each haul, so that, by the end of the working day, after eight hauls or so, they'd have a profitable catch. By the time Cecil himself was skippering seine-netters, in the 1960s, that bank had been so depleted of turbot that only an 'odd one' would come up in the net.

The biggest turbot Cecil ever saw was taken while single-boat pelagic-trawling with the *Brighter Morn* in the deep waters of the Kilbrannan Sound about 1990. It was a Friday night and the crew was ready to finish for the week. There was a south-westerly gale blowing, so he decided to tow the heavy gear into the lee of Kintyre and lift there rather than out in the channel. They towed in for the south side of Tor Mór, heaving in by degrees, and about half-a-mile from land decided to lift. As they 'birled roon' to leeward, a turbot was noticed in one of the wings of the net. Where the fish had stuck, the meshes were 64 inches from top to bottom, stretched. He was certain the fish would drop out before the net reached the power-block, but it didn't. It weighed almost four stone and sold for £330. 'A lovely big fish.' [Cecil Finn, 2003]

The biggest turbot Robert Ross ever netted weighed four stone. It came up in a seine-net hauled at Pirnmill and 'nearly lifted wee "Kinnon" ower the side'. The big flat was buried under four or five boxes of mixed fish and when Iain McKinnon jumped into the fish-pond to start boxing, the turbot gave a flap and 'lifted him up in the air'. [Robert Ross, 2003]

Sole

Two species of sole – the lemon *Microstomus kitt* and the Dover or, locally, 'black' *Solea solea* – occurred in the waters around Kintyre. Each makes superlative eating and commands a high price on the market, but, of the two, the 'black' has always been by far the rarer and could be counted by individuals caught, not by boxes filled. Many fishermen believed that black sole 'went in pairs' and were consequently often taken together. The same, incidentally, applied to turbot and halibut.

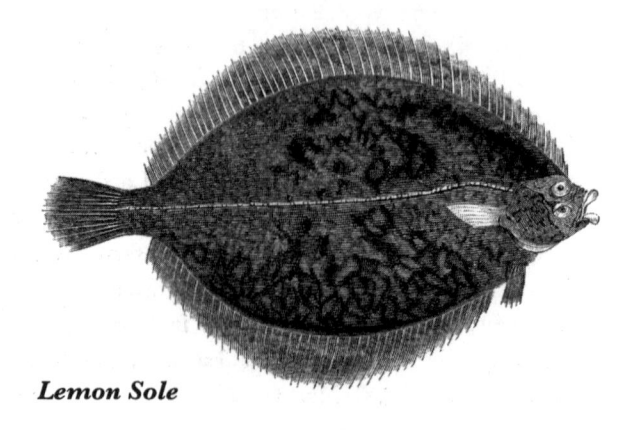

Lemon Sole

Fish-prices dropped in summertime, but, when running to Ayr to land six or seven boxes of lemon soles and perhaps 40 boxes of codling, for two days' fishing, the shot of sole would fetch a higher price than the shot of codling. These sole – which were 'reddish' on the back – were fished on corally sea bottom south of Ru Stafnish. After a week's work there, Cecil Finn recalled, 'when it came Friday, ye wid squeeze the point o yer finger an ye'd take the blood oot it, the four fingers, workin wi the grit. Jeest worn away between liftin the rope an guttin wi the grit'. At that time, there were no gloves for handling ropes and fishermen would rub their fingers with methylated spirit to try to 'firm them up' for the next week. A seiner would wear out 30 coils of manilla rope in a year's work, particularly when fishing frequently over the Ru grounds. [Cecil Finn, 2003]

These sole must have been the 'rid sole' which John McWhirter remembered taking in the small – and illegal – otter-trawl decades earlier. From a stone to a stone-and-a-half of these fish could be caught in a single haul with a low-powered engine. He would head through the Lodan, in the direction of Ailsa Craig, to 'open the Second Waters', shoot the net and then tow towards Auchenhoan Head, from about 16 fathoms of water into 7 or 8, to 'cant her gradually aweh up for the *coves* o the Island*; ye could take her all that distance'. 'A grett place for rid sole. Of coorse, that's afore they're cleanin up stuff; afore everybody wis at it ye'd get fish anywherr. A mind o plenty rid sole.' [John McWhirter, 1974]

* *The caves on the south side of Davaar Island.*

Henry Martin also recalled otter-trawling for lemon soles south of the Lodan, specifically off 'The Watters'*. The trawl, he said, had to be

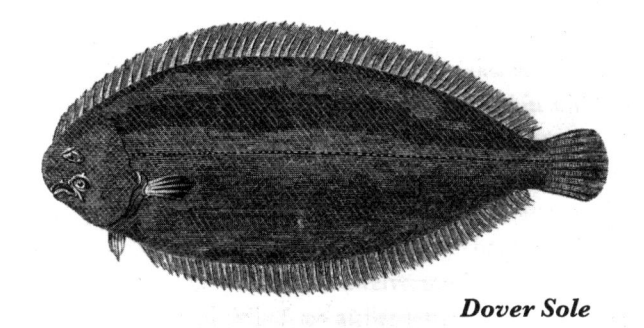

Dover Sole

towed slowly to pick up the sole; and in that area 'clabby doos' (p 76) would clamp on to the netting and fray it. Sole always fetched a 'scatter o shillins' more than plaice, and there was one fish-buyer who would be on the point of Campbeltown Quay every day when the *Fame* came in from fishing, calling: 'Mertin, A'll gie ye such an such a price for the lemon soles!' One day, when sole weren't to be got, the *Fame* went elsewhere and got a fishing of plaice, but that buyer declared, 'A'm naw wantin them', and walked away round the fish-shed. [Henry Martin, 1974]

* *Second Waters, the stream that flows through Balnabraid Glen and enters the sea at The Brig; but there is another stream, the First Waters, further north on the Learside coast.*

One night the *Fame* went into Port Righ and 'tried a *dreg*' of the otter-trawl, heading south for Isla Ross. Another skiff shot abreast of the *Fame* and towed along with her; but off Mecky's (Ugadale Point) both trawls 'got fast'. When the *Fame*'s crew lifted their trawl – 'she wis a wile strong net' – there was a boulder in it and no fish; but the 'Ould Fella' said, 'There used tae be plenty lemon sole doon along here', so they shot again and 'got a grett haal an when it cam dehlight in the moarnin we had a good fishin'. They went close inshore and rid themselves of the boulder by rolling it over the side using a staging-board. 'Ye wid aye get fish efter ye wid lift a big stone lik that. Maybe that wan stone wis makin the grip. We took a wile loat o rid sole oot o that place. Doon at the Watters tae.' [Henry Martin, 1974]

Plaice

The plaice *Pleuronectes platessa* is *leabag* in Gaelic, but is generally – and confusingly – referred to as the *flounder* or *fluke* in Scots. Its red-spotted back makes it one of the most distinctive of flatfish and it has long had a high commercial and culinary value. It feeds on worms, small crustaceans and molluscs. A tagged 'flounder', caught by George McEachran and crew off Auchenhoan Head on 9 March, 1900, had been 'liberated by the Fishery Board's steamer *Garland*' exactly four months earlier in Machrie Bay, on the opposite side of the Kilbrannan Sound.[8]

One September, John McWhirter tried otter-trawling off Keil, Southend, in the hope of taking a fishing of plaice there; but he was disappointed. A fisherman in Campbeltown, known as 'The Dog'*, had told him 'it used tae be a grett place for tryin the *screenge*' (p 52). John shot there in 'eight tae ten fadom', towing for almost 'two mile o a streetch'.

'An it wis supposed tae be a famous place for *flounders*. We hardly got any – a stone or two. They wirna in it. Och, that wid've been afore everythin wis cleaned.' He continued west, almost to the Moil Light, 'tryin a wee *dreg*' in every bay he supposed was sandy-bottomed, but 'got nawthin but wee skate'. In the morning, he headed north to the West Bank, but 'got fast' and tore the net, so he 'never went nae merr efter that'.

A more regular haul was to shoot in 12 fathoms off the Arranman's Barrels buoy and tow north, in 8 and 9 fathoms, until Davaar Lighthouse was opened. There was one snag off Allan's**, on which his gear 'got fast' several times during flood water, but never during ebb. Once the reef below Allan's had been rounded, he'd tow into a 'wee bight' frequented by turbot. When he first trawled that coast, in company with five or six other skiffs, the cod-end of the nets would 'blow on the top o the watter wi codlin an fish – och, an flounders, thon big rid-spotted yins'. [John McWhirter, 1974]

John Cameron, born in Southend, the son of John Cameron and Rosetta Fullarton. He had four brothers – Alexander, James, Charles and Archibald – who were also fishermen in Campbeltown.
**Feochaig, which was farmed by Allan McLean in the mid-nineteenth century.*

Plaice

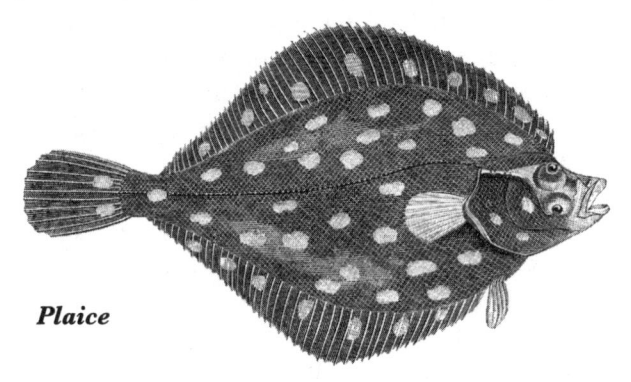

In February, flats came off the shore to congregate and spawn on muddy bottom. There were certain localities which yielded good catches, such as Skipness Bay, a 'corner' at Sgolaig, a *trink* (p 71) at 'the Moil' (Maol Dubh), and a 'wee shot' off Innellan in 40 fathoms of water. Robert Ross recalled a notable catch of plaice taken in a seine-net haul, with four coils a side, at Ettrick Bay, on the west side of Bute. 'Oor keel,' he said, 'wis rubbin in the sand in the heid o Ettrick Bay.' Archie 'Tar' McDougall had been there, trawling, the day before, and got two boxes of 'nice flounders'. Thus encouraged, Robert shot and lifted twenty boxes of fish, six of haddies, four of codling and ten of big plaice, some of them nearly the length of a fish-box and four inches thick in the body. [Robert Ross, 2003]

'Roon the Ru', or south of Ru Stafnish, was a common otter-trawling ground. The plaice caught there were so large that two of them would often 'make a stone', and it was the practice to finish the day's work with a haul further north in the Lodan for smaller plaice in case these were needed to make up weight. Of these giants, Henry Martin remarked: 'They must've been livin there, them flats, fae the beginnin, they wir that big. Well, ye can say it wis cleaned, an we tried it a wheen o times efter, but ye never wid get a fish. Grett big things. They wir big wi half a stone in wan.' [Henry Martin, 1974]

Jenny Lind's Bay, Arran, was a resort of huge plaice, the length of a fish-box and with spots the size of ten pence pieces, 'big grunkeepers' (p 61), as Lawrence Robertson's father called them. Generally, a seine-net haul would yield from three to five of these big fish, after which the fishermen would leave the spot 'for another day'; but Lawrence recalled the Whitehills seiner *Lochie* landing, one night in Campbeltown, c. 1952, some ten boxes of these giant flats from Jenny Lind's. 'Wee Joe', the *Lochie*'s skipper, must have got his net into a bit of clean ground 'amongst the stones' and managed to haul it without breaking a rope or suffering some other mishap, though the day was thick with mist. When boxing these plaice, fishermen would turn the uppermost fish 'white belly up', and that fish would practically cover all the others beneath it. [Lawrence Robertson, 2003]

One Friday, on his way south from hake-fishing at Skipness, Cecil Finn decided to try a 'quick haal' in Carradale Bay in the hope of netting a box of *flukes* to 'make up the pack'. At that time of year – end of August, when farmers on the upper Clyde islands would 'cut the hervest' – the inshore grounds would begin to clear of wrack and, breeze-assisted, it would wash ashore. Too much weed lying on the seabed caused the ropes to become 'glutted up', and hours would be lost cutting the tangles clear. The day was bright and the sandy bottom visible, so Cecil said to his crew: 'We'll steam roon the bay furst an watch for tangles an see if it's thick.' His mother's brother, Archie Blair from Tarbert, was on the bow watching and presently came aft to the wheelhouse and said to Cecil: 'Come on up tae ye see this. Aweh ye go – A'll steer her up.' Cecil duly left the wheel and went forward to look. 'Here wis the flounders, swimmin aheid o the boat, a dozen o them, flappin aweh, the whole wey up intae the bey. The place wis full o flounders.' They shot away and hauled eight or nine boxes of plaice. 'Ye'll naw see that noo.' [Cecil Finn, 2003]

One winter, the *Felicity* of Campbeltown was seining from Tarbert. The weather was 'hellish bad' – south-east wind and snow showers – and her crew 'wirna getting oot'. They were fairly acquaint with the Clyde and ended up in Loch Long, but had to shift from there, possibly owing to submarine activity. The regular skipper, Jock 'Knuckler' Robertson, was ashore for a month and Cecil Finn was in the wheelhouse. He and Jamie McKinven used to ring for mixed herring on the clean ground off Carrick Castle, at the mouth of Loch Goil, so they tried there and hauled 'a scatter o boxes' of fish. The boat's provisions, however, were exhausted, and the crew had decided to return to Tarbert, when Cecil remarked to James: 'Dae ye ever mind o getting the *flukes* up at the heid o the Loch, Jamie?' They used to ring there, too, in the mornings, and would lift a scoopful of plaice. 'A mind we used tae get them, right enough, Cecil.' – 'A wonder wid it be worth gan up a wee run an tryin it?' Cecil continued. James, however, was doubtful on account of the wartime acoustic mines that might be encountered there. 'We'll go up a run an try it,' Cecil decided. They did just that and, with reduced rope, netted a couple of boxes of flukes and a box of big *plowt*, or freshwater flounders, which had roe in them, but which they didn't keep, owing to their low value. The *Felicity*'s crew took fifty boxes of *flukes* out of that spot in a week's fishing. [Cecil Finn, 2003]

The Boat, near the mouth of Loch Caolisport, was a good spot for plaice. Robert Ross got a box there prawn-trawling one day in the *Dalriada*. 'Peggy's Joan' (John Black: his mother was Peggy MacAlister) was aboard with them, filling in time until 'Bibie' (Iain McNab) had his new steel boat, the *Girl Seona*, built*. Robert took the *Dalriada* into Scotnish to lie the night there, and on the way in John gutted and boiled a 'braw male o flounders'. By the time they moored, the meal was ready. When Robert went down into the forecastle, he found the table 'laid out beautiful' with a big flounder on each plate. 'The smell,' he said, 'wis gan roon ma hert.' As Robert began eating, John gave him a sly wink before turning to the other crew member, Malcolm 'Tamar' Johnson, who was 'awful finicky' when it came to food. 'Well, A always mind, there wis wan thing old "Poogie" (Archie McDougall) used tae say: "Wan fish that wisna worth eatin roond here wis a flounder. There a taste o wreck (seaweed) off it."' This remark had the desired effect – 'Tamar' began spitting out the fish and finally 'clattered the plate over the side', declaring: 'Aye, fuckin wreck – there's a taste o wreck off it! "Poogie" wis right!' [Robert Ross, 2003]

*She was launched in 1968.

Witches

The witch *Glyptocephalus cynoglossus* is a thin, insubstantial flatfish and poor eating. When Campbeltown and Ayrshire boats began working the Gigha grounds, c. 1950, 10 boxes of witches for two days' fishing was not an unusual landing (p 22). 'If ye go tae Gigha noo, A doubt very much if ye'll see wan witch for a week. They wir there then, before the boats started on them.' [Cecil Finn, 2003]

Freshwater flukes

The flounder *Platichthys flesus*, also known as the *freshwater fluke* or *plowt*, and, among Tarbert fishermen, the *black mole*, is the one native flatfish which is tolerant of fresh water and can be found in estuaries, rivers and burns, and in such bodies of fresh water as Loch Lomond.

They could be got in the Dubh Chaol-linn in East Loch Tarbert, Fairlie Sound, at the mouth of Inverkip and elsewhere, but were an unattractive fish – black-spotted on the underside and 'muddy' in the flesh – and seldom fetched more than a 'couple of bob a stone' in the market. [Robert Ross, 2003] The week that the *Felicity* took 50 boxes of plaice from the head of Loch Goil (p 93), about the same quantity of flounders came up in the net; but many of these fish, having little market value, had probably been taken and released repeatedly. 'They wir lik blottin-paper,' Cecil Finn remarked. 'Och, ye'd eat them right enough if ye'd naethin else tae eat.' [2003]

Flounder

Spearing

Flatfish, being the shape they are, present an easy target for the spear. The 'flounders' here referred to were probably primarily *Platichthys flesus*, which delight in shallow water, unlike plaice. 'Tramping' flounders in shallow water required bare feet. 'You feel with the feet as you might feel with the hands,' Bob Smith explained. 'You touch it, pin it with your foot, inspect it for size, and, if it's big enough, spear it. A sharpened stick is enough, but with that you have to stab the fish in a small and exact spot. A two- or three-pronged *leister* (spear) is more efficient, and that's what's used from a boat.'

From a boat, 'dead calm and a suitable angle of light' were requisites, though a spear-fisher could 'work away in a slight ripple'. In calm conditions, a solitary man could fish by 'drifting about', but the operation was more efficient with two men aboard, one to manoeuvre the boat and the other to wield the *leister*, its long shaft heavily weighted with lead just above the spear itself. [Bob Smith, 2003]

Dick Gillon in Southend was 'a great man for spearing flounders' to sell around the village. Young Hugh McShannon often took Dick's boat and fish-spear and went out into Dunaverty Bay and along Keil shore, punting the boat along with the spear on the sandy bottom. On a quiet day, the fish lying half-buried in the sand were quite visible in water 12 or 15 feet deep, but it was necessary to 'creep up very slowly to them because ye wid upset them, ye wid startle them, an they wid be away before ye got near them'. It was no difficult matter to spear half-a-dozen flounders during one outing and Hugh considered it 'a great sport'. Spears were made by local blacksmiths and consisted of an iron socket with a 'little barb' forged on to it about two inches from the point. The wooden shaft, on to which the spear was fitted, was as long the boat. [Hugh McShannon, 1982] As a boy, Donald MacDonald of Gigha speared flounders by wading out over the sandy seabottom at Port nan Cudainnean, where he was brought up. His spear was a length of wire and he watched for fish 'working, the sand being shifted, an just plonk it down an get them caught on the barb'. [1978]

'Back to the old days'

When Bob Smith, during his time at Auchindrain Museum (p 54), wanted flounders, he would go to Brainport bay and fish for them – with rod, line and lugworm – 'on the face of the incoming tide'. The way along the beach to the bay took him past the bottom of some gardens, and one day an old woman, who was tending her roses, 'nailed' him for a blether. When he told her he was 'after a flounder or two', she begged him to give her some, if he had any to spare, saying that she hadn't tasted a locally-caught flounder in over fifty years. Bob duly handed her a pair on his way back, and when he returned about a fortnight later, to catch the same tide, the woman was waiting for him. Her sister, she said apologetically, would like a flounder as well. 'It's jist that it takes us back to the old days,' she explained. He got a half-bottle of Bell's whisky thrust on him and, as he remarked, 'far better than that, the information that many households had a *leister*. Bob was eventually able to acquire several of these fish-spears for the museum. [Bob Smith, 2003]

References and Notes
1. *AH*, 9 May 1868.
2. *CC*, 5 April 1879.
3. *Ibid.*, 25 Feb 1882.
4. *Ibid.*, 11 July 1891.
5. *AH*, 15 Feb 1913.
6. Campbeltown Fishery Office records, 29 March 1913.
7. *Scottish Fisheries Bulletin*, No 18, p 26.
8. *CC*, 24 March 1900.

Skate and Ray

Skates and rays, though flat like flatfish, are actually closely related to sharks; indeed, they evolved from the sharks some 100 million years ago. That evolutionary process adapted the skate and ray for their particular hunting strategy, which is to lie flat on the seabed, camouflaged and watchful, and capture passing prey by swooping over and covering it. This strategy required a further biological adaptation: the skate, when half-buried in mud, is able to take in clean sea-water through the spiracle, or nostril, on the top of its head instead of through the buried mouth.[1] There is no biological difference between skates and rays – the simple distinction is that the ray is short-nosed and the skate long-nosed. The so-called 'wings' of the fish – actually the pectoral fins – are the only marketable parts.

After mating, the female releases eggs contained in flat, leathery pouches, which are shiny black when weathered. These capsules – not to be confused with the small, elongated amber-coloured cases produced by the spotted dogfish *Scyliorhinus stellaris* and *S caniculus* – can be found washed ashore, in which innocuous state – empty after hatching – they are romantically known as 'mermaid's purses'. Some fawn-coloured fibre-coated specimens encountered on the Atlantic coast of Kintyre are of remarkable dimensions, up to 10 inches by 6 in their moist state, excluding the mooring tendrils at either end. I sent an example to the Natural History Museum in London, but the Department of Zoology there admitted the impossibility of identification. 'There exists no comprehensive literature which could be used as a reference. Only a few

Skate

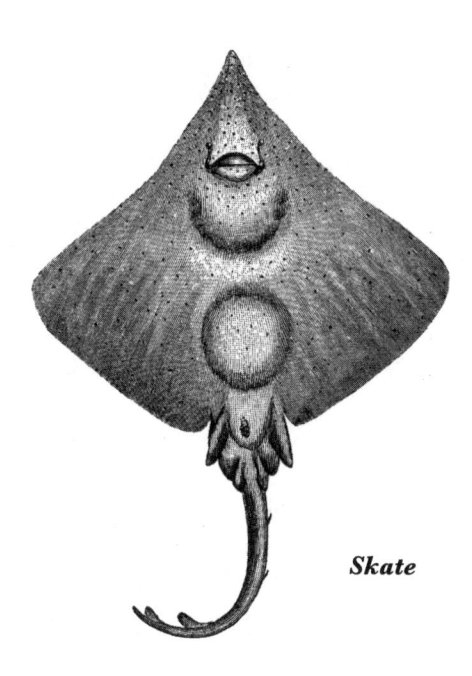

have been described and identified with certainty.'[2]

All skate are of the genus *Rajidae*, but the species this chapter deals with is principally *Raja batis*, the common skate, also known as the 'grey skate' or 'blue skate', but not by the generality of fishermen, who have their own regional names. To many East Coast fishermen a large, long-lived skate is a *barndoor* (across the Atlantic, in New England, the name for *Raja laevis*), but in Kintyre alone there are two names, in Tarbert *gobach odhar* and in Campbeltown *dunny*. *Gobach* relates to the fish's long nose and *odhar* to its coloration – tawny, yellowish, pale, dun, etc. – which latter term might just link with the otherwise obscure *dunny*.

The dimensions of these large skate have been well documented, as the following catalogue shows. In September, 1894, one of the Largs, Ayrshire, fishing-boats landed and despatched to Glasgow a skate measuring 7 ft by 5 ft 1 in and weighing about 10 stones. The record skate 'for these waters' was understood to be a specimen weighing 14 stones landed by Billy Blair, 'the famous old-time yacht-sailing master'.[3] Another giant skate, 6 ft 9 ins long by 5 ft 3 ins broad, was taken on a long-line at the mouth of Lowlandman's Bay, Jura, by D Galbraith in June 1906. 'The combined strength of three men aboard the small craft was required to land the monster. Its great weight almost capsized the boat.'[4] In July, 1913, a Carradale fisherman, Lachlan Paterson, recorded in his notebook, 'Caught a skate 170 lb. in the Trammel Net'.[5]

Lifting a house

When hauling big lines, if a large skate would take the bait, 'ye'd be as well tae try an lift a hoose'. 'There's a gobachoar on!' would be the cry. A combination of weight and flatness of form made the big skate a difficult fish to raise. 'Ye'd think the lines wir fast on the bottom,' Hugh MacFarlane of Tarbert recalled. When the skate would 'nose up' from the seabed and the line lose its tension, the crew would haul in that slack until the skate stalled again. When the fish would give another 'jump', that would be more slack line to take in, and so the struggle would continue until the giant was brought alongside. [Hugh MacFarlane, 1978]

The yarns of Hugh's older brother, Sandy 'Fadye' MacFarlane, were legendary. One day he was telling Sandy Sutherland of a skate he caught that was so big he couldn't tow it round the perch at the entrance to Tarbert harbour. One wing got stuck on the perch and the other got stuck on MacArthur's Island* and the crew had to 'wing it' – cut off the wings – before they could reach the quay. Sandy listened to this and then dismissed it with the words: 'Ach, that's naethin at all.' A skate caught in the Pentland Firth was so big that 'we had tae put a mastheid light an a port an starboard light on it when we wir towin it'. Sandy Sutherland was a native of Findochty, in Moray, who came to Tarbert during the Second World War with his three brothers in the *Lassie* and returned year after year. [Robert Ross, 2003]

Named after a MacArthur who kept a goat on the island.

When Cecil Finn was 13 or 14 years old, a Campbeltown seiner, the *Betty*, owned by Tommy Meenan, caught a huge skate at the Brown Head. The fish was stuck in the mouth of the net and the crew just 'whipped' net and skate aboard. When laid across the hatch of the *Betty*, the tips of its wings were said to have just cleared each rail of the boat, the beam of which exceeded 13 ft. The crew landed the skate on the quay at Campbeltown and with hatchets hacked its wings into chunks, which filled, Cecil thought, no fewer than 14 boxes. [Cecil Finn, 2003]

A distinctive fish

These skate had negligible commercial value, and it was the practice among most fishermen to release them once they had been freed from the net. Fishermen were quite certain that many of these fish were caught and released repeatedly and this was proved, to Cecil Finn's satisfaction, in the Sound of Sanda. A *dunny* there, distinctive by a ring of copper piping which had been placed over its tail and become embedded there by successive growth, would be netted 'nearly on a weekly basis'. 'Here we go again!' the crew would complain when the net came up with the skate in it; but it would always be liberated. Then a day came, when, on the quay at Campbeltown, Cecil and his crew saw the fish in a box. 'Somebody had knifed it.' [Cecil Finn, 2003]

No market

In Lawrence Robertson's earliest years seine-netting, *dunnies* were taken quite frequently between the Ru and Feochaig. Once aboard and freed from the net, they would be 'winged' and landed – each wing would yield about four stone of flesh – but finally there was no market for them and they would be released. [Lawrence Robertson, 2003]

Giving assistance

Dunnies were particularly thick in the sea-lochs north of Gigha. 'If ye got one, ye got bugger all else,' Cecil Finn said. 'The net jeest stopped workin.' When Cecil got his steel boat, the *Gleaner*, in 1968, she proved unsuited to seine-netting, for which she had been built. 'The hydraulics,' he said, 'wir overpowerin the engine', and he wasn't able to work at seining until an auxiliary engine was installed to drive the seine-net winch. In the interval, he went prawn-trawling 'roon the West Side'. One night, after he had hove up his trawl, Archie 'Tar' McDougall – a Tarbert skipper and cousin of Cecil's mother – called him on the radio. 'Cecil,' he said, 'will ye come an gie us a hand here?' – 'Whoot is it?' Cecil enquired. 'A big gobachoar. A canna get the bastard oot. He's stuck in the middle o the net.' Cecil went at once, thinking it would simply be a case of going alongside the *Trustful* and giving Archie 'a pull'; but the skate was 'massive' and required both Archie's and Cecil's derricks combined to lift it out of the water and cut it clear of the net. 'There wis quite a good list on us tae get him up,' Cecil recalled. 'God knows how many times he'd been lifted.' [Cecil Finn, 2003]

Working big lines in the early twentieth century, Hugh MacFarlane saw huge catches of skate of marketable size. 'Skate wis terrific at thon time,' he recalled. 'Ye wid get wan every hook near o skate. That's when we used the *cleep* (gaff). If ye'd get them now, ye'd make a small fortune. A seen us haevin tae take two runs wi the boat wi skate an eels.' The conger eels weren't so welcome, but the skate fetched two shillings a box, which was little enough considering the quantity a box was forced to hold. 'Two shillins for a big box, an eight-stone box, an they'd be wi thir feet, the buyers, *champin* (stamping) them into the box. Two bob – that's what we wir getting!' [Hugh MacFarlane, 1976]

Rays

The thornback ray or roker *Raja clavata* does not attain anything like the dimensions of the common skate, but it has commercial value and Kirkcaldy-registered long-liners fished it annually off Gigha during February or early March. The last to work there was probably the *Silver Chord* in about 1950.[6] Robert Gillies has seen 10 to 12 boxes of thornbacks taken daily in September on the fishing grounds around Gigha – he consigns his catches to Fleetwood market, where higher prices tend to prevail – and in September, 2003, the Tarbert prawn-trawlers *Fionnaghal* and *Frigate Bird* were catching up to 40 boxes daily at the mouth of Loch Stornoway, Kilberry; but that abundance lasted only a few days. The blonde ray *Raja brachyura* and spotted ray *Raja montagui* are also caught locally and marketed. [Robert Gillies, 2003]

Thornback Ray

As food

Skate, as a locally-consumed food resource, figures but scantily in oral tradition. In Pirnmill, Arran, however, the fish was favoured among fishing families. In spring, the heads and tails of line-caught skate would be cut off and the remaining 'wings', still joined, suspended from a clothes-line by a string tied around the middle. They would be allowed to hang for up to a fortnight, then taken down, broken apart, skinned and parboiled before frying. 'It was lovely,' Margaret McBride recalled, adding: 'I never ever remember seeing maggots in them.' [Margaret McBride, 2003]

References and Notes
1. J Crompton, *The Living Sea*, London 1957, p 132-35.
2. A Martin, *The Kintyre Magazine*, Campbeltown, No 31, pp 18-19.
3. *CC*, 15 Sept 1894.
4. *Ibid.*, 30 June 1906.
5. Notebook in possession of Lachie Paterson, Carradale.
6. Jim Tarvit, letter to author, 10 May 2003.

Other Species

Anglerfish

The anglerfish *Lophius piscatorius*, which can exceed 6 ft in length, is locally referred to as a 'monk', but the true monkfish *Squatina squatina* is a fish of temperate seas and related to the sharks. Robert Ross, however, recalled seeing, on Tarbert Quay in the 1960s, a specimen of *Squatina squatina* which Ronnie Johnson had trawled up in the Clyde. [2003] The anglerfish, it has to be admitted, is one of the ugliest of fish, appearing to be all head and mouth, but it does have a short, tapering tail of delicious white flesh, much prized in restaurants. It takes its name from its habit of lying concealed in mud and agitating its rod-like fore dorsal ray, which has a growth of shiny skin on its free end, to lure unsuspecting fish towards the lurking maw.

In Robert Ross's earliest years as a fisherman, there was no market for monks and they'd be returned to the sea. He recalled one individual, caught in the *Psyche's* seine-net off the Red Wharf at Skipness around 1946, which was almost 6 ft in length and took four men to heave overboard. Some fishermen would place a large, square biscuit-tin in the mouth of a big monk just to see it crushed in the powerful jaws, and in the 1960s Willie Dickson, part-owner of the *Gleaner* of Tarbert, had his foot bitten by a monk which 'snapped at him like a dog'. [Robert Ross, 2003]

The name 'miller's thoomb', for the anglerfish, is practically obsolete and appears to have been chiefly used among Campbeltown fishermen.[1]

Anglerfish

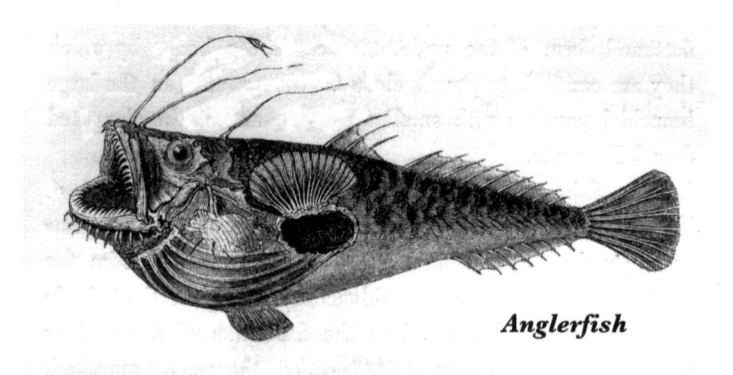

The name is normally applied to the tiny freshwater bullhead *Cottus gobio*. In Tarbert, the anglerfish is 'craig-goo', Gaelic *creag dhubh*, 'black rock'.[2]

When James 'P O' Morrans crewed with Robbie McKellar on the *Royal Burghs* of Campbeltown, it was his job to tie the cod-end of the net after every shot. One morning, P O neglected to tie the string, which was greased to render the knot easier released should the cod-end come up heavy. When the bag did come up, after the haul, 'the cod-end string wis flappin aweh' and the bag was, of course, completely empty. Nothing much was said about this oversight of P O's, but later in the day, when work was in full swing, he walked aft to the wheelhouse and addressed his skipper: 'Robbie, A've been worryin all day how that cod-en string wis open. A know now whoot happened.' – 'What's that, P O?' said Robbie. 'Well,' James continued, 'see when the cod-en lay on the bottom, wi the grease on the rope there wir a miller's thoomb* came along an caught the rope an opened it.' [Robert Ross, 2003]

**Cecil Finn heard another version of that story, in which the culprit, attracted to the grease, was a seal.*

On breezy mornings, when boats couldn't put to sea, there would be a movement of men to certain forecastles, where, packed tight, they would drink tea and exchange stories. Willie Wareham, who fished for many years with his kinsman, James Wareham, in the *Jessie* of Campbeltown, was 'good wi the yarns' and loathe to allow anyone to better him. During one of those sessions, somebody told of a miller's thoomb that was so big, 40 fathoms of gut was unravelled from its belly. 'Ye wid hardly believe that,' some credulous soul remarked. 'Well,' Willie said, 'I can believe it,' then proceeded to tell of a specimen caught one day in the Lodan. 'There wis a box-an-a-half o haddies in him,' Willie assured his audience. [Cecil Finn, 2003]

Gurnards

In Gaelic, both the grey gurnard *Eutrigla gurnardus* and red *Aspitrigla cuculus* are known as *cròdan*, widely corrupted into *owdan* in South Kintyre. These colourful fish, with their big armour-plated heads and spine-like pectoral fins, are unmistakable. On the Scottish East Coast the gurnard is known as the *crooner*, among other related names, owing to the groaning noise generated by certain muscles in the walls of the swim-bladder, which vibrate rapidly when contracted.[3] 'Ye wid hear the kinna syllable, a growl comin oot it. Croothan the ould men called it. It's a very stabby fish. They kinna girn right enough when ye wid lift them up… Ye wid feel the vibration in the fish.' [Hugh MacFarlane, 1976]

Localised gurnard fisheries have been recorded. At Craignish (p 51), in the mid-nineteenth century, it was fished 'to the west in summer', the 'natives' having recently 'become fond of the fish'. As a by-product, oil was extracted from its head and intestines.[4] There was a gurnard fishery using ring-nets at Duart in the Sound of Mull. The fish fetched four or five shillings per 'drywood' half-barrel, which was the container in use at that fishery. [Hugh MacFarlane, 1976] A ring-net fishery was also prosecuted in Skye waters for several years, until the gurnards suddenly disappeared.[5]

One day, in November, 1905, the beach at Bellochantuy, on the west side of Kintyre, was found to be 'literally covered' with in excess of three tons of gurnards. There were 'many conjectures', locally, as to how the fish came to be stranded there, but the generally accepted theory was that they'd been caught and discarded by the crew of a steam trawler which had been seen working offshore on the previous day. The fish, being 'quite fresh and good', were gathered up by the locals, 'who were not slow in taking advantage of this unique opportunity of obtaining a good supply of fish for nothing, "oudans" being very palatable'.[6]

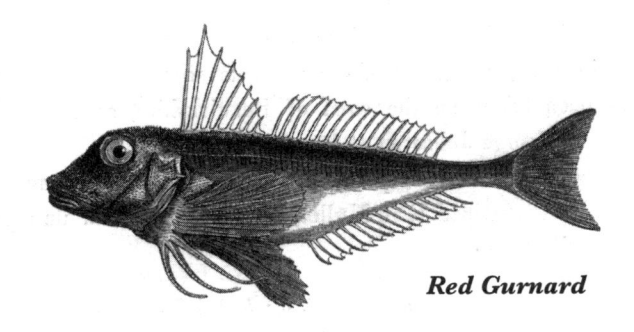

Red Gurnard

Lt. Sydney Jinks, Royal Naval Reserve, who died in 1965, was a Fleetwood trawler-skipper who was stationed in Campbeltown during the Second World War. Like Jack Dansey, a Hull trawler-skipper who also found himself in Campbeltown, Sid met and married a local woman – Jessie McKay – and remained after the war, forsaking distant-water trawling in steel for ring-netting in wood.

Syd had command, during the War, of one of the armed Norwegian whalers which escorted convoys entering and leaving the North Channel. James Macdonald crewed with Syd on the *Golden Hind* in the early 1950s and Syd told him that, when fishing Icelandic grounds between the wars, if a trip had failed to meet expectations, perhaps owing to bad weather, on his passage home to Fleetwood he would go into Machrihanish Bay and tow for gurnards to 'top up the trip'. [James Macdonald, 2003]

The only bulk of 'croodans' Robert Ross ever saw was taken by seine-net north of the buoy at Skipness in the summer of 1946 when he was a boy aboard Angie 'Molly' Johnson's *Pysche*. They had four or five boxes of the fish, which they landed in Tarbert. 'We gutted them an when we took them in we wir told there wir money for them if they wirna gutted!' [Robert Ross, 2003]

George Newlands considered them 'grett tae eat' and recalled taking some home and showing his young wife, Jeannie, who was 'keen on guttin the fish', how to manage the owdan. It had to be skinned, but being 'aa spikes thegither, ye'd tae be very very wary'. George would fry or steam the fish, just as he would a haddie. 'A lovely fish, a lovely taste off it. In fact, I'd sooner have an owdan as a haddie. Ye never wid get many o them, though.' [George Newlands, 1976]

While seining in the Sound of Sanda, c. 1958, the *Felicity*'s crew got talking to Billy Gilchrist and Duncan McKerral, who were creel-fishing for lobsters in the same area with a small motor-boat. They were getting some lobsters but complained of lack of bait and asked the seiners to keep unwanted fish for them. There were no small fish at all in the Sound at the time, only a 'scatter' of owdans. 'Ye aye avoided them,' Cecil Finn said, 'because ye'd get a nesty jag off them. Anyway, we *clatted* (gathered) them up this deh for them an gied them a couple o boxes o owdans.' A few days later, off the Ru, they encountered the lobster-boat again and went alongside. Billy and Duncan had 'a hoora dose o lobsters aathegither' boxed in the boat and said that they had never before seen a fishing like it, which they attributed to the 'grett bait'. Cecil would eat an owdan occasionally, fried, but only the big, bright-red ones, which were about a foot in length and quite fat. The flesh was very white, but rather too sweet for his taste. [Cecil Finn, 2003]

Ling

The ling *Molva molva*, cod-green and eel-long, is a solitary deep-water fish, traditionally caught by long line for salting and drying. In the 1780s, Campbeltown fishermen were instructed in long-lining by fishermen from Port of Rush, Ireland, and in 1787 exported no fewer than 27,390 dried ling to Spain.[7] Ling remains a favourite among the older generation, and the occasional trawl-caught fish is eagerly received for salting and hanging to dry. Among Tarbert fishermen, the ling was prized in its fresh state. 'That wis the one fish they wid take home aheid o any other fish,' Robert Ross remarked. [2003] Robert Gillies is of a similar mind. He considers ling 'the cleanest fish in the sea', and, aboard his *Morning Dawn*, to this day, the regular Thursday dinner at sea is fresh ling boiled and eaten with white sauce and potatoes. [2003]

Ling

Pouting

The pouting or bib *Trisopterus luscus*, known in Kintyre by its Scots name *gildee* – 'gold eye', from its large glowing eyes – is invariably discarded when caught in trawls. At an earlier period, they were taken on small lines, but, having no commercial value, would be left on the hooks and 'throwed in the *troch*' with the tangle of hauled lines. Hugh MacFarlane considered them 'better than whitins' and would 'go through the troch for the gildees, string them up an I'd have a *touch*. Many a time I've strung a dozen o them on a string an got a bob (shilling) or more'. They were a small fish, except in West Loch Tarbert, where 'fine big ones' could be taken. [Hugh MacFarlane, 1976]

Ballan Wrasse

Known throughout Kintyre as 'creggag', 'craigach' or 'criggach' – Gaelic *creagag* – the wrasse *Labrus bergylta* were quite plentiful among the wrack of rocky coasts. Hugh MacFarlane fished them 'many a time' from the Perch rocks, at the entrance to Tarbert harbour. 'An odd fella wid take the bait. Ye wid catch them wi the hook. Kinna riddish an some o them kinna blueish. But a very very wee mooth, more jeest sookin the bait. Quite edible; big eyes lik a *gildee*.' [1978] Robert Ross saw a few taken in splash-nets hauled on the West Shore and Erines shore. They'd be up to 3lb in weight and old John Weir would take them home and cook them. [2003]

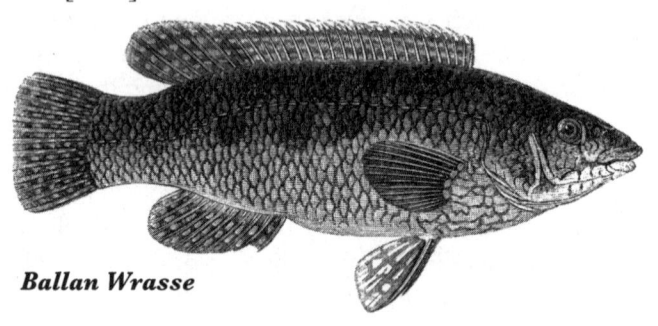

Ballan Wrasse

Basking Shark

The basking shark *Cetorhinus maximus* is the second largest fish in the sea, after the whale shark of the Pacific. From its high dorsal fin came both its Kintyre Scots name *sell-fish* (sail-fish) and its Tarbert Gaelic name 'sholltar' (*seòldair*, sailor). Particulars of maximum weight and dimensions vary wildly from source to source – suffice to say that six tons in weight and 30 ft long might not be far off the mark. It feeds by straining plankton through the comb-like gill-rakers of its immense gaping mouth and is therefore inoffensive to all but the minutiae of sea-life; yet by its sheer bulk alone it can endanger small boats and damage and destroy nets.

The basking shark's huge oil-rich liver made it a target for opportunistic harpooners on the west coasts of Ireland and Scotland. The Welsh naturalist, Thomas Pennant, in his *A Tour in Scotland and Voyage to the Hebrides* (1772), penned a vivid account of shark-fishing from Arran. While visiting Lochranza he was able to examine the carcass of a 27 ft 4 in-long shark which had been harpooned several days before. He also took the trouble to sensitively and accurately record the Arran islanders' fishing practices:

> They are very tame or very stupid; and permit the near approach of man: will suffer a boat to follow them without accelerating their motion, till it comes almost within contact when a harpooner strikes

his weapon into the fish as near the gills as possible; but they are often so insensible as not to move untill the united strength of two men has forced in the harpoon deeper: as soon as they perceive themselves wounded, they fling up their tail and plunge headlong to the bottom, and frequently coil the rope round them in their agonies, attempting to disengage themselves from the weapon by rolling on the ground, for it is often found greatly bent. As soon as they discover that their efforts are in vain, they swim away with amazing rapidity and with such violence that a vessel of 70 tuns has been towed by them against a fresh gale: they sometimes run off with 200 fathoms of line, and with two harpoons in them; and will find employ to the fishers for twelve and sometimes twenty-four hours before they are subdued. When killed they are either hauled on shore, or if at a distance, to the vessel's side. The liver (the only useful part) is taken out and melted into oil in vessels provided for that purpose: a large fish will yield eight barrels of oil, and two of sediment, and prove a profitable capture.[8]

Basking Shark

In the early nineteenth century, the Commissioners and Trustees for Fisheries, Manufacturers and Improvements in Scotland encouraged fishermen to compete for premiums – up to £14 for the greatest quantity produced – on both shark ('sun or sail fish') and dogfish oil and advised on how best to produce that oil: '... to free it of dreg and any putrid smell, the liver of the fish should be melted the day the fish is caught. The quantity of salt to be put into the kettle along with the liver, should be in the proportion of half a pound to ten English Gallons of Oil. And as soon as the Oil comes to be boiling, it should then be taken off the fire, and allowed to cool.'[9] The decline of the primitive and dangerous shark-fishery began with the withdrawal of that oil bounty and was compounded by the appearance of the paraffin-lamp, which effectively ended reliance on fish-oil as a lighting fuel.

Nonetheless, shark-hunting was revived in the Clyde in 1938 by

Anthony Watkins, who established an oil-processing factory at Carradale, and, following the wartime hiatus, resumed operations in 1946 employing local fishermen to crew three harpoon-boats and a steam-drifter converted to serve as a floating factory. His adventure, which paralleled that of Gavin Maxwell in the Hebrides, is related in *The Sea My Hunting Ground*, which appeared in 1958 and has tended to be overshadowed by Maxwell's *Harpoon at a Venture*, published six years earlier.

Donald McIntosh, who was born in Carradale in 1893, maintained that there were 'very few [sharks] comin in' when he first went to the fishing in about 1907. 'It wis efter the Furst World War, that's when they became more numerous.' When the wind was from the north, an 'awful smell' from Watkins's factory pervaded the village, and the carcasses, dumped offshore to lie and rot on the bottom, released an oily slick to the surface and could be smelled for months afterwards. [Donald McIntosh, 1974]

Still another revival in shark-fishing – this later one attracting the critical attention of conservationists – was initiated in the late 1970s by an Ayrshire fisherman, Howard McCrindle, as a seasonal alternative to trawling, and ended in 1993 with the breaking up of his vessel, the *Star of David*, under the Government's 'decommissioning' scheme.[10]

Traditionally, basking sharks were seen by fishermen only in summer and mysteriously disappeared before the arrival of winter. With the onset of high-powered deep-water fishing, however, that perception altered. During the winter herring and hake fisheries of the 1970s and '80s, sharks were frequently lifted from the seabed within the Clyde, particularly in October and November. Though often 'lively' enough when brought to the surface, the fishermen's belief was that these sharks had been 'lying ticking over' on the bottom. [Lachie Paterson, 2003]

In one of Ronnie Johnson's fishing diaries, he records two sharks caught within a week in January, 1975, while mid-water trawling for herring with the *Taeping* in lower Loch Fyne. On Wednesday 22nd, he noted: 'Shark in net in 6 a.m. haul. Towed it to the Moil bay and got rid of it.' On the 27th: 'Tow, north of Tarbert harbour. Shark in net again!'[11] It was generally believed that unless a net, in which a shark had been caught, was thoroughly cleaned after mending, the smell of the slime would soon attract another shark to the net; and it was not uncommon to see two or three shark-damaged mid-water trawls at a time laid out for repair on Tarbert quay. [Peter McDougall, 2003]

On account of the sheer bulk and weight of the basking shark, the general inconvenience and specific damage to gear entailed in netting one was frequently such an annoyance that some vindictive skippers would have the hapless beast hoisted aloft and killed by severing its tail. The putrefying carcasses of these giants – brought up already dead in pelagic trawls and dumped, or despatched in the settling of scores – were occasionally lifted from the seabed in prawn-trawls, with harrowing consequences for the unlucky crews.

Live sharks were also taken in prawn-trawls. Peter McDougall, in the *Silver Spray* of Tarbert, lifted one from 70 or 80 fathoms depth between Skipness and the Cock of Arran around Christmas c. 1970 and towed the carcass to Tarbert harbour to dispose of it. [2003] A shark James Macdonald got in the 1970s off Machrie Bay was a summer fish, netted as the *Crimson Arrow*'s prawn-trawl was being raised to the surface. The shark, still inside the net, was winched tail-first to the top of the 20 ft gantry; then the wings of the net were let go with 56 lb weights attached, and the big fish dropped back into the sea from the cod-end. Its nose was rubbed raw by the synthetic twine stretched tight around it, and none of the crew expected the shark to survive its half-hour manhandling. Having hit the water and sounded, however, the shark soon reappeared astern and burst clean out of the water; and it leapt and plunged away through the Kilbrannan Sound until out of sight. There was a trainee fisherman aboard, whose first day it was on a fishing-boat, and he was wide-eyed with astonishment at these goings-on. [James Macdonald, 2003]

The *Crimson Arrow* (built in Campbeltown in 1970) was sold in 1974 to Dugald Coutts Campbell in Carradale and became *Dawn Carol*. Thereafter, acquired by Howard McCrindle, she was the shark-catcher *Star of David*.

When Alasdair Macleod and his son Donald were out hand-lining for saithe or mackerel in Loch Fyne, for several years in the mid-1960s they encountered basking sharks. The sharks, which arrived in Upper Loch Fyne in late July or early August, appeared to be curious and would follow the boat, with the consequence that no fish could be caught. Alasdair Macleod, however, solved the problem. 'He carried a five-gallon drum of waste tractor-oil and when a shark started to follow, poured the black oil on the sea. The shark soon was off!' [Donald Macleod, 2003] Ring-net fishermen used diesel-oil to deter sharks from entering their nets.[12]

The basking shark is now unquestionably in serious decline. No longer are great shoals seen, such as the 43 counted by Sir Alister Hardy in Loch Fyne in 1952[13] or the 26 congregated at the mouth of Carradale harbour one evening in the summer of 1978 or '79.[14] A solitary shark, sighted off

Carradale harbour in August, 2003, by a visitor, merited a report in the *Campbeltown Courier* under the headline 'Shark Spotted at Carradale'.[15] In the previous year, only one basking shark was reported off the entire Scottish coast![16]

Basking sharks, unlike the whales and dolphins with which they share the sea, are not mammals, i e warm-blooded and 'brainy' like ourselves, and their plight has failed to evoke the emotive response which made 'Save the Whale' such a powerful ecological rallying cry. Yet, through accidental netting, tactical persecution and commercial exploitation – not least by Norwegian interests – in the last century, the basking shark, which remains very much a biological enigma, has been declared 'vulnerable'. It is to be hoped that the statutory protection now afforded them is effective in regenerating the stock.

Dogfish

Two species of these small sharks were commonly encountered, the spurdog *Squalus acanthias* and the lesser-spotted *Scyliorhinus caniculus*. The former moves in large predatory shoals and is fished commercially, by net and line, though generally marketed under fictitious names to disguise its shark identity. Its chief characteristics are the spikes or spurs (hence the name 'spurdog') on the fore end of the dorsal fins, and the sharp nose, or *gob*, from which it derives its Gaelic name – *gobag* – in Tarbert.

Spurdog

The spikes of large dogfish will penetrate the sole of a rubber seaboot and a jag from one can cause poisoning serious enough to require medical attention. Spurdogs were sometimes taken among herring in ring-nets, and if a fisherman discharging a catch suffered a jag while working in the hold, the standard advice was to rub the wound with methylated spirit, which was kept for igniting the primus stove. [Robert Gillies, 2003] One jag Robert Ross received while discharging herring from the *Elma* of Carradale in 1954 left him with a stiffened finger for a week. He believed the poison from the spike of a dead dogfish to be more potent than that from a living one. [2003] Our ancestors, however, saw in these spikes potential tools. When excavated archaelogically in the 1970s, King's Cave on Jura yielded, among its organic artefacts, 14 dogfish spikes, one of which had been worked into a tool and showed signs of use. A similar spike excavated in Denmark, and dated to around 5000 years ago, had apparently been used as a combined awl and needle.[17]

The spurdog is viviparous and can give birth to up to a dozen pups, on occasion when writhing helplessly on the deck of a fishing-boat. When encountered in packs on herring-fishing grounds, dogs could badly damage nets by their habit of snatching an enmeshed fish and taking away a piece of netting with it.[18] Until the nineteenth century, spurdogs were extensively fished in summer around the Scottish coasts for their livers, a score of which could yield four pints of fine oil for household use.[19] A spurdog tagged 15 miles west of Cape Wrath on 10 December, 1962, was recaptured three years and eight months later off Newfoundland – on the other side of the Atlantic![20]

On one occasion, at Claonaig, the *Nancy Glen* netted 110 boxes of spurdogs, always a severe test on account of their sheer dead-weight. Fortunately, the weather was perfect and there was a small boat close by to assist. John McPherson was out in the family launch, the *Elf*, jigging for mackerel, and came alongside. The bag of the net was cut open and the catch removed by hand. On the following day, at Sgolaig, the *Nancy Glen* netted another bag of dogfish, but had no success. 'We never got them. We jeest gied it up an they burst away.' [Peter McDougall, 2003]

The local record catch of spurdogs was almost certainly that taken by Tommy Finn's *Gleaner* of Campbeltown while seine-netting on the King William Bank off the Isle of Man in May 1998. Some 720 boxes of large dogs were landed at Ramsey, whence the unmanageable net was towed, strapped to the boat's side, and emptied within the harbour at low water. That haul alone earned each crew member £1700, a sum which would have been greater had more favourable market conditions prevailed. [Lachie Paterson, 2003]

When the big spurdog fishery in the Sound of Gigha was at its peak in the early 1980s, Angus MacAlister counted some 30 boats off Tayinloan, ranging in size from 12 ft punts to forty-footers. With the *Golden Promise*, he and his son John worked two lines, each bearing 50 hooks spaced 7 yards apart, to minimise the risk of entanglement. While Angus hand-hauled, John unhooked the fish and re-baited. The standard bait was herring, a box of which would be delivered to Tayinloan each morning from McFarlane and Jackson, fish-salesmen in Tarbert. Daily catches might range from 25 to 30 boxes of dogs (at £1 a stone) plus a couple of boxes of roker (£1 25p a stone). It was a handy and profitable fishery while it lasted, but, as Angus remarked, the crews were 'working night and day'. He'd land his catch at Tayinloan at 5 p m, cross to Gigha and have a meal at home, then go back out to shoot the lines and lie until daybreak, when the constant effort of shooting and hauling would begin all over again. [Angus MacAlister, 2003]

The lesser-spotted dogfish, locally known as 'moorlach' (Gaelic *mùrlach*), has no commercial value, but before sand-paper became available, Kintyre fishermen used a dried-out moorlach to scrape their boats preparatory to re-varnishing.[21] The moorlach was put to the same use on Gigha, and, more ignominiously still, cleaned the chimneys of fishing-boats. As Willie McSporran explained: 'They took him live an tied a string on him an, ye see, he went doon an he wis squirmin aboot an he cleaned the chimney.' [2003]

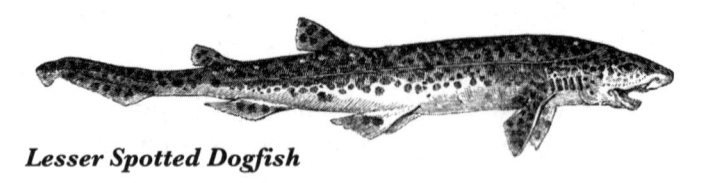

Lesser Spotted Dogfish

On Jura and Colonsay, in the late eighteenth century, 'a very delicate fish that may be had through the whole year, called by the country people murlach' was evidently stripped of its 'very rough skin, like shagreen', and eaten.[22] When Robert Gillies was a young fisherman, he encountered a superstition among some of the older men. They maintained that the moorlach was the 'nurse' that looked after the other fish in the sea (certainly, 'nursehound' is one of the names its larger relative *Scyliorhinus stellaris* is known by). 'Ye wid get a row if ye wir bad tae them. Put them aweh back intae the watter as quick as possible.' Nowadays, however, he keeps them and gives them to crab- and *buckie*-fishermen for bait. [Robert Gillies, 2003]

Conger eel

The conger eel *Conger conger* – Gaelic *easgann* – is generally a fish of rocky coasts, reefs, piers and submerged shipwrecks, but can also be taken numerously in open waters, as the accompanying stories show. It can grow to immense and fearsome proportions and exceed 100 lbs, and its life-history resembles that of the smaller freshwater eel in that it undertakes one vast journey to the deep waters close to Madeira, where it spawns and then dies. After hatching, its larvae drift in a north-easterly direction for two to three years in warm ocean currents to arrive on the coasts of Europe, where, in littoral waters, they complete their meta-

Conger Eel

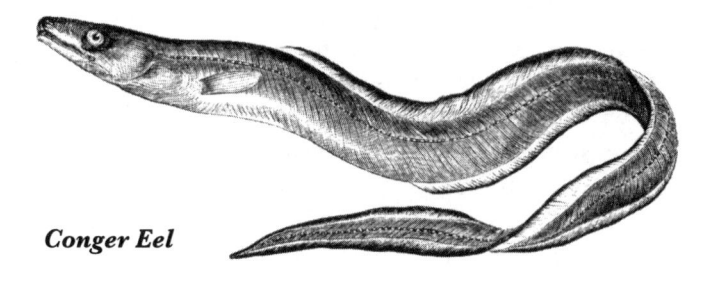

morphosis. The adults feed nocturnally on fish, lobsters and crabs.[23]

Though the conger's flesh has its devotees, locally there is little tradition of eating the fish, perhaps owing to its serpent-like appearance and consequent grim Biblical resonances. The commercial value of congers has always been limited, and fishermen, in any case, find them troublesome creatures to contain, not least on account of their near-indestructibility. Fisheries have, however, been recorded, for example at Inverchaolain in Cowal, where, in the mid-nineteenth century, congers – 'numerous and of a large size' – were caught 'in great quantities for the Liverpool market'.[24] After the Second World War, large quantities of congers were landed into Tarbert and despatched to Billingsgate in barrels. Long-liners from the Scottish East Coast joined local boats in the fishery. [Robert Ross, 2003]

One morning, John McWhirter and his crew were working big lines between the Claits, on the south end of Arran, and Ailsa Craig. The weather had been breezy and they hadn't got to their lines on the previous day. They were hauling away, getting 'an odd fish', when it became apparent that they'd 'hit a school o eels' – there was one on every hook. John had a big Gighaman, Calum MacNeill, crewing with him, 'an he could fairly haal lines – his big erms wis takin a fadom every time, an every haal he had, always an eel'. John himself was standing behind the pump-beam and *gybing* – removing the hooks and passing them to another man who then put them in a basket – while the fish were dropped down into the hold, from which one hatch-board had been removed.

The work was going with a swing until a big unmanageable eel came inboard. It gave one 'waggle', that almost knocked John down, then disappeared, writhing, into the engine-room. It took the line with it, and the line snagged on the coupling of the engine, which was running at the time and which began winding in the line. Line and eels began flying over the rail at an alarming rate. In a panic, John ran aft and his crew ran forward. They could only watch helplessly until the engine finally 'choked hersel'. Between lines and eels, 'what a mess, an the job A had getting them clear!' By reversing the fly-wheel by degrees, they eventually freed the lines from the coupling.

'So that wis the best haalin ever we had. A never seen haalin lik thon. An such an *eye* o eels – A don'know how many we had. The pletform wis feet deep wi eels an lines. Och anee anee! We dinna know whoot tae dae. We jeest gied her the sell an got her heid for Campbeltown an worked aweh the whole wey in.' [John McWhirter, 1974]

When Tommy Ralston first went great-lining for hake with his father in the *Golden Fleece* around 1952, they shot the lines with no bottom floats on them; consequently, the entire line had been on the bottom, where the congers were. 'We had a big shot of really large conger, over 50 boxes as I recall, and thought that we would "never be poor again". One shilling a stone (around 1p per kilo) was what we got for them from MacMillan in Ayr. Conger were really difficult to handle. They were so slippery that they were almost impossible to grip and when they got their tails through the stringer, their strength was such that the only thing you could do was to let them go until the whole fish had threaded itself through, *snood* and all. If the eel had the hook stuck down its throat, which was quite common, we had to use the "rummler" to get it out. This was simply a broom-handle that was thrust down the poor fish's throat and was then held, with the *snood*, while the fish was whirled around until the hook was torn out. Cruel work!' [Tommy Ralston, 2003]

A 'fight between an otter and a conger eel' was observed by lightkeepers on Davaar Island in July 1877. While sitting quietly in one of the houses, they heard 'splashing and struggling going on in the water below them'. Looking out, they saw a large otter with a conger eel. At first the eel was managing to 'hold its own', but the otter finally gripped the eel by the head and succeeded in dragging it on to a rock-shelf*, only for the eel to struggle back into the sea. Again the otter dragged it ashore and again lost it. At last, with the eel's resistance weakening, the otter landed it for a third time. By then, however, one of the keepers was approaching cautiously with a gun, intent on having a shot at the otter; but it was 'too wary' and, abandoning its prey, swiftly retreated. The keeper instead shot the eel, which measured 5ft 8 ins. 'This is the third eel landed of late by otters on this reef of rocks of which the lightkeepers obtained possession.'[25]

**Oitir Buidhe.*

Mackerel

The mackerel *scomber scombrus* – in Gaelic *reannach* – belongs to the tunny family. With its shining metallic blue-green back, patterned by wavy black lines, it is one of the most beautiful of fish, though its beauty fades rapidly after death. Essentially an oceanic species, in early summer shoals of mackerel move into coastal waters to feed, departing as winter approaches, though some lean individuals may linger in enclosed waters throughout winter and be taken in trawls.

Mackerel

Traditionally, there was little local interest in the fish as a food – it was unjustly branded a 'dirty feeder' – though, as Robert Ross put it, 'If ye hanna a herrin, a mackerel wid do.' [2003] When, in 1957, Donald Macleod, a Skye-born farmer (p 150), took a trip to sea on Duncan McAlpine's *Maireared* of Tarbert, he sat down at about four o' clock in the morning to a feed of freshly caught mackerel fried with sliced onions in a big cast-iron pan. The fish had been taken in the first ring of the night, near Skipness. There were no herring in the net, though these were to come later. In the following winter, he heard that the *Maireared*'s cook, Donald 'Mickey' Johnson, had fallen overboard and drowned north of Otter Spit. [Donald Macleod, 2003] As John H Smith remarked of Lochfyneside, and the same applied in Kintyre: 'The majority of… people will not eat this fish. They look upon it almost as orthodox Jews look upon pork.'[26] There was often little market interest either. 'They dinna lik tae see the *reannach*,' Hugh MacFarlane said. 'They winna get tuppence for the full o the boat.' [1976] Until modern times, the tendency of mackerel to rapidly lose its freshness has militated against its marketability.

The total catch of mackerel in Loch Fyne in 1893 was just over 60 tons with a value of £977, taken mainly in ring-nets, but also in 'nets set along the shore'.[27] In the 1890s and early 1900s, however, a lucrative trade in cured mackerel for the American market flourished, but that fishery, on the Clyde, was practically confined to the Ayrshire fishermen.[28]

During the Second World War, with its food shortages, mackerel fetched good money. The *Irene* of Arran, on 31 July, 1941, at Ayr, landed 13 baskets of herring and nine of mackerel, taken by ring-net off Whiting Bay, and received £1 a basket for the mackerel, against £1 4s 6d for the herring; and 84 baskets of mackerel taken at Fairy Dell, Arran, on 25 August, fetched 19s a basket from a 'steamer' in Lochranza.[29]

Post-war, a small summer mackerel fishery developed using a string of multi-coloured feather lures. The lines were operated by hand with a jerking motion, hence the name *jigs* for the lines and *jigging* for the technique. The method was also called *darras* or *darrows*, which is the term used by Donald McDougall in his notebook entries in 1953. End of June: 'Good wages with darrows.' July 21–25: 'Some boats working darrows owing to scarcity of crews.'[30]

The mackerel is one of the fastest swimmers in the sea, as ring-net fishermen would confirm, for mackerel were notoriously difficult to surround, and a fast-moving shoal would be described as 'flying'. Among Tarbert fishermen, there were two Gaelic words – 'revick' (*raibheic*) and 'garr' (*gàir*) – describing the noise generated by a mass of mackerel rushing on the surface, particularly when migrating out of Loch Fyne. 'In my day,' Dugald MacFarlane recalled, 'ye winna hardly get sleepin when they went tae go away doon here, the roar that wis off them.' [1978]

Since the late 1970s, the migrating mackerel shoals have been subject to ruthless pursuit in their deep-water winter habitat, where, hitherto, they found immunity from human predation.

Garfish

The streamlined and highly predacious garfish *Belone belone* was called the 'mackerel guide' because fishermen believed that where garfish were, mackerel too would be found. It has been taken in ring-nets and mid-water trawls during spring and summer, but is a rarity. Its most obvious feature is its long, thin beak equipped with needle-sharp teeth. Though excellent eating, garfish have green bones and therefore tend to be regarded with suspicion.

Sturgeon

The primitive-looking sturgeon is extremely rare and most fishermen die without ever seeing one. The species encountered in local waters,

Acipenser sturio, is a native of the Baltic. Sturgeon are essentially marine fish, but, like salmon, travel up rivers to spawn. The roe of certain species is famously marketed as caviar, of which the finest quality Russian product comes from the Beluga *Acipenser huso*, which can exceed a ton in weight. Famously, too, the sturgeon is classed as a royal fish, though this prerogative – dating to the reign of Edward II in fourteenth-century England[31] – has been allowed to lapse.

Sturgeon

The last locally-caught sturgeon despatched to Buckingham Palace was probably one taken in the summer of 1954. It came up in the *Annie*'s seine-net during a haul in the Sound of Sanda and, when noticed 'wallopin aboot' on the deck among the other fish, it puzzled the crew. As Davie Robertson, whose father owned and skippered the *Annie*, admitted: 'We dinna even know hoot it wis.' At Campbeltown Quay, however, the local fishery officer, John Rioch, was later able to identify it. [Davie Robertson, 2003]

That sturgeon was bought by Campbeltown fishmonger, Donnie Gilchrist, who despatched it, packed in a mixture of sawdust and dry ice, by British Road Services at a cost of 18s 6d. The letter of acknowledgement, dated 31 May, 1954, from the Master of Household at Buckingham Palace, was framed along with a photograph of Donnie's 11-year-old son, Alistair, holding the fish, and hung in the fish-shop in Longrow South until the business was taken over in 1988 by Archie Bob and Helen McMillan of Carradale. Alistair recalled seeing a photograph, taken c. 1920, of his fisherman grandfather, William 'Oakie' Gilchrist, standing on a stool holding a sturgeon.[32]

James Macdonald in his *Crimson Arrow* took a sturgeon in deep water off Kilberry around 1972. The fish – about 3 ft long – was purchased by a Campbeltown fish-buyer, Malcolm McMillan, and ended up on the menu of the Central Hotel, Glasgow. [James Macdonald, 2003]

The last locally-caught sturgeon was probably that taken by Kenny Brown of Tarbert when prawn-trawling off Gigha in the *Caledonia* in 1992. The fish was still alive when it emerged from the net, and he decided to preserve it in one of the holding tanks for live prawns. His hope was that a contact ashore would arrange for the fish's transfer to some sea-life centre, but in the end he was disappointed and the fish was auctioned on Tarbert Quay. Afterwards, he remarked to his crew: 'I wish I'd thrown that over the quay.' [Kenny Brown, 2003]

Documentary records, however, are few. Thomas Eaglesome, Peninver, took one – 6 ft long and weighing over 60 lbs – out of a salmon-net in August, 1887.[33] A specimen, between 5 and 6 ft long, was caught in Carradale Bay in December, 1893, by the crew of a skiff belonging to Archibald Keith, Campbeltown, and despatched to Glasgow market.[34]

The largest fish recorded locally was speared in the River Fyne in July, 1871. Though measuring over 10 ft and weighing 102 lbs, it scarcely bears comparison with another nineteenth-century specimen, landed at Grimsby, which exceeded 11 ft in length and weighed 623 lbs.[35] The trapping and killing of the big far-travelled sturgeon makes rather sad reading. Nowadays, even a gamekeeper would probably observe and admire it; but an Inveraray fish-curer paid £2 – which was wealth at that time – for the dead fish. The sturgeon was noticed, in a pool about half-a-mile from the mouth of the river, by the Ardkinglas Estate gamekeeper, Hector Urquhart, who hurried home for assistance, leaving another man to guard the fish.

'As the party was returning in hot haste with net and spear, they espied the person in charge making frantic efforts by stone-throwing to prevent the escape of his prisoner downstream. The tide was ebbing fast, and the big fish was beginning to make a determined set for the river mouth. The gamekeeper's party succeeded in running their net across the stream just in time, and after an exciting struggle, in the course of which the fish charged furiously at the net three times, it was speared and brought to the land.'[36]

John Dory

The John Dory *Zeus faber* is of singular coloration and form – deep and narrow – and has long been prized as a food. Neil Weir, when a schoolboy in Tarbert in the 1880s, was catching John Dory with hand-lines in Toll a' Choilich, beyond the red perch at the harbour entrance, and earning £1 a box for them in the local market. More recently, in about 2000, Neil Prentice in the *Silver Line* was taking some with a pelagic trawl north of Tarbert harbour. Robert Ross – who occasionally caught these fish at seine-netting, and kept them for eating – got 'a meal or two' from Neil. [Robert Ross, 2003]

Salmon and sea trout

Economically and culturally, the Atlantic salmon *Salmo salar* ranks high in historical importance, only the herring approaching its status. Its complex life-history, stated with utmost simplicity, is: born in a river, migrates into oceanic waters and returns to its native river to spawn and, generally, die. Returning fish were vulnerable to human predation, and a host of devices – from crude spears to elaborate traps – came into being.

Ring-net and, later, mid-water trawl fishermen would occasionally find a salmon or two in a catch of herring. By law, these fish should have been returned to the sea, but naturally they seldom were and became a perquisite of the crew. Some ring-net crews, indeed, encircled the mouths of such salmon-rivers as Carradale Water in the pretence of 'shooting' on a spot of herring, but the real purpose was to try for salmon or sea-trout, and fish would be smuggled ashore, perhaps inside a seaboot. Yet, the name 'salmon' was a taboo word in the fishing community and would be referred to as a 'billy', 'red fish' or 'queer fellow'. A few especially superstitious skippers would not tolerate the fish itself aboard their boats.

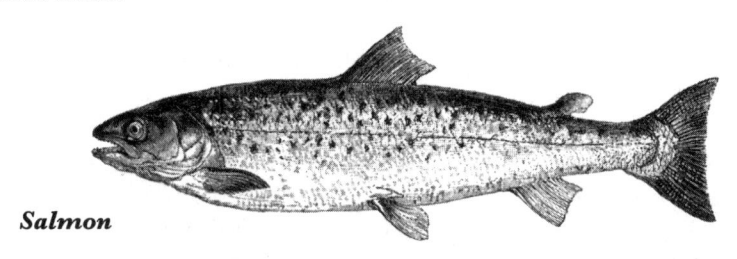

Salmon

Salmon were taken both legally and illegally in rivers and burns, and poached along the coast using small beach seines known as 'splash-' or 'plash-nets'. One Campbeltown 'worthy' operated within the Loch and would sell his catch around local hotels, resisting the beating down of his price unless a glass of whisky and a glass of beer were forthcoming. Donald Macleod, using a gill-net stretched out from the concrete support of a sewage-pipe, to which it was tied, and anchored at the outer end, could take from eight to 10 salmon in a season from Achnaba on Lochfyneside. His biggest fish weighed about 10 lbs. [Donald Macleod, 2004]

Commercial salmon-fishermen, however, employed the offshore 'bag-net' – secured by poles to the seabed – into which the migratory salmon were guided by a wall of netting, or 'leader'. Fishing rights were leased from landowners or from the Crown. This feudal ownership, established in the early Middle Ages, proceeded from the fact that until the discovery of the salmon feeding grounds off Greenland and the development of the nylon monofilament net – both in the 1960s – nobody knew where salmon went or what their migratory routes were. They came seasonally, year after year, and the typical landowner's attitude was that since these valuable fish appeared close to his estate and ran up his river, they must – like the deer, hares and wildfowl – belong to him. And as Bob Smith points out: 'Since salmon fisheries had to be leased, just as was a farm, this put salmon-fishers into a social grouping quite different from that of any other fishers.'[37]

Robert Wylie and his brother-in-law, Jimmy Rae, held differing theories concerning the migratory route of salmon. They agreed that fish entered the Clyde from the North Atlantic and passed around the Mull of Kintyre, but Jimmy believed they then proceeded straight up Kilbrannan Sound, while Robert reckoned they crossed to the Ayrshire coast and came around the Cock of Arran into the Sound. The most salmon Archie Graham took out of a bag, in one visit, was 40, and his biggest ever fish, caught at Ugadale, weighed 42 lbs. The salmon-fishing season generally lasted from mid-May until August. [Archie Graham, 2003]

Salmon-fishing stations were established around the Kintyre shores, probably in the nineteenth century. Before motor boats and cars facilitated the checking of several nets in the course of a day, fishermen occupied huts on the shore adjacent to their net. At Crossaig, for example, the Wylie brothers had a hut in which they could cook and sleep, and Jimmy Rae, indeed, built his house at Brucefield, Ugadale, so that he could give his best station constant surveillance. It was there that he devised and erected his anti-shark fence, a galvanised wire barrier which ran parallel to the leader-net and helped divert destructive basking sharks from his gear. [Archie Graham, 2003]

Hungry seals, having no understanding of the concept of ownership of fish, were the other main pest in the salmon-fishermen's life and were routinely shot. In the late nineteenth century, when seals were apparently still relative rarities, James Rae, salmon-fisherman at 'Salt Pans', captured a large one in his net, brought it to land and confined it in a 'large tub of water, where the strange-looking animal kept swimming and plunging about for a long time, and was visited and examined with great interest by a number of people from the town'. Unfortunately for the seal – and possibly, too, for some of its urban admirers – Rae 'had at last to shoot it, as it was getting so troublesome, and might escape again into the water and continue its depredation amongst the salmon.'[38]

The sea trout *Salmo trutta trutta*, like the salmon – from which it can be near-indistinguishable, large ones being often mistaken for small salmon and vice versa – is a migratory fish which spawns in rivers. Donald

Macleod and his father, Alasdair, could enclose up to two dozen 'nice fish' – from 2 to 3 lbs in weight – working a splash-net along the shore at Achnaba. They'd try a haul on chance at times, but, on a still evening, the fish – which did not arrive in Upper Loch Fyne until the latter half of May and tailed off in July – could be seen and heard jumping to catch midges and flies. [Donald Macleod, 2004] Angus McBride's diary (p 128) records '5 doz. trout the size of a herring' caught off Pluck in the *Irene*'s ring-net on 30 June, 1941.

Sea scorpion

The fish which Donald Macleod knew in Gaelic as the *greusaiche*, or cobbler – almost certainly the long-spined sea scorpion *Cottus bubalis* – was a frequent pest when entangled in the splash-net, but his father had 'a great respect' for the small fish and wouldn't allow them to be harmed. Certain individuals, which Alasdair Macleod recognised as surely as he could recognise one of his own sheep, would be caught repeatedly in the same spot and liberated time and again. [Donald Macleod, 2004]

Squid

In common with the octopus (p 40), squid and cuttlefish are invertebrates, that is, have no backbone. The so-called 'cuttlefish bone', which can occasionally be picked up on local beaches, is actually an internal shell. It is commonly seen stuck in the bars of budgerigar cages, to enable the birds to trim their beaks, but its fine texture also makes it a superlative material for casting silver. That internal shell is substantially-formed and as white as chalk, whereas that of the squid is both delicate and transparent; but the cuttlefish is seldom encountered by fishermen.

When Tarbert fishermen could not obtain herring for 'big line' bait, one of their alternatives was squid* which could be caught in ring-nets and, when the 'bone' was removed, cut into strips. In summer and autumn, shoals of squid, or *gibearnach*, could, like herring, be seen in the sea-phosphorescence; but fishermen knew them from herring by their much slower movement. [Hugh MacFarlane, 1978]

In his *Dialect of South Kintyre*,[39] Latimer McInnes defines *squeeb* as 'Cuttle Fish'. He may have been correct, or partly correct, but in more recent times, *squeeb* certainly relates to 'squid', of which it is surely a variant, and I suspect that the two species have tended to be confused. Squid – of which several species (*Loligo, Alloteuthis, Todaropsis, Illex* and *Todarodes*[40]) are caught in Scottish waters – are also termed 'inks', for 'ink-fish', from

---

* *Informant says 'cuttlefish' and refers to removal of the 'big white bone', which indeed suggests that cuttlefish is the correct identification, yet such concentrations of an otherwise locally uncommon species seem questionable.*

Squid

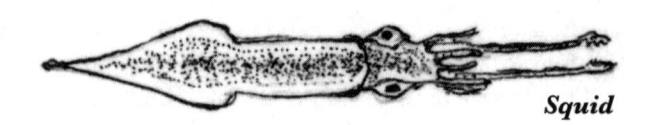

their habit, shared with the cuttlefish, of ejecting when alarmed a cloud of black sepia, behind which they may retreat (p 40).

James Macdonald [2003] recalled the waters off Ru Stafnish as yielding two or three boxes on occasion, and in the 1960s the Maidens ring-netter *Saffron* caught a score of baskets off Garroch Head and sold them for £1 a basket at Ayr. [Robert Ross, 2003]

A remunerative post-war market developed for squid, but prior to that, local fishermen had no notion of their culinary value. The Italian community in Campbeltown certainly had, and Leo Grumoli of the harbourside Royal Cafe – where many crews divided the week's earnings on a Saturday morning – used to collect unwanted squid from trawlers landing catches in the evening. Squid, for him, was *calamari* and an everyday food in his native country. The tubular body of the squid, and its tentacles too, would be cut into rings about half-an-inch thick and either fried in seasoned flour or batter or else stewed and served with vinaigrette sauce or Salsa Verde.

Leo's grandson, Ronald Togneri, explained the importance of seafood in his family: 'My Italian relatives and forebears came from a valley in the Apennines 50 miles or more from the coast, yet had an abundance of fresh fish and shellfish on offer at local markets or from weekly fish vans. Any town in Italy or France, no matter how far from the sea – and I would include the French Massif Central – can offer in its market fresher fish in greater variety than the best fishmonger in our cities or, dare I say it, our fishing towns.'

The 'favourite imported fish' in Ronald's grandparents' part of Italy, incidentally, was *baccala*, or salt cod, from Scotland. It required much steeping and changing of water and, when eventually cooked, was 'done in a rich tomato sauce'.[41]

The *Alliance* was present at a brief but lucrative squid-fishery on the west side of Kintyre in October, 1982. It happened 'nearly by accident' when a Carradale skipper, Lawrence McBride in the *Altair*, took his prawn-trawl into 30 fathoms water and found himself among them. Daily catches exceeding 40 boxes were not uncommon during that fishery, which lasted less than a fortnight and extended south from Cara Island over sandy seabottom. The squid fetched around £8 a stone. [Robert Gillies, 2003]

References and Notes
1. The *CC* of 19 Oct 1907, reported a 'Miller's Thumb', 16 inches across the mouth, ashore at the Quarry Green in Campbeltown Loch.
2. Derivation confirmed by George Campbell Hay, 14 May 1979.
3. A L Wells, *The Observer's Book of Sea Fishes*, London, 1962 edition, p 128.
4. *New Statistical Account*, Vol 7, p 50.
5. A Martin, *The Ring-Net Fishermen*, Edinburgh 1981, p 200.
6. *CC*, 11 Nov 1905.
7. A Martin, *The Ring-Net Fishermen, op. cit.*, p 181.
8. T. Pennant, *A Tour in Scotland and Voyage to the Hebrides*, 1772, pp 169–70.
9. Broadsheet of *Premiums on the Fisheries*, dated 182[blank] and signed William Arbuthnot, Sec.; in the possession of Bob Smith, Linlithgow.
10. A Martin, *Fishing and Whaling*, Edinburgh 1993, p 14.
11. In possession of Mrs Margaret Johnson, Lochgilphead.
12. A Martin, *The North Herring Fishing*, Colonsay 2001, p 46.
13. *Fish and Fisheries*, London 1959, p 71.
14. Judy Martin, pers comm, 1992.
15. 22 Aug 2003.
16. *West Highland Free Press*, 5 Sept 2003.
17. A Martin, *Fishing and Whaling, op. cit.*, p 11.
18. A Martin, *The North Herring Fishing, op. cit.*, p 152-3, and *Herring Fishermen of Kintyre and Ayrshire*, Colonsay 2002, p 122.
19. A Martin, *Fishing and Whaling, op. cit.*, p 11.
20. *Scottish Fisheries Bulletin*, No 27, p 28.
21. A Martin, *The Ring-Net Fishermen, op. cit.*, p 94.
22. *Old Statistical Account*, Vol 12, p 322.
23. M Pritchard, *Fresh and Saltwater Fish*, Glasgow 1986, pp 130-31.
24. *New Statistical Account*, Vol 7, p 11.
25. *CC*, 7 July 1877.
26. John H Smith Manuscript, c. 1930, deposited in Argyll & Bute Council Archive, Lochgilphead.
27. *Fishery Board for Scotland Annual Report*, 1893, p 196.
28. A Martin, *Fishing and Whaling, op. cit.*, p 46.
29. Notebook of Angus McBride, Pirnmill, in possession of Mrs Margaret McBride Harvison, Pirnmill.
30. Notebooks in possession of Mr Peter McDougall, Tarbert.
31. E L Gordon, *The Secret Lives of Fishes*, New York 1977, pp 98-99.
32. Alistair Gilchrist, pers comm, 30 August, 2003.
33. *CC*, 3 Sept 1887.
34. *Ibid.*, 9 Dec 1893.
35. M Pritchard, *op. cit.*, p 22.
36. *AH*, 22 July 1871.
37. Letter, 16 Dec 2003.
38. *CC*, 26 July 1873.
39. Campbeltown 1934, p 9.
40. J Kinnear, Marine Laboratory, Aberdeen, letter to author, 21 Jan 2004.
41. R Togneri, letter to author, 22 Sept 2003.

Scallops

There are four species of scallop in Scottish waters, of which two are commercially fished, the big *Pecten maximus*, generally known in Scots as a *clam*, and the dainty, brightly coloured queen *Chlamys (Aequipecten) opercularis*, known as a 'queenie' or 'crechan' (Gaelic *creachann* and in Tarbert also *creachal*).

Clams are hermaphrodite – each is both male and female – and reach sexual maturity between the ages of two and three years. They spawn twice a year, in spring and autumn. The fertilised eggs develop into minute free-swimming larvae, which eventually settle on seaweed, to which they become attached by a sticky thread, or byssus. Finally, they leave the weed and continue their lives on the seabed. The age of a clam can be calculated by counting the annual white growth-rings on the shell. Given the chance, they can live beyond 20 years.[1]

Far back in prehistory – Mesolithic times – the lower, concave shell of the clam was in domestic use, probably as a scoop and container, and, in more recent times, as a milk-skimmer in butter-making and as a receptacle in whisky-drinking.[2] Empty shells could be collected from beaches, but clams themselves would seldom be found, even with the biggest of spring tides; and the native oyster *Ostrea edulis* – historically abundant in most sea-lochs – was both a common food, from prehistory onward, and a commercial resource long before the clam. 'Otter oysters' were gathered in the nineteenth century on the south side of Otter Spit, Loch Fyne,[3] and in 1887 Messrs William Hay and Co., Tarbert, began commercial oyster-cultivation in West Loch Tarbert by depositing 'about 700,000 gathered at great expense from lochs and creeks all along the West Coast'.[4] At its peak, the fishery employed three or four crews of dredgers and supplied markets in Glasgow and Greenock at 10s per 100 oysters,[5] but by the 1920s the industry had declined to insignificance.[6]

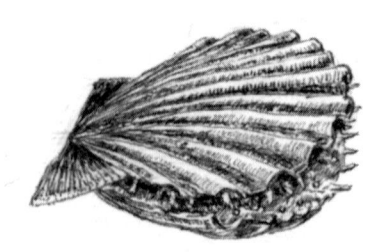

Scallop

The main method of fishing clams is by dredging, though smaller quantities are collected commercially by divers or farmed by growing them in mesh-bags. The clam-dredge is a triangular iron frame with a toothed crossbar, or *sword*, set at an acute angle for raking the shells out of the seabed and into a bag, the belly of which comprises steel rings for durability. Initially, owing to the abundance of the shellfish, only one or perhaps two dredges were towed per side, but, as stocks dwindled and, in compensatory fashion, engine-power increased, greater numbers of dredges were employed, now shackled in a line to a hollow steel 'bar'. The traditionally-minded Carradale clam-fishermen still work from five to seven dredges per side, but elsewhere, among the highest-powered boats, working long trips and fishing 'round the clock', 12 and even 18 dredges a side are not unknown.

The origin of commercial clam-dredging in Scottish waters can be dated to January, 1935, when an Irish skipper, Alexander Davidson of the *White Heather* of Bangor, crossed the North Channel to Campbeltown with his crew, Jack McManus and Jack Brierly. They were immediately storm-bound and only managed out on the 11th day, a Sunday. After about nine hours' dredging at the back of Davaar Island, they returned to port with 400 dozen clams, only to be confronted by a deputation of local fishermen objecting that 'Campbeltown was never a port for Sunday fishing' and insisting that Davidson donate his catch to charity. This he refused to do: 'They all knew how long we had been lying in port. I and the crew all had dependants to support.' The deputation then left, but returned soon afterwards in conciliatory mood. Davidson assured them that the Kilbrannan Sound 'must be full of scallops' and undertook to put his four dredges on to the quay so that interested parties could take them to a blacksmith who could 'copy the pattern'.[7]

The value of the entire Scottish clam catch in 1935 was just £176, but in the following year – 'several beds of clams located in the Firth of Clyde' – the value increased to £2,008. The clams, which were despatched to English markets, fetched from 3s to 3s 6d a dozen.[8] A year on, in 1937, another leap in value was recorded: 13,413 cwts, valued at £14,745, from the coasts of Arran and eastern Kintyre.[9]

Initially, clam-dredging – in common with seine-netting and prawn-trawling – was merely a seasonal alternative to herring-fishing, providing a small but useful winter income, but in the 1960s the establishment of processing factories in Scotland overcame the problem of keeping alive consignments of clams sent 'in the shell' to Billingsgate, and fishing could now continue through the summer months.

Another development of the 1960s was the export by air of clam-meats, fresh or frozen, to markets in Europe, chiefly France, and America. As these markets expanded and fishing effort intensified, Clyde clam stocks became depleted and fresh grounds were progressively opened up, off Gigha, Colonsay, Jura, Islay, north-west Mull and beyond. That rapid expansion is shown in the following simple statistics: from a quantity and a value, in 1967, of 19,850 cwts and £122, 892, the catch and value increased in 1969 to 110,755 cwts and £598,349.[10] Of these landings in 1969, almost 50,000 cwts were caught by Clyde boats, but a sudden decline set in and catches fell to 23,000 cwts in 1971 and 10,500 cwts in 1972, owing to the development of a fishery on queen scallops[11] in which small trawl-nets, equipped with foot-rope 'bobbins' (heavy rubber rollers, for bouncing over hard ground), replaced dredges. In one two-minute haul with a 6 ft dredge in the Clyde, the fisheries research vessel *Mara* lifted 10,000 queenies – abundance indeed![12] This new queenie fishery, which was short-lived, saw the hasty establishment of several factories in Campbeltown, providing employment for squads of piece-workers, chiefly women.

Both the clam and the queenie are free-swimming; by clapping their shells together they produce a kind of liquid jet-propulsion. Shoals of migratory queenies were occasionally taken in ring-nets. Sometimes a mass of them would 'show up lik herrin in the water' when, in late summer and autumn, fish were located by the phosphorescent flash they generated ahead of the searching boats.

In the 1930s, when Archie Carmichael of Tarbert was in the first *Village Belle*, the crew shot on a deep flash in the 'burning' off Lagan. 'Ye wid think ye wir in for a shot o herrin, an it wis crechans ye had.' On that occasion, there was a 'good scatter o baskets' of the shellfish in the net. The crew let them go. [2003] The available evidence suggests that the abundance of queenies experienced post-war in the Clyde can be attributed to a dramatic increase both in the density of the stock and in the localities colonised by the species. Certainly, John McWhirter, who was born in 1886, could say that the 'only place' he ever saw queenies was in Skipness Bay, where they would 'play', or flurry noisily, on the surface. [1974] It was there, too, that Tarbert line-fishermen, in the same period, dredged the shellfish for line bait (p 134).

First dredging from Campbeltown

Clam-dredging from Campbeltown began through Irish boats working clams in the Lodan. Then there was 'a race tae get dridges' and all the town blacksmiths were kept busy. A ring-net winch was used for hauling. Henry Martin's first experience of clam-fishing was with the skiffs *Lady*

Charlotte and the *Lady Edith*, which neighboured each other at ring-netting. One crew wanted to try clam-dredging and the other didn't, so the willing crew went into the Lodan with dredges and did well that week. A row broke out, however, when it became apparent that the reluctant crew was to receive a share of the week's earnings. [Henry Martin, 1974]

Condemned at the market

One crew tried dredging in Campbeltown Loch, from the red navigation buoy opposite Maxwell's Planting to Isla Hattan. They were lifting 'grett big clams' from previously untouched beds and got a good fishing. The 'whole fleet' was there next day, but when the *Lady* Henry Martin crewed on went to Campbeltown quay to land, the crew was told to go and dump the catch because the previous day's landing had been 'condemned' at Billingsgate and there was no market for the Loch clams. This reverse was attributed to the clams' being contaminated with sewage from the town. 'The smell that wis off the ropes wis something terrible.' A haul was later tried off Askomil shore, but the ropes were polluted with mud there too and the crew had to go out into the Lodan and 'dreg them' clean. [Henry Martin, 1974]

In an obvious reference to the same ill-fated fishery, Cecil Finn recounted that during the Second World War some 2000 dozen clams dredged from the Trench Point outward were unsold at Billingsgate owing to their being 'too muddy'. They wouldn't travel, he said, but had they been processed locally would have been 'as fresh as paint'. [Cecil Finn, 2003]

From Tarbert

Archie Carmichael's earliest experience of clam-dredging was while crewing on the first *Village Belle* of Tarbert before the Second World War. Herring fishing had suffered a slump and 'everybody wis at the clams'. The first dredges were Irish-made and were tried out while the *Village Belle* and her neighbour-boat were in Oban waiting to get out to fish for herring in Loch Buie, Mull. Off the quay at Oban, the fishermen were 'fillin the droadges' with coal that had fallen into the water from boats loading and unloading there. When they started fishing in earnest with the dredges – towing one per side – they were filling them with clams. 'Och, they wir thick. Nobody had ever touched them. A seen us wance at Pirnmill near fillin the two boats.' The catch was put in the hold to be bagged later at the 'Ootside Pier' at Tarbert. 'Ye had a job tae get bags,' Archie explained. 'Ye had'ae depend on the bakers tae get the [flour]bags in them days.'

Clam-fishing grounds were close to home at first – outside the harbour, the West Shore and the Kerry Shore – and on sandy ground to preserve the dredges from damage on rocks. Towing-ropes, too, were liable to damage, and each dredge had a 'marker' – a couple of *arcans* (cork floats) on the end of a rope – attached to it so that, if the towing-rope snapped, the dredge could be recovered using a grappling-iron. Dredges were hauled using the McBain ring-net winch and the ropes were hand-coiled. The next dredges were bought from Girvan and were smaller and of different design. In post-war years, the number of dredges towed per side increased and boats sought clams beyond the Clyde. [Archie Carmichael, 2003]

Some indications as to the peripheral role of clam-dredging in the yearly round of the typical herring-orientated skipper appears in Donald McDougall's notebooks (p 80). In November, 1941, there was 'nothing doing' among the Tarbert herring fleet, so on 1 December Donald 'started clam fishing'. The weekly divide on Saturday 27 December was £7 per man, with £7 5/- deducted for expenses. In 1944, he started clam-dredging early, on 12 September. In January, 1947, the complaint again was 'nothing doing' and on 4 February he 'started clam fishing'. On 31 March, 1951, he reported: 'Some boats stopped clams as money poor; not worth working at.' Early in February, 1952, he noted 'puckles' of herring fished at Otterard, Culzean Bay and the Ballantrae Banks, adding: 'Some boats at clams owing to poor fishing.'[13]

Arran

Angus Martin McBride (1907-1972) of Pirnmill, Arran, also kept records of fishing, mixed in with everyday diary material. When his father Willie died in 1937, the family boat, the *Ella*, was sold, and Angus transferred to the *Irene*, owned by Willie Kerr, Lochranza – also skipper – and John Currie, Pirnmill. She partnered Donald McAnsh's *Betty* of Torrisdale at ring-netting. When herring-fishing was slack, Angus gathered winkles, fished with lines or found seasonal employment heather-burning, sheep-dipping, marking lambs and potato-planting on local farms. After the *Irene* – the last full-sized fishing boat in Arran – was sold c. 1947, Angus 'got a job on the roads', gathered winkles and hired out bicycles to summer visitors to Pirnmill.[14]

Of greater interest here, however, is his account of clam-fishing in 1942. The *Irene*'s crew started on 12 January with 'three dregs at the Cock', but 'only got about 3 doz altogether' and finished at Corriegills with about 17 dozen clams. They lay in Brodick Bay that night and 'sent away a bag from Brodick pier in the morning'. That day they tried

Corriegills again, but were dissatisfied and shifted south to Whiting Bay, finishing there with about 50 dozen and anchoring for the night at Lamlash. On Wednesday morning, they worked again in Whiting Bay, but were disappointed, so despatched three bags – '15 doz in each bag' – from the quay there. A strong south-easterly breeze put them to Brodick Bay, where they 'worked off the pier till dark' for about 35 dozen. Next morning, they left their anchorage in the bay and 'sent 2 bags away' from the pier. By then, the wind was 'blowing hard so made for Lochranza got in behind the castle as soon as we reached there; home about 3 oc, afternoon Thur 15th'. Their week's catch of 91 dozen clams, at 7s a dozen, gave them a wage of £4 10s a man. Freight per bag amounted to about 8s.

On the following Monday, 19 January, a hard-blowing wind kept them in, but on Tuesday they managed out in the afternoon and got 20 dozen clams at 'the Cairn Lochranza'. Gales of wind and snow confined them 'in the boat all week, behind the Castle'. Their clams weren't sent away until Saturday because 'the bus couldn't manage over' until then.

On Monday 26, they were back at the Cairn, Lochranza, for 42 dozen clams, which were 'sent away with bus next day'. The wind was 'blowing hard' on Tuesday and they weren't out, but they worked all Wednesday – 'a wild cold day, with heavy snow showers' – at the Fairy Dell, north of Lochranza, and got 50 dozen. By Friday, they had moved south to 'Caticol cairn', but the fishing there was 'no use'. With 147 dozen clams fished and a wage of £8 1s 6d that week, the crew 'put dredges and ropes ashore on pier, as we heard from the Polly Cook* there was 800 bks (baskets) of herring [caught] at Brown Head'. On Monday 2 February, Angus significantly heads his entry, 'Starting fishing again' – the *Irene* was going back to the herring: real fishing![15]

*Originally Mary Sturgeon *of Dunure and acquired in 1933 by Angus Cook and Gilbert McIntosh Sr of Carradale.*

Ronnie Brownie

Ronnie Brownie's father, Fred Brownie, was of Aberdeenshire agricultural stock and came to Carradale around 1920 to work on a farm, but he married into a local fishing family, the McIntoshes. Ronnie was to become the only full-time clam-fisherman in Kintyre, dedicating himself entirely to the method from 1974 until his retirement in 2000. He himself admits that there was a lingering stigma attached to clam-fishing. The fishermen of his generation were locked into the herring tradition and regarded all other pursuits as inherently inferior, to be suffered only when ring-netting was uneconomic. He recalled one Campbeltown skipper boasting to him, 'Never at clams in ma life – we never had tae,' the insinuation being that the only men who went to clam-fishing were those who couldn't make money at herring. Nonetheless, Ronnie Brownie made plenty of money at clams, though he didn't himself say so. Another factor, prejudicial to clamming, was the herring skippers' pride in their boats, for iron dredges are sore on wood.

Ronnie Brownie's first experience of clam-dredging was in 1964 aboard the *Sunshine* with his elder brother Fred and an uncle, Denis McIntosh. They towed three 6ft 'Rothesay dredges' on single ropes over the port quarter. To lift the dredges, the engine would be thrown out of gear and each man would go to a rope and haul in the slack astern. Each dredge, in turn, would then be raised using the ring-net winch, hoisted out of the water on the brailer-pole – another piece of ring-net equipment – and emptied on to the deck. At that time, a clam-boat's woodwork was protected by nothing more than strips of old winch-belting attached to the rail with slate-nails. Five years later, in 1969, when Ronnie bought the *Brighter Hope* from Shetland, she was already 'rug' for clam-dredging, having customised protective steel 'sheathing' on her sides as well as a trawl-winch for spooling in steel warps.

In the mid-1960s, Ronnie said, the Rothesay and Kyles fishermen were the 'top clam men on the Clyde'. Most of their boats had twin derricks and they towed two dredges per side. 'All the Clyde men, bar the Rothesay men, only went tae clams if there wis no herrin in it. The Rothesay men made a career o it.' They would begin clamming at the end of September and continue until April, at the latest, by which time prices had fallen owing to the diminution or disappearance of roes from the clams, a market restriction which no longer prevails.

When Ronnie started clamming, dredges were 4 ft across and some boats still dragged a *pailin-stab* (fence-post) stapled to the back of the chain-bag, a crude device that was soon entirely replaced by circular steel piping. The original dredges had no chain-bags on the bottom, only wire-netting. The $2^{1}/_{2}$ ft-wide dredge, which came into use about 1980, proved itself more efficient and remains the standard model. [Ronnie Brownie, 2003]

'The Other Side'

'Roon the other side', to Kintyre fishermen, was the west coast of the peninsula and Gigha, Islay and Jura. The virgin clam beds there were first exploited, Ronnie Brownie believed, by Manx dredgers, operating off Islay and Machrihanish, and landing into Red Bay on the Antrim coast of Ireland. The clams, he said, were 'as thick as the grass', and 100 bags for two or three hours' towing in 'Port Ellen Bay' was not exceptional. These Manxmen were followed, in the mid-1960s, by Solway Firth skippers John King (*Ranger*), Jackie Johnston (*Radiance*) and Hughie Campbell (*Adoration*). By the late 1960s, the Clyde clammers were fully engaged, operating from Crinan south to Machrihanish, and working both sides of Jura. [Ronnie Brownie, 2003]

Robert Ross remarks, however, that the Jacksons, in the *Village Belle* and *Village Maid*, went through the Crinan Canal in the late 1930s to dredge clams off Tobermory, Mull; and he himself clammed in Loch Melford in 1946 with Angie 'Molly' Johnson's *Silver Spray*, one of several Tarbert boats which operated there rather than risk the Minch herring-fishing. [2003]

Colonsay

Tarbert crews established a clam-fishery off Colonsay in about 1964, following on the example of two East Coast crews which had operated there, netting clams with otter-trawls. The *Destiny* (Ronnie Johnson), *Dalriada* (Robert Ross), *Caledonia* (Peter Brown), *Nancy Glen* (Duncan McDougall), *Our Lassie* (Iain McNab) and *Fionnaghal* (Peter McDougall) all participated in the early years of that fishery, working in two combinations of three boats, so that every third day a different crew in the partnership would have its turn at running the combined catches to port, leaving the two other crews to continue fishing. Robert Ross was teamed with the *Nancy Glen* and *Caledonia*, whose port of delivery was Crinan, whence the catches were carried by lorry to Eyemouth for processing. The other combination landed to a processor in Oban, Crofter Seafoods.

The boats towed either three or four dredges on nylon ropes, with 15 fathoms of wire between the rope-ends and the dredges. It was a spring fishery over an area of ground, 'paved' with clams, extending from Scalasaig north for about a mile. When Robert first arrived on the ground, he decided to work through the night to make the quota of 600 dozen clams per boat, but in unfamiliar waters and with hail showers battering repeatedly out of the darkness, it 'seemed a long night'. The clams were of the highest quality. Scientists from the Marine Laboratory at Aberdeen, who accompanied Robert during dredging operations, found that 'every clam wis ten years and upwards'. For Robert, however, as for many of his contemporaries, clamming was only 'a kinna pastime when there wis nothin else doin'. He spent three or four springs at Colonsay, after which he never returned. [Robert Ross, 2003]

Sanda

The clam-fishery at Sanda was initiated by a Peninver fisherman, John McKerral. While fishing lobsters there, he was finding big clams clipped on to the back-ropes of his creels. Later, while himself clam-dredging, he returned to the spot in a breeze of south-west wind, shot in the lee of the island and took a 'hell of a fishing' of big clams. He didn't, of course, have the spot to himself for long. Ronnie Brownie went there with his *Brighter Hope* and joined a big fleet of boats in 'wan wee bit', extending from the Scart Rocks to the Arranman's Barrels. [Ronnie Brownie, 2003]

It was in the autumn of 1969, in his small *Sapphire*, that John McKerral got the clams on his creel ropes, and in the spring of the following year, with the *Girl Ann*, that he first tried the Sound of Sanda for clams. On the previous day, he had received word from his buyer, George McAulay in Glasgow, that no further supplies were wanted that season. John towed between the Scart Rocks and Glunimore, and, when he lifted, the dredges were crammed 'tae the swords' with 'great big clams'. His initial reaction was disbelief – 'They must've been knee-deep' – and when McAulay received that day's consignment, which contained 'enormous roes', he quickly reversed his earlier instruction. The message from Glasgow was now: 'Get as many as possible.' John reckoned that the Sanda grounds until then had remained untried for clams owing to the strength of the tides there. That fishery engaged a fleet of clammers for several weeks in succession until the virgin stock was effectively exhausted. [John McKerral, 2003]

Once that spot had been cleaned up, Sanda was virtually forgotten by clam-fishermen until Ronnie Brownie quite unexpectedly set another fishery in motion. It happened in February, 1988. He had been working off Sgolaig, south of Tarbert, and decided to head round the Mull of Kintyre and finish his week on the west side. He left Carradale about 5 o'clock on a Wednesday morning and, realising that the tide wouldn't suit at the Mull for a further hour, decided to pass the time with a haul at Sanda. A 'dose o big clams' came up in the dredges, so he worked that day and the following day with great success and decided to work Friday too, reasoning that: 'There'll be a fleet here next week.' There was, and the spot of clams was soon fished out, but for the three days he dredged there alone, the *Bonnie Lass III* grossed about £6000. [Ronnie Brownie, 2003]

Retaining a catch

Another memorable episode in John McKerral's career occurred on

Christmas Eve, c. 1970, when, in the *Girl Ann*, he took an exceptional fishing from 'a wee corner' of the Bight of Isla Ross; but the market had closed for Christmas, so the clams were transported by lorry from Campbeltown and the bags emptied in the Geelot – the rock-bound tidal channel off Peninver – where, contained in a laced-up sheet of netting, they remained for some four days until the market re-opened and he was able to bag them again and sell them. [John McKerral, 2003]

Marking the ground

Before Decca Navigation and track-plotting, clam skippers, in common with other fishermen, relied on landmarks to get them where they wanted to be and to keep them out of trouble after they had got there. Most clam skippers in the early years also used what might be termed 'sea marks' to give them more precise points of reference. These devices were simply assembled – an empty lubrication oil-drum or 'bow' (net-buoy) on a line held to the seabed by a clam-bag loaded with stones from the dredges – and served both to indicate peaks of hard ground, located by echo-sounding, and as marks to be towed around or to and from. On occasion, for example in Ardminish Bay, Gigha, as many as six cans could be in simultaneous use. Ayrshire clammers were known to have used *winkies* – the flashing buoys which marked the outer ends of ring-nets – for night dredging in Ardneil Bay, north of Ardrossan. Cans, being replaceable at no cost, could be left out overnight, but the more valuable buoys would be retrieved at the end of a day's fishing and marks taken on the land in the hope being able to find the exact spot again. [Ronnie Brownie, 2003]

Sharp marks

Ronnie Brownie tells a story about his brother Fred, who was, by inclination, more a herring- than a clam-fisherman. 'Froonky', as Fred was universally known, was clamming in Killean Bay with his *Silver Cloud* one Thursday and struck a good spot. It was his last tow of the week and he radioed John McConnachie in the *Numora* to report 'a braw mark there for Monday'. – 'Well,' John advised, 'leave the *bow*.' – 'Aw, naw, sherp marks,' Fred assured him. When he returned the following week, however, Fred had 'no idea wherr he wis' and was 'nearly makin oot at last the peak had moved, he wis that adamant!' [Ronnie Brownie, 2003]

Coal

More than clams came up in dredges. There were stones raked from the seabed, often in back-breaking quantities for those on the deck who had to shovel them back overboard. Coal spilling from the upturned dredges was a more welcome sight and some crewmen would 'keep every lump'. When clamming back and forth off the entrance to Ardrossan harbour in the mid-1960s, the *Sunshine* of Carradale in one week lifted around four tons of coal, which was flung into the hold to be bagged and shared among the crew when they returned home. When clammers began working Lamlash Bay, they dredged up an abundance of coal, but: 'Wi all the dridgin it got an men takin the coal home, ye'll har'ly see a lump in it now. Before, ye'd get bagfuls o it.' [Ronnie Brownie, 2003] In the 1980s, Ronnie Brownie's nephew, Robert Gillies, lifted 40 bags of coal there one day, dredging inside Holy Isle. There was a stove aboard the *Alliance*, so after the boat's coal-locker had been filled, the remaining coal was divided among the crew. Robert's wife, Valerie, however, disliked the 'foul' smell that the stored sea-coal gave off. [2003] Billy Wareham lifted over 40 bags of slow-burning coal in one day's dredging in Lamlash Bay with the *Boy Stewart* in the 1970s. Coal could also be brought up south of Brodick, but it was 'wee nuts'. On the west side of Ailsa Craig, entire gannet eggs – dislodged from nests on the cliffs – were picked up in dredges. [1997]

Fish

Fish, too, could be taken in notable quantities on certain spots of ground. On Skelmorlie Bank, off Largs, around 1970, before robust 'hopper-nets' had depleted the fish stocks there, cod, haddock, plaice and lemon sole in marketable quantities could be lifted in the dredges. In Machrihanish Bay, two boxes of 'monks', or anglerfish (p 101), could 'quite often' be gathered in a day's dredging. At Dunan Hole, south of Ballantrae Banks, a couple of boxes of skate, plus turbot and lemon sole, was not an uncommon daily by-catch, and, on the 'outside' clam-grounds off Sanda, a box of skate could be taken in a day, at first anyway. South of Lendalfoot, on the Ayrshire coast, Colin Campbell's *Silver Fern* dredged up two boxes of fine plaice in a day. Working off Loch Ranza in his low-powered *Brighter Hope*, Ronnie Brownie was marking a turbot most days. As he remarked: 'They must've been thick.' [Ronnie Brownie, 2003]

Crechans

Tarbert small line fishermen fished the queenie, or crechan, for line-bait. They could go into Skipness Bay and fill a boat in a couple of hours, towing a triangular dredge, about three feet across the spear, and with a woven bag of netting to gather the catch, the whole thing so small and light that 'ye'd swing it on yer wee finger'. With two men pulling on oars and a man standing aft holding the tow-rope, and giving it a *chug* (tug) now and again to judge when the dredge had filled, they'd 'get the full o the net ev'ry time'. Each of the crew of four got four boxes of crechans apiece, and 'that wid do the week's bait'. [Hugh MacFarlane, 1976]

Sudden abundance

In the late 1960s, the brothers John and Lawrence Robertson with the *Felicity* were 'weeks on end' working the same inshore ground at Pirnmill for flatfish and codling. One morning, as they 'bighted away in' – put an arc on the ropes – they noticed some small yachts at anchor off the slip at Pirnmill, but didn't think the gear would be near them. But when they picked up the *dhan* and began winching on the ropes, they quickly discovered that the boat was 'moored solid'.

'We must've got wan o their anchors,' John speculated. 'We'd better go back.' First, however, they gave the engine 'full bit' – maximum speed – and managed about 30 turns of rope in; then she stopped dead again. 'That's enough!' John decided. They then hauled back on the ropes until they reached the net, but they couldn't raise it. More puzzled than before, they had to resort to *fleeting* – gaining the net by degrees, while moving into shallower water – and when they finally got to the net, they discovered that there was a queenie clamped on 'every mash' from wings to bag, and that the bag itself held five or six hundredweights of the shellfish. That accounted for the unexpected heaviness of the net, but it didn't explain how the scallops came to be there. 'Where did they come fae, overnight?' That unwanted catch started a fishery there. A Carradale boat, John Ramsay's *Golden Sheaf* – skippered temporarily by James Macdonald of Campbeltown – came across to the Arran shore, and, towing one dredge per side, began exploiting the stock. A 20-minute drag was sufficient, and the boat would lie, with one of these big dredges hanging over one side, while the other dredge was emptied and its contents bagged.

For some 15 years, Lawrence had fished that area with seine-nets without encountering queenies. His only previous experience with the shellfish happened in the mid-1950s, when the *Felicity*'s crew went into Lochranza to rid the net of a heavy object and then moored at the quay to mend the net. Having cooked a meal, Lawrence went up on deck and told his shipmates: 'Yer dinner's ready, boys.' He remained on the illumined deck, mending, when, 'There wis this noise an A looked ower the side an there they wir in the lights – ye could see them comin right up tae the surface, scores o them, flappin away'. This was a shoal of queenies and he 'dinna even gie it a thought'. [Lawrence Robertson, 2003]

The *Golden Sheaf* had been clam-dredging further north when the spot of queenies came on at Pirnmill*. 'The queenies wir runnin ower the *swords*, runnin oot the dridges, grett big queenies.' Having landed the catch at Tarbert that evening, James Macdonald returned to Pirnmill the following morning to resume dredging. At that time, a group of Rothesay boats was already queenie-fishing, and he had just 'arrived back' when he 'saw this fleet comin, this wis them comin – they got win o it right aweh'. The Rothesay crews tried to exclude the Kintyre men from the queenie market, so to maintain their own monopoly on landings, but the attempt – which breached the regulations of the Clyde Fishermen's Association – failed. [James Macdonald, 2003]

* *Ronnie Brownie, Carradale, dates it to autumn 1969.*

North of The Brig

Remarking on their abundance, from Loch Fyne to the Solway Firth, Billy Wareham recalled catching twelve bags of white-shelled queenies on a spot of clean ground north of the Brig at the Second Waters, where he hadn't expected to find them and never found them again. He was trawling in the *Girl Aileen* at the time and took her into that spot – familiar to him as a seine-net haul which formerly yielded a box or half-box of 'big brute flounders' – and towed round and round in the hope of netting some codling and other fish. [Billy Wareham, 2003]

References and Notes
1. J Mason, *Scottish Fisheries Bulletin*, No 6, p 11.
2. A Martin, *Fishing and Whaling*, Edinburgh 1995, p 51.
3. *New Statistical Account*, Vol 7, Kilfinan, p 363.
4. *Fishery Board for Scotland Annual Report*, 1888, p xxv.
5. *Ibid.*, 1896, p 199.
6. *Ibid.*, 1921, p 26.
7. A Martin, *The Ring-Net Fishermen*, Edinburgh, 2nd edition 1996, p vi.
8. *Fishery Board for Scotland Annual Report*, 1936, p 35.
9. *Ibid.*, 1937, p 34.
10. *Scottish Fisheries Bulletin*, No 28, pp 21-22.
11. *Ibid.*, No 39, p 40.
12. J Mason, *ibid.*, No 46, p 3.
13. Notebooks in possession of Mr Peter McDougall, Tarbert.
14. Bill Harvison, letter to author, 8 Oct 2003.
15. Notebook in possession of Mrs Margaret McBride Harvison, Pirnmill.

Silvercraigs

'The anchorage of Silvercraigs, near Loch Gilp, is one of the most striking and picturesque in Loch Fyne, from the intricacy of the several creeks and bays, and the lofty and rocky promontories by which they are separated.'[1]

Jessie and Maggie Campbell were raised at Silvercraigs, on the north side of Loch Gilp, an inlet of Loch Fyne. The original name for the district was Aird, Maggie said; then it became Castleton. Silvercraigs in Gaelic was Creag an Airgiod. Nearby, there were four crofts at Baile Beag, but only gardens at Baile Mór. In her schooldays, the post office – a purpose-built shed – was at Baile Mór. Fishermen once lived in Ardnaherir, Achalephin and Drum Fuar, which all became ruinous. In the time of the old drove road from Lochgilphead, at Achnaba there was an inn called Cossack Inn. Maggie 'always wondered at the name', particularly since there is a Cossack Street in Lochgilphead; but the explanation seems to lie in the popularity Cossacks enjoyed after Napoleon's disastrous Russian campaign of 1812. These old settlements were close to Allt Oigh, which entered the sea below Silvercraigs, and Maggie and companions 'used to follow the burn' inland.

The parents of Jessie and Maggie were Duncan Campbell and Jane Blair. Duncan was a fisherman, but he 'went to sea' in his youth and when fishing was slack. He also had a stake in the land, which, if it did not quite amount to a croft as properly defined, afforded him and his family a supplementary livelihood which allows him to be classed loosely as a 'crofter-fisherman'. In the Census of 1881, he appears, aged 22, living with his parents, Hugh, aged 60, and Sarah (*recte* Mary) MacLarty, aged 40, and a brother, Donald, aged 24. Father and two sons were all described as fishermen.

Duncan and Jane had 10 children: Dugald, Hugh, Neil, Duncan, Donald, Archibald, Mary, Jessie, Jeannie and Margaret, who was known as 'Maggie' or 'Meg'. Maggie, born on 5 April 1899, was the youngest, and the one who remained at home to care for the old folk. She never married and, when she 'slept away' painlessly in the winter of 1998, in Ardfenaig nursing home, Ardrishaig, she was just months short of her

100th birthday. When I met her for the first time, in 1977, she had already left the croft at Silvercraigs and was living in a farm cottage at nearby Castleton.

Maggie's older sister, Jessie, whom I also tape-recorded in 1977, was 92 years old when she died in Campbeltown. She had married an Ardrishaig policeman, Colin MacBrayne. He was posted to Campbeltown, c. 1919, when the oldest child, Jean, was two years old, and they settled into a room and kitchen in Gayfield Place, Dalintober. After Jean came Nan, then Duncan, Mary, Colin, Campbell, Netta, Willie and Margaret. The link with fishing continued in Campbeltown. Colin and Campbell became fishermen and two of the girls, Netta and Margaret, married fishermen (Denis Meenan and Joe Brown, respectively).

Of the oldest children in the MacBrayne family, Nan, Duncan and Mary were most familiar with Silvercraigs. They spent summer holidays there, in company with Campbell cousins from Greenock (Archie, Mary, Sheena, Elspeth and Myrtle) and from Clydebank (Duncan, Colin and Chrissie). At that time, Maggie shared the house with her Uncle Archie and brother Duncan, who, in common with another brother, Hugh, had worked as a mason. She looked after them and also tended the croft.

Morning and evening, old Archie would preside over a religious service in the house. He would read, in English, a passage from the Bible, followed by a prayer in Gaelic, of which, as Mary MacBrayne remarked, 'we never understood a word'. He also took the Sunday morning Gaelic service in the Free Church at Lochgilphead, which the whole family attended, walking there and back.

The Campbell line-skiff featured prominently in holidays at Silvercraigs. The children would fish from her; there were trips to Port Ann for gravel to lay on the path to the crofthouse, and to Otter Ferry, on the opposite shore of Loch Fyne, to gather driftwood.

Duncan and Jane Campbell were Gaelic speakers, but neither Jessie nor Maggie attained fluency, though they understood much of what they heard. 'All the fishermen would meet an they would be in the house an they'd be talkin Gaelic together,' Maggie recalled. 'An then we'd be askin for Gaelic words. No use o talkin if ye're answerin in English. However, ye understood it an learned to speak some of it.'

At Aird Public School, to which Maggie went in 1904, the children's lack of English was repeatedly complained of in the 1880s. On 5 May, 1883, for instance, the teacher remarks in the school log-book: 'The imperfect knowledge of English (consequent on the habitual use of the Gaelic language) possessed by the children makes the work of teaching them laborious and discouraging in the extreme.'[2]

Also at Silvercraigs in the 1881 Census (p 137) – and in subsequent censuses – were three families to which Maggie and Jessie frequently referred, the Sinclairs, MacEwans and Whytes. The head of the Whyte household, Alexander, aged 79, is described as 'farmer of 50 acres, of which 10 arable'; but his three unmarried sons, Peter (43), Malcolm (41) and Alexander (37) are described as fishermen. Neither Peter nor Malcolm was mentioned by the Campbell sisters, but Peter is of special interest here because in 1892 he gave evidence to a Royal Commission on the Highlands and Islands (see Appendix), and that evidence provides a valuable insight into the living conditions of crofter-fishermen of the time.

The crofthouse in which the Whytes had lived was ruinous by the time Mary MacBrayne began visiting Silvercraigs, but Maggie talked of that idiosyncratic family and told Mary how she had once asked Mary Whyte, who was a great age: 'How on earth do you manage, Mary?' The answer was: 'I'm methodical, Maggie, methodical.' There were still MacEwans there and two MacGougan brothers, who seemed 'ancient'. Mary remembered the old MacCall sisters, Bessie and Lexie, who lived 'under the Barr'. Lexie had 'worked away in service' and retired to the croft at Silvercraigs. Bessie kept goats and would 'come out screeching for them' until the animals came 'charging down'.

Some 20 years ago, Murdo MacDonald, at Baile Mór, went across to Silvercraigs with his neighbour, Hughie MacArthur, and had a 'prowl around' the derelict MacCall crofthouse. Deterioration of fabric and furnishings aside, it was little changed since the sisters' time there. It comprised two rooms: the basic kitchen – with two box-beds, a wooden dresser, cast-iron cooking range, and wooden chimneypiece with brass rail and smoke-board – and the parlour, with sofa and a 'grand fire-place with tasselled mantle-covering'. The photographs which Hughie MacArthur took that day show an upended sewing-machine, crockery still on the dresser and the pot-chain and hook still hanging from the chimney above the range. A bungalow now stands there.[3]

Duncan Campbell was originally a drift-net fisherman and would talk of when there were small boats in every creek on both sides of the Loch. As Maggie said: 'When the fishin was there, they just launched all these boats out – there was really no expense attached to it – for the herring was just at their door.' As drift-netting declined, Duncan Campbell turned to ring-netting and had the *True Love* (built in Ardrishaig in 1893) which he worked in partnership with the *Silver Craig* (built in Ardrishaig in 1900) belonging to a neighbouring family, the MacEwans, three of whom – brothers – later emigrated to Sakatchewan, Canada. Their tenancy was taken up by a family of Grahams from Lochgair, who were draining-contractors and occasional fishermen. Calum MacCall, another neighbour, was a fisherman, but Maggie didn't remember him. 'There was five of a family there. There's none of them left now.' He kept his boat at the Cottages and may have partnered the Sinclairs, none of whom Maggie remembered being at fishing. 'But I remember their boats being drawn up on the beach. And they left them there jeest. They had something against selling a boat. They thought it wasn't lucky. A superstition attached to that. Half o the fishermen were lik that. If they met a red-headed woman, they would turn back.'

When the *True Love* was replaced by the *Aliped*, bought from Girvan, she was the last boat in Silvercraigs and took a neighbour-boat in Ardrishaig, the nearest village. The Campbells went often to Ardrishaig, especially on Saturdays in the boat. Maggie: 'Ardrishaig wis a great place. The steamer came in then, when we were over. We went over tae meet all our friends comin for the Glasgow Fair. It wis a great place in these days.'

The Silvercraigs boats were generally anchored in the Wee Harbour, but in good weather they could be left in the Big Harbour. Punts were used to ferry the crews to and from the skiffs.

The men fished from home for a great part of the year. In January, they sailed for 'the Banks of Ballantrae' on the Ayrshire coast, remaining there, and living aboard the boat, for some six weeks. In May, they would leave for the 'North' summer herring fishery in the Minch. Maggie: 'We used to go away up in the skiffs, oh, a crowd of us. We used to go up to Crinan an walk back. We had a gay time of it, you know. We dined aboard the skiffs. It was great. The whole family went. An we walked back or else got a lift back – it was vans in these days. It was a great occasion, that. We saw the fishermen off just at the sea-lock there out at Crinan. They would all be away till on at the end of June. When they came back, they were bronzed. As sure as ever – of course, it's the strong air. They were terrible sunburnt when they came back.'

Jessie had earlier memories of the *True Love* and the *Silver Craig* sailing north to the drift-net fish fishery at Loch Boisdale. 'It used tae be such a busy time getting them ready for the North – the buzz was terrible.' Jerseys would be knitted and several shifts of clothing made ready. Provisions would include coffee, which was very popular with Silvercraigs fishermen, hard sea-biscuits, bought by the bag from MacDonald the baker in Ardrishaig, and butter which came in lidded earthenware crocks. On the day of the fishermen's departure, schoolchildren would be granted a holiday. Jessie recalled going with her mother and Aunt Maggie and her family 'the length o Cairnbaan' in the skiff and walking back home by the road. Tea and buttered sea-biscuits were served on board. The boats were drawn through the Canal by a single horse, led by a man. The earliest family boats she remembered at Silvercraigs were the small, open skiffs *Clio* and her Uncle Peter's *Scarba*.

The fishermen could be heard, by the sound of their leather seaboots, returning home in darkness. 'We used to hear them comin in, perhaps if they'd come in through the night,' Jessie recalled. 'We would be up in the loft, in bed; we used to hear them, the rattle of the big boots as they came through the garden at the end of the house.' When they arrived in, Maggie would ask: 'Any fishin?' – 'No.' – 'Oh, you are awful. You never really can get a fishin!' Then her father would command her to welcome the fishermen. '"Fish or no fish, welcome home, the fishermen" – say that.' And the greeting would be recited quickly.

The men made the creels to catch *buckies* for line-bait (p 64) and also the wooden *trochs* for holding the lines. The creels, baited with fish, were set at the 'back of the Craig'. Duncan Campbell broke the buckie-shells with a mallet, sliced them into sections and passed them to his brothers, Donald and Archie, who baited the lines with them. On a sunny spring day, the men would bait out of doors at the end of the house; otherwise, they sat in a heated shed at the back. Jessie remembered filling clay-pipes with tobacco for them, so dirty were their hands. 'I think it wis the nicest thing tae see a line baited,' Maggie remarked. The line-skiffs, built in Ardrishaig, were pointed at each end and four-oared, and would be sailed or rowed to Otter Ferry, where the lines were set. The biggest catch that Maggie recalled seeing was 60 stone of cod. 'That line-skiff was down to the gunnel.' Some of the fish and roes were given away and Dan Hamilton, a fish-buyer and herring-curer in Ardrishaig, came and took the rest. At her mother's anxious insistence, Jessie would run uphill on stormy days to watch for the men returning.

Fish

The staple diet at Silvercraigs was fish. In summer, fresh herring, coated in oatmeal, were fried; in winter, *sgadain saillte*, salt herring, were boiled and eaten with potatoes, perhaps twice a week into the spring. A barrel of herring would be cured, but no earlier than November, because if any fat remains on the fish 'they resist the salt'. The herring were first *roiled* (turned in salt) then pickled in brine. If a potato would float in the pickle, then it was strong enough for curing purposes. Besides the fish caught commercially by the menfolk, there was the children's contribution taken with rod and hand-line. Codling could be caught, from an anchored boat, by jerking a hand-line weighted to reach the sea-bottom. These would be eaten fresh and a portion of the catch distributed to neighbours. Small saithe – *cuddies* and *peuchties* – were fished by rowing a small boat back and forth through the Dorus at evening, with perhaps six rods inserted into a portable wooden beam, or *sgathach*, at the stern. Sometimes shoals of cuddies would be seen 'playing', or flurrying, on the surface. These small saithe would be salted on the bone for winter provision. The large saithe (*stanelock*) and cod that the men caught in spring were also cured, in big wooden tubs, then laid on slatted frames on the roofs to dry. When dried, they were hung indoors, and, as required, would be steeped overnight in cold water, 'tae get the salt out them', then boiled. 'They were beautiful with butter an potatoes,' Maggie recalled.

Shellfish

Spoot-fish (razor-fish *Solenidae*) were gathered during 'spring ebb', when the tide 'ebbed almost to the Point – it had tae be before ye got them'. Some folk dug out the spoot-fish with a *graip* (fork), but others – Maggie and Jessie among them – used only their hands to catch the top of the shell. 'There's a knack in it,' Maggie said. 'They go down very quickly.' The shellfish were prepared for cooking by placing them in a basin and scattering salt over them, 'so that they would throw out the sand'. Next day, boiling water would be poured over them, the shells removed and the 'top' cut off the fish itself. Fried in butter, spoot-fish would constitute a meal – either breakfast or 'tea' – 'but if anybody said they were tough, well, that was a sign they dinna jeest care for them'. *Clabba-doos* (p 76), Maggie said, could be collected off the Wee Harbour. 'The tide had to be very far out to get them.' *Wilks* weren't eaten by the Campbells, but they gathered them, to sell to MacVicar in Ardrishaig, on local shores or else took the line-skiff to Otter.

Wells

The Campbell well at Silvercraigs was 'cut out a rock, more or less'. It was deep and lined with *chuckies*, quartz pebbles. 'Ye scrubbed these chuckies out quite often. Lovely water. It came down the Craig,' Maggie said. Jessie recalled its being 'as cold in summer as it was in winter'. Flagstones were laid all round the well and, in early spring, the path from house to well would be strewn with white shells gathered from 'banks' that came ashore. 'They were beautiful at night; ye could see it as plain,' Maggie remarked. A trout from the burn would be placed in the well to eat flies and grubs and so keep the water clean, and the family would 'put down a worm or two' for the fish, which would 'come out quite the thing'. The postman, too, always had a tit-bit for the trout when he called with mail. The last trout was accidentally removed from the well in a *stòp* – a narrow-mouthed wooden water-container – and, when it was emptied, the fish was found dead. Afterwards, a cover was placed over the well to prevent cows from going there to drink. Two stops were generally carried at a time, for balance. One of the Silvercraigs stops, which had been bought at Inveraray, was donated to Auchindrain Museum. The Campbells had a second well, in the garden, for washing purposes. There was a basin beside it in which all the members of the family would wash their faces in cold water, summer and winter. Beyond the house there was another well which was used by visiting fishermen for refilling their casks.

Butter and buttermilk

Butter was churned on the croft at Silvercraigs, but the quantity made was insufficient to last the year. Jessie's mother had a large urn-shaped crock for holding cream, which was skimmed from the milk every morning. If the day was cold, the churn wouldn't 'do so quickly', so the crock would be left by the fire, covered, 'to heat a bit, and that would make the butter come quicker'. The first churn that Jessie recalled seeing in use was of the 'plunger' type. When the butter 'broke', the buttermilk would be removed, the butter cleaned in water, patted into shape and finished with a thistle-design print on it. A paddle-churn – placed on a chair for ease of operation – was later acquired. When the butter was made, the buttermilk would be drained into a dish, cold water from the well poured into the churn, and the churn activated again to clean the butter. A part of the produce was used fresh and the remainder salted. The elderly Whytes, who lived 'across the burn', habitually put coarse salt into their butter. 'An they'd give us a *piece* on butter wi a big lump o coorse salt in it!' When there was no milk at Silvercraigs, supplies could be bought at Castleton Farm, along with 'lovely buttermilk' at twopence a can. It was used for baking – 'sweet milk' never was – and some of the older folk were fond of pease-meal with buttermilk. The meal – bought a stone at a time – would be put into a bowl, perhaps with a little salt added, and boiling water poured over it.

The pig

A pig was kept on the croft at Silvercraigs and killed at six months old. Some crofters fed their pig on raw potatoes, but the diet of the Campbell pig was boiled potatoes, buttermilk and milk. When butchered, its flesh would be cured in a tub of brine, rolled into hams and hung for winter provision. Neighbours might buy parts of a butchered pig for curing and hanging. A side of beef, mutton or pork could be purchased from a butcher and cured; but meat was seldom eaten and was generally reserved for week-ends.

Oatcakes and bread

Oatcakes and scones were made on a girdle hung half-way up the chimney from a pot-hook and chain. After removal from the girdle, the oatcake would be crisped in front of the fire, on a toaster which attached to the ribs of the grate, then hung from one of the varnished kitchen rafters in a flat home-made basket. Each cake was about two feet long. 'I don't know how she handled them yet,' Jessie said of her mother. The ingredients were simply oatmeal, salt and water, flattened using a special 'nicked' roller which 'left these marks on the oatcakes'.

Jane Campbell always wore a white apron when baking. When flour-bags were empty, they would be split open, washed and rubbed with 'salt-soap' from a tin. They were then spread out on heather and left until they were bleached and the brand-names faded from them, then Jane would sew them into aprons.

When Jessie was a girl, at her father's suggestion she would practice making 'bonnachs' – cakes – with the clay that was dug from the shore for 'claying the step' at the door of the house. The clay was blue at first, but turned white, and she amused herself by making fancy designs round the edge of her clay cakes. After school, on Tuesdays and Fridays, the children would buy perhaps six loaves from a bread-van and carry them home in a white sack. Later, a grocery-van called. Gulls' eggs, for baking, were gathered on the Big Island and 'n Eilean.

Potatoes

The potatoes grown on the Campbell croft at Silvercraigs were dry-textured owing to the sandiness of the soil. Seed-potatoes were planted from a *poca-bratain*, or bag-apron, cut from a jute sack and tied round the waist with hay-rope. The harvest was gathered into home-made willow baskets and emptied into a long *pit* in the field, trenched around to 'let the water run off it'. When the potatoes had dried, the heap would be 'ridged up' to form a shape that would shed rain, then covered with bracken, followed by a light covering of earth. A week or two later, more earth would be added and 'clapped' well with spades to firm it. The crop remained in that pit, protected from weather, until the last of the supply was used in spring. Potatoes for immediate domestic use were stored in the barn, in a large lidded *kist* which Maggie reckoned must have held about five hundredweights. When exhausted, that supply would be replenished from the pit. In April, Duncan Campbell would select the next season's seed-potatoes from the pit, 'watching where the eyes were' and splitting the bigger ones. The whole plot of land was originally dug and planted by hand, but latterly the farmer at Castleton, Archibald MacArthur, would plough with a horse and then turn the rigs after the potato-seed had been planted.

Champed potatoes and *brochan càil*

When the Campbell children were young and money scarce, potatoes 'champed', or mashed, with a wooden *champer*, would be served in an *ashet*. Everyone had a bowl and helped themselves to the mash, to which milk would be added. Jessie's Uncle Alex would have cheese with his. *Brochan càil* – curly kail cooked with a handful of oatmeal – was 'really a soup', as Jessie commented. 'If ye went over, the old Whytes wid have the pot half-way up the chimney. It seemed always to be there. An, of course, ye got a bowl of that.'

Hay-making

The hay-crop, for cattle fodder, was cut by scythe. The whole family would be out in the field at three or four o' clock on a summer's morning, for children had to help as soon as they were old enough. For refreshment, the common drink was *fuarag*, oatmeal and water mixed in a can. The hay, when cut, was left to the sun and air and raked from time to time. Then it would be lifted, shaken well and made into cocks, or heaps, two or three feet high. The simple cock was known as a *coil*, but a smaller one, called a *prapag*, could be made by folding a bunch of hay into 'lik a muff, wi a hole at each side'. 'That was a lot more work,' Maggie said, 'but if ye took the trouble tae do it, they dried awful quick; see, the air was going through them.' These small heaps, when dry, were gathered into *rucks* in the field and netted with ropes and stone-weighted rope. Still later, MacArthur at Castleton would send over a hay-cart to transport the rucks to the back of the house, where a single large house-shaped stack would be built. This was communal work and neighbour would assist neighbour with the stacking of the hay, which was constantly tramped to 'keep it firm'. The stack would be thatched with rushes, cut and 'tied as ye tie sheaves o corn'. First one side, then the other, would be thatched from a ladder and covered with an old piece of herring-net. When cutting a section of hay from the firmly-packed stack, a long-bladed hay-knife was used. Cattle were also fed on cut grass and oat-straw: 'They beat the corn off the straw, and they fed that to the hens, the corn. Then they fed the straw to the cattle.'

Oats

The fields at Silvercraigs were ploughed and harrowed by a horse loaned from Castleton Farm, for which service the crofters would give the farmer their labour at harvest-time. The main fertiliser was *wreck*, or seaweed, which was forked into a wheel-barrow and taken straight to the field where it was to be spread. Wreck-gathering was men's work, but they didn't have to leave the bay to obtain the quantities needed. Oats were sown with two hands, casting the seed to left and right, alternately, from the belly of a white sheet of unbleached cotton, knotted around the neck. After the district harvest had been taken in, a Harvest Home was held in the barn at Castleton Farm and 'all the folks' invited. A supper was provided and the company danced to the music of fiddle and melodeon on the swept-out stone floor. Whoever got the 'end of the harvest' – the lucky last sheaf, or *Cailleach* ('Old Wife') – would keep a bunch of it and hang it, formed into a cross and tied with ribbon, in the house.

Thatching

The byre at Silvercraigs would be re-thatched every autumn with rushes, but there were no rushes at Silvercraigs, so the Campbells went 'wi the boat' to West Otter Ferry and cut rushes there with a scythe. There was a stone pier and two houses there, now in ruins. In droving times, cattle were ferried from there across to East Otter, on the other side of the loch, and then on to Dunoon.

Once the top layers of the old thatch had been stripped off, the new was 'put on fresh' in strips, working from the bottom of the roof upwards, and pegging it to the underlying turf. A sheaf at a time was shouldered up the ladder, and the band loosened out to lay on the thatch, the 'growing end' laid upwards. Once on, a net – secured to iron pins in the walls of the byre – would be put over the thatch as protection from gales: 'We got east wind terribly there, very bad east wind.' The thatching of the byre was a day's work, more or less, and 'it was lovely to look at when it was done'. The last thatched dwelling-houses – two together under one roof – that Maggie remembered in the district were in nearby Baile Mór.

Fuel

There was a 'peat-moss' at Silvercraigs, but in Jessie Campbell's time there it was flooded and no tradition survived in her family of peats having been cut there. There were few trees in the district, but a boat would be taken across the loch to East Otter and filled with driftwood there. Burnt heather – *falaisg* – was gathered for kindling, along with small sticks from the shore and *barrlach**, the twigs from larches, gathered at Baile Mór. Whins, which grew on the Craig and at Garbhard and Barr, would be burned in February or March and gathered the following spring, when breakable. These could mostly be broken by hand or over a knee, but thicker stems had to be cut with an axe, all of which was children's work, unless the men had time to give to it. Baking by girdle was always done over a whin fire – 'Ye wid get a fire in a minute or two' – whins being 'clean' and their heat easier to 'regulate' than that of coal. In April, when the weather had improved, the Campbells and MacEwans would sail to Greenock in skiffs and load up with ten tons of coal. One of Duncan Campbell's sons, Dugald, who was a captain in the Merchant Navy and had a house in Greenock, would order coal from a merchant there and it was 'down in the docks ready for them when they went'. When the skiffs returned to Silvercraigs, they were brought into the harbour at high water and the coal unloaded into small boats and landed on the beach. From there, it was brought up in bags or barrows, or by pony-drawn cart, and piled at the back of the house to form a coal-heap, or *gualag*. Other local families had their coals delivered by cart from Lochgilphead and, latterly, the laird arranged for a smack to bring in supplies, which could be bought from him.

*Standard Gaelic barrach, *top branches of trees, brushwood. Not gathered by the Campbells, but by other families.*

Sabbath in Aird

'They were good-living people here,' Maggie said. 'They were great church-going people in Aird. The road was black with people goin up tae church.' Church was the Free Church in Lochgilphead, where three services were held – the morning service in Gaelic and the afternoon and evening services in English. 'Folk walked up an down that road thinking nothing of it. Four mile from our place. An then they used tae come down an hold perhaps kitchen-meetings, our ministers.' No work, 'but what was necessary', was done on the Sabbath. The meal would be prepared on Saturday and pots of water filled from the well; ashes weren't put out; 'the dishes weren't washed, even'.

The Whytes

The Whyte family at Silvercraigs had radical leanings and hated 'wars and the Crown'. In the anecdote below, Mary's gesture inland may be interpreted as an implicit reference to the land the Whytes lost by eviction (p 188).

'Mistress Jock', wife of the local laird, John Campbell of Shirvain, and a bossy, interfering woman, approached Mary Whyte prior to a general election and instructed her: 'Now, Mary, you must remember to vote for your country.' – '*I* have no country,' Mary replied. Mistress Jock was very perplexed. 'I used to have a country,' Mary continued, waving a vague hand towards Ach' an leth-Pheighinn. [Maggie]

Military Medal

An Ardrishaig fisherman, Angus 'Fetty' Law, appeared one day at Silvercraigs with Alan Campbell, the son of a shopkeeping family in Ardrishaig. 'Do you know this man has the Military Medal?' Angus remarked to Sandy Whyte. 'Och,' said Sandy, 'throw it in the watter.' Angus was 'very deflated'. [Maggie]

Sandy's bees

Sandy kept bees at Silvercraigs and used to leave over a comb of honey at the Campbell croft. The combs were well-liked, but the boys would say: 'They're quite nice apart from the wee bees in them.' During the First World War, when sugar was scarce, Sandy would go into Lochgilphead and try all the shops for sugar to give to his bees. When asked, 'How many of a family do you have?' his reply was invariably: 'Thousands.' [Maggie]

An ominous dream

Jessie Campbell's father believed in dreams, but he didn't like to tell them. There was one dream, however, which troubled him and of which he did speak. He was with his son, Duncan, who at the time – the First World War – was on active service with the Argyll and Sutherland Highlanders. They were walking together over a hill in Cowal and there was an inn nearby. When he looked at his son 'there was blood on his mouth'. Soon after the dream, word came that Duncan had been wounded in action. [Jessie]

'Tory Jock' Orde

'Tory Jock' was the derogatory name by which Sir John Orde of Kilmory was known. A hated landowner, whose style was that of an English squire, he was responsible for a series of drastic evictions from his lands (p 188) and was no friend of the fishermen. The contempt in which he was held emerges in two fragmentary stories.

'He used tae come out at the Clock Lodge an drive his carriage an pair right across there. There was a causeway right across the ebb tae Ardrishaig. Me father used tae always tell us aboot "Tory Jock", how the wee boys were runnin after the carriage, an how the whip, whippin roon the wee boy's neck, near killed him. However, he got off with it.' [Jessie]

The incident happened on 1 November, 1870, while Orde was 'proceeding in his coach at a smart rate' along the public road near Ardrishaig. He 'struck with his whip at some children who were standing on the roadside, and who were doing nothing to provoke him in any way. The lash of the whip caught around the neck of one of the little boys, and he was pulled to the ground, and dragged for several yards along the rough road, whereby he was bruised and cut about the head and neck. Sir John's groom, who was sitting behind the coach, deponed on oath that his master struck at the little boy quite gratuitously, and that when told that he had lassoed a child by the throat, he merely gave a mocking laugh'. Orde appeared in Inveraray Sheriff Court, in April of the following year, on a charge of assaulting a four-year-old boy. Orde's defence, that the boy had been throwing stones and frightened the horses, 'causing them to shy and plunge', evidently satisfied Mr Spiers, interim Sheriff Substitute, who decided that 'the occurrence was purely accidental' and found Orde not guilty.[4]

'Stand back, stable boy'

'That was when Queen Victoria was goin through the Crinan Canal. "Tory Jock" went first, tae bow tae the Queen, an this other toff said tae him: "Stand back, stable boy." He wis higher up than "Tory Jock".' [Jessie]

Orde's humiliation before Queen Victoria may be fiction or may be grounded in some real incident, for another version of the story has Orde and the other principal local landowner, Alexander Campbell of Auchindarroch, jealously trying to brush off each other as they moved forward to greet the Queen, who, during her tour of her kingdom in 1847, landed at Ardrishaig to sail through the Canal on her way to Oban. The Queen, in her published diary, records only that Orde lent her his carriage 'and was extremely civil'.[5]

[All material from Jessie and Maggie Campbell, 1977, and Mary MacBrayne, 2003, unless otherwise indicated]

References and Notes
1. John MacCulloch, *The Highlands and Western Isles of Scotland*, London, 1824, p 62.
2. Argyll and Bute Council Archive, Lochgilphead, Log Book 1875-1939, CA/5/198.
3. M MacDonald, letter to author, 4 April, 2003.

4. *AH*, 29 April 1871.
5. M MacDonald, Archivist, Argyll & Bute Council, letter to author, 18 March 2003.

Kames

Walking the coast from Silvercraigs north to Kames involves a distance of just over five miles. Once, for the sake of seeing the old ferry quay at West Otter, I did the walk and thought nothing of it; but Donald and Margaret MacVicar at Kames were astonished that anybody would come by such a rocky way when a road existed. Yet, both Silvercraigs and Kames are practically hidden from the main road and one would never know they existed unless directed to them or discovering them by chance. Until 1977, I was unaware that so many corners of natural beauty and historical interest lay concealed on that stretch of coast.

In that year, Murdo MacDonald, Argyll and Bute Council archivist, who lives in Baile Mór – another picturesque, secluded spot – invited me to meet Maggie Campbell, by then settled in a cottage on Castleton Farm. I also met the farmer in Castleton, Donald Macleod – born in Skye and raised on Mull – and it was he who suggested a retired forestry worker, Donald MacVicar in Kames, as a source of material for the book I was then researching, *The Ring-Net Fishermen*. Donald Macleod's first language was Gaelic, and in Gaelic he would converse with Donald MacVicar – who was one of the last few native speakers left on Lochfyneside – whenever the two met.

I duly met Donald MacVicar and his wife, Margaret Bell, who belonged to nearby Lochgair, and so began a productive association, maintained by occasional visits and correspondence. Their cottage, in which Donald was born on 7 February, 1898, was built above the stony beach beside a wooded burn. It was dark and cluttered, a veritable living museum, but enriched by the old couple's kindness and hospitality.

Kames represents Gaelic *Camus*, a bay. Old maps show roadside communities at West Kames – evidently removed in the 1930s when the A83 was re-aligned – and Middle Kames. East Kames – closest of the three to Lochgair – was built beside the shore and the MacVicar cottage was there, though Margaret always used 'Low Kames' as her address. The burn beside their cottage was called Eas Dubh ('Black Waterfall', undoubtedly from the upstream waterfalls) and, where it entered the sea,

Allt a' Chrè (Clay Stream, from the clay obtainable at ebb-water). On the shore below Middle Kames, there had been a 'navigation school' kept by an elderly retired seaman. That school was known as The College, and some of the students there jokingly 'christened' the hill above it University Hill, a name which persisted, for Donald knew no other.

Donald's father was John MacVicar and his mother, Mary, was a MacVicar too. The only English he heard spoken as a boy was in school, where, 'If you were heard talkin Gaelic, ye got a clout on the jaw without bein spoken tae'. Donald remembered some 60 pupils in Lochgair School when he attended. There were 40 when Margaret went first and 24 when she left. The school was closed in 1928, but reopened briefly in September, 1939, for child war-evacuees from Glasgow.[1]

The Lochgair School log book is singularly lacking in social information, but those for Minard School, some six miles north along the lochside, contain a wealth of lively notes on the extra-curricular activities of fishermen's children. The withdrawal of 'older boys' to 'follow their occupation as fishermen' is remarked upon in April of successive years, but on 8 July, 1881, the following observation was logged: 'The Herring fishing being remunerative in the near neighbourhood has drawn away a number of the older boys, while some of those who are yet in attendance prosecute the fishing during the night which renders them unfit for school work.' On 5 May 1882, the schoolmaster complains: 'I regret the loss of a few advanced pupils who have joined the fishing fleet and gone to Stornoway.' In March, 1883, many pupils were 'away gathering whelks (winkles) and other shellfish for the market', while others were collecting wrack for their gardens. At the end of the following month, attendance was poor owing to peat-cutting, and, in February, 1886, had become irregular 'owing to some of the scholars having to go to the wood for white grass for thatch'.[2]

Donald fetched water in buckets from a well, and even after a supply was piped to the cottage in 1980, the well remained in use for drinking-water, tea-making and cooking. The MacVicars kept hens, until foxes destroyed them, and it was a delight to sit at the narrow kitchen window, with its view across the loch, and dine on several big eggs, red-yolked from the hens' foragings in the seaweed. My vegetarianism perplexed poor Margaret, who was ever uncertain that a meal of eggs – supplemented perhaps by Donald's home-grown potatoes – was adequate for me.

Donald and Margaret had no children, and Donald's only extended absence from Kames was during the First World War. He was shot through an ear – the bullet left a distinct notch – but he spoke little of those years. He gave unstintingly of his knowledge, a slow release as he translated Gaelic into English in his head. At times he'd fall asleep while I tape-recorded him, and waken after a few minutes, mostly unaware that he'd been gone. In 1978, I began collecting Gaelic vocabulary from him. Donald was no storyteller, but a scrupulous witness to the life of the community he was born into and of which, after the death of his sister Janet, who lived in a cottage across the burn, he was the last surviving representative.

Fishing at Kames

The four fishing families at Kames were MacVicars, Turners, MacTavishes and Murrays. Donald MacVicar's own family was in the district for at least four generations, he said. His father left the fishing when Donald was young. 'They couldn't make a living. Boats lay on the shore. Nobody would buy them.' Before Donald's time, the fishermen around Lochgair had smacks for drift-netting, but these proved 'too big tae pay'. A greater number of men was needed to crew a smack than to crew a smaller skiff and 'the upkeep was too heavy'. Many boat-owners discarded the smacks. 'I know there were a few rotted up on that shore in Loch Gair, burnt an rotted; couldn't get them sold, and they couldn't keep them.' Smaller open boats, which carried a brazier for heating, were more economic to work. The boats Donald remembered in use were skiffs, quarter-decked to form a small forecastle, or *den*, which contained *bunkers* on each side, doubling as seats and beds and providing storage space 'in below the lids'. A small stove was fitted for heating the den and for cooking on. The main cooking utensil was the fish-pan, which was in two parts: the main pan and an inner container – made by tinkers – which had a perforated bottom and a curved wire handle. 'Ye could catch it an lift it out, an by the time ye had it up, there's no water in it; ye put the herrin dry on the plate.' Tea was drunk from bowls.

In summer and autumn, crews fished with drift-nets for herring, changing in winter to cod-netting. The *lìon-gruund*, or ground-net, had three to four-inch meshes and was 'great for big cod'. It would be let down in deep water, on long buoy-ropes, with just enough corks strung on the back-rope to 'keep them off the bottom'. These nets were assembled by stretching the ropes from trees or 'stance-poles', which were the uprights of the net-drying frames.

Selling in Lochgilphead

The Kames fishermen sold what fresh cod they could and salted the rest.

They would hire a horse and cart and drive the fish to Lochgilphead and sell it though the streets. Fresh cod would fetch 'a penny a pound' and the salted and dried product 4d a pound. In the salting process, the cod was first beheaded and the greater part of the bone removed; then the fish, layer upon layer added daily, were steeped in a tub of brine until ready to be laid in rows on the roofs of the houses, drying 'where no beast could get at it'. Cod-heads would be boiled in a pot and the flesh eaten off them, while the juice that remained was made into a soup.

Hauling up the boats

All the Kames fishing-boats would be hauled ashore on a single day in the 'back end', after the gear had been removed for storage and the ballast dumped on the shore. From 10 to 15 men, spread along both sides of a boat, could drag her ashore; the smaller boats could be lifted bodily by up to 20 men. 'There wir that many folks, it wis a great day, drawin up the boats.' The boats were left on the beach until spring, when they would be cleaned and tarred for the start of the fishing season. The hulls were tarred from keel to waterline, and the upper hull coated with linseed-oil boiled with *roset* (resin) melted through it. Tar was obtained from the gas-works in Inveraray or Lochgilphead or else imported in barrels from Greenock.

Housing

The earliest houses were drystone-built – 'you would see through the walls' – and thatched, but these began to be replaced, Donald thought, about 1900. Rushes were gathered on a hill about a mile away and stored until sufficient for thatching. 'They wirna supposed tae be goin there for it', so they went by moonlight and carried the bundles of thatch on their backs from the hill. Fire in these old thatched houses was originally contained in an iron creel – *creathal* – set on a flagstone in the middle of the floor and with a hole in the thatch above for the smoke to escape. Later, when chimneys came into being, a fireplace would be built with stones or bricks and with four iron bars to form a grate, the whole cemented with clay 'out the shore', and overhung with a pot-hook and chain attached to an iron bar built into the gable.

Fuel

Kindling at Kames was, as at Silvercraigs, *falaisg*. When farmers burned coarse heather in spring, the 'strong shanks', or *cowes*, would remain, and during the summer or 'back end' these would be pulled from the ground, gathered into big bundles and tied with rope, then carried home for stock-piling. 'The best o stuff tae kinnle a fire.'

Peat was the main fuel at Kames, but families there had to go 'two miles above Knock Farm hill' to cut in the spring. Gaining the year's fuel supply was an effort that involved the whole family. Food would be brought and 'peat tea' brewed on the hill. An ordinary spade was used for removing the top turf at the peat-bank. The peat-spade was called a *torbhsgian* and sometimes a cow's horn would be mounted on the shaft as a handle.

As the cutter placed the wet peat-blocks on the edge of the bank, they would be lifted and 'put out' – spread on the heather – by children, if there were children. If they 'had far to go' to the spreading ground, then a peat-barrow would be used. Once spread – 'ye caught them wi the two hands so that they wouldn't break' – the peats would be left for perhaps eight or ten days until dry enough to be fitted together in clumps – *tein-nteanan* – of four or five placed upright, with one laid longways on the top.

When dry – perhaps after a fortnight, 'maybe longer, dependin on the weather' – all the peats would be gathered and built into stacks, about 6ft high, broad at the base and tapering to a single row of peats at the top, so that they 'shed the rain'. For that reason, too, the stack-builder always tried to 'keep the peat at a slant' when forming the walls. Peats, in bags or in home-made creels, were carried off the hill when needed, perhaps a creel in the morning and another in the evening, but the people would try to take home a 'good puckle' so that 'in bad weather they would have it'. These extra peats would be piled in some corner outside and covered with a piece of sail, perhaps, to keep them dry. When opening a new stack on the hill, it would be broken at one of the ends, so that 'it wisna harmin the stack for standin'. Peat-cutting in the Kames area began to decline about 1920.

Peat-torch

If some one had to go out on a very dark night, he would look for a long peat and stick an end of it into the fire 'till it got goin'. Hand-held and with the wind keeping it alight, that single peat served as a torch, providing the distance – to a neighbour's house, say – wasn't far. On arrival there, the peat would be 'stubbed out like a cigarette'; then, before leaving to go home, it would be placed in the neighbour's fire until lit again, 'an ye had it comin back'. If the light began to dim, 'give it a bit shake an it wid flare up… the peat wou'na go out'.

Ghosts

In Donald's youth, there were folk who would 'hardly go about in the dark' for fear of meeting a *bòcan*, or ghost, which might in reality be 'only a bush'. Others would 'travel from dark till daylight and they wouldn't see anything'. Some pranksters enjoyed wearing a white sheet and presenting themselves to nervous travellers who 'were seein this *bòcan* an turnin back as hard as they could'.

Fertiliser

The fishermen would till their plots of land in spring, but when absent during the week, the women performed such tasks as weeding. Dung was in short supply at Kames, so basically it was 'seaweed for everything', gathered in creels from the shore in spring, a labour which involved whole families. When seaweed was scarce locally, the cottars and their families would go off in small boats to a more distant shore and spend an ebb tide cutting weed from the rocks with old 'hooks' (sickles), for that kind of work would 'spoil' a new tool. With a good ebb, from 30 to 35 creel-loads might be gathered and left in heaps along the high water-mark to drain before spreading.

Shellfish

Winkles (*faochagan*) were gathered commercially and fetched from 8s to 10s a hundredweight, but razor-fish – s*poot-fish* or *spooties* – were gathered as a food, as at Silvercraigs. The presence of a *spootie* was betrayed by a small dent in the sand or by an inch or two of the upper shell's protruding, but, as Donald put it: 'Ye had tae be nimble… Ye had tae be very quick tae press them wi yer two fingers that they winna get away down. Ye wid need tae take yer time takin them up, unless ye wid lose the meat – they wid break, because they kept a hold in the sand.' They could also be located by the 'spoot' – or spout – of water they put up when disturbed – hence their name – but by that time it was too late: 'They were away.' To avoid cutting his fingers when grasping the shells, Donald very often used a 'piece of flat iron' for digging out the shells. Three or four dozen *spooties* would suffice to make a meal. They were placed in boiling water to remove the sand and then broken from their shells and cleaned, but 'it didn't matter how ye cleaned them, ye got sand when you were eating them'. They would be fried, but not for too long because, as Margaret MacVicar observed, 'The longer ye cooked them, the tougher they got'.

[All material from Donald MacVicar, 1977 and '78, unless otherwise indicated]

References and Notes
1. Argyll and Bute Council Archive, Log Book 1874-1928, CA/5/106.
2. *Ibid.*, Log Books 1871-1888, CA/5/245.

Food

The themes of food and eating recur abundantly throughout this book, but this chapter attempts to present, largely through childhood memories, elements in the diet which, for the most part, are now obscure.

Mary McGeachy

Mary McGeachy was born on 7 August, 1910, in Dalintober, and lived at 17 High Street. Her father, John Edward McGeachy, was a successful fisherman, and his family – there were 10 children – 'never really went hungry'. Breakfast was a bowl of porridge, and 'if ye dinna eat yer porridge in the mornin, it wis waitin on ye at tea-time'. Some mornings Mary would be at the house of her father's cousin, Sweeney McGeachy, and would be served breakfast there. When she'd go home, her own 'crowd' would be sitting eating porridge and Mary would boast: 'I had an egg this moarnin!'

There was always plenty of fish, especially herring, which would be salted in a *kit* or *firkin* for winter and served once a week… 'an if there wir naething else, ye'd tae put up wi them twice a week'. In summer, there would be fresh herring ('diced', or notched, along the back and dusted with oatmeal and flour) that 'fried in their own fat'. Her father would occasionally go to 'the hill' and shoot rabbits to put meat on the table. At school, a '*piece* on jam' at 'race-time' – or play-time – was the sole sustenance.

Having gone for a neighbour's shopping, Mary would sometimes be rewarded with a sixpence. At about the age of 10, with just such a sixpence, she bought three cakes of cream chocolate at twopence each 'an I ett them all an I was seeck for a week'. But 'luxuries' were rare, and when interviewed, at the age of 91, Mary still had her own teeth. [2001]

Nan McKay

Nan McKay, through her mother, Flora McGeachy, was related to Mary McGeachy, above, and was also brought up in High Street. On a

Saturday morning her mother would make batches of scones, potato-scones and pancakes, and these would constitute the 'tea-dinner' that evening, which Nan hated: 'I laiked ma potatoes at dinnertime.' The table would be laid out with bread, butter and jam in addition to the baking, and she was the one who 'got the rows' when she would bypass the bread and put a hand out to take a scone or pancake. 'Packin furst!' her father would scold. Her mother always made clootie-dumplings as a birthday treat, one small – which was eaten hot – and one large, which would be sliced when cool. Grated carrot, for moisture, was always included in the mixture and a few threepenny bits, wrapped in grease-proof paper, added as surprises. [2003]

Archie Carmichael

Archie Carmichael of Tarbert wasn't fed salt herring until about the age of eight years; children had potatoes mashed with milk. For 'sheep's heid broth', the head was first singed bare at the smiddy. Dead hares would be dumped at the Fountain* after a shoot over a local laird's land. 'If ye wir quick, ye ran doon an grabbed a hare.' Many folk at that time, however, wouldn't eat a hare. Witches were supposed to be able to turn themselves into hares by night, and there was a story told of a hare being wounded by a shot and an old woman, next morning, being seen limping with an injury to the same leg. [2003]

*Sited at the harbourside, close to where the burn enters the sea, it was an ornate metal structure with iron cups for drinking. It was knocked down and destroyed by a lorry in the black-out during the Second World War.

Groceries

At Port Righ, Carradale, most of the groceries – lentils, barley, biscuits, etc. – were bought from travelling vans. May McDougall remembered Lipton's van coming from Campbeltown on a Friday or Saturday when she was a girl. Ginger snap biscuits would be weighed in the van and sold in paper bags. 'We used tae say, if ye got one an ye hit it on yer elbow, if it broke intae three that wis luck.' Renton the butcher and Hoynes the baker sent vans from Campbeltown, and Campbell the grocer and Paterson the baker in Carradale also ran vans. Sometimes she would be sent to Airds to buy butter and bread – which was usually ready about mid-day – at the baker's shop. 'Ye used tae go up for the new loafs. When ye wir goin through the village, ye could smell the bakin. It wis a lovely smell.' [May McDougall, 2003]

Oatcakes

Before she got married, May McDougall would make oatcakes on the griddle for her father, Charlie, at Braemar. 'He loved oatcakes,' she said. 'I wid make them an he wid sit toastin them in front o the fire.' He simply held them to the range, and when they had curled a little at the edges, he would spread them with butter and perhaps add cheese. She remembered, as a girl, seeing in the cottage next door, in which her grandmother Mary McDougall lived, a 'lovely barrel' standing at each side of the old black range. Each barrel – one for meal and the other for flour – was glossy with varnish and had a wooden lid with a gold-coloured glass handle on it. May's father was very fond of peasebrose, and would cook it in a pot and eat it with milk on a Saturday or Sunday night when he was home from the fishing; but none of the children liked it. [May McDougall, 2003]

Vegetable garden

Braemar had a substantial plot of land attached to it and Charlie McDougall kept a good vegetable garden, growing potatoes, carrots – which were always a success, owing to the sandy soil – cabbages, curly kail, turnips, parsnips, beetroot and parsley. After his own produce had been used up, he would bring home bags of potatoes and carrots from Creggan Farm, near Skipness, and store them in the small summer house out the back, the carrots in a sand-filled galvanised bathtub. [May McDougall, 2003]

Clootie dumpling

When May McDougall's father and the crew of the *Clan McDougall* went to the North fishing (p 168) they would take with them a big clootie dumpling which her mother had made. May did the same for her husband, Johnny, when he went North. 'Well, ye jeest kinna followed on whoot yer folk did.' Her dumplings would be five or six pounds in weight – 'as big as yer pot held' – and cooked in a pillowslip kept especially for that purpose. In her mother's time, these *cloots*, or cloths – and many another article, such as aprons and pillowslips – were sewn from cotton flour-bags obtained from the baker in Carradale and split, washed and then laid on the grass to bleach until 'snow-white'. [May McDougall, 2003]

Sea biscuits

These biscuits – manufactured in bakeries using flour, water, salt, sugar and (optionally) lard – served fishermen as a 'stand-by' when the supply of bread was exhausted, though some claimed to prefer them to bread. They would be carried to sea by the stone and, to keep them crisp, stored in special metal containers or net-bags close to the stove-pipe. There were many names for the biscuits. In English: 'sea-biscuits', 'ship-biscuits', 'butter-biscuits', 'crackers' and 'bulwark-biscuits', which was the variety formed with a rim, or bulwark, all round. In the Gaelic of Lochfyneside, they were *briosgaidean cruaidhe*, 'hard biscuits', and on Gigha *briosgaidean Tobar Mhoire*, 'Tobermory biscuits', or *briosgaidean madaidh*, 'dog biscuits', from the habit of the 'old laird', Colonel Scarlett, of feeding them to his 'great pack of hounds'. Donald MacDonald, Gigha: 'That was my dinner at one time when I was at school there, coming over from the west an going to school. If I hadn't a piece with me for my dinner, maybe have a ha'penny to buy a hard biscuit in in the shop there. Dog-biscuit for a dinner till A would go home about five o' clock, or after [supper] in the evening again.' [1978]

Winkles

Wilks were gathered at Port Righ Beag, the small bay north of Port Righ, and round the Point, to the south. May McDougall's mother would put the wilk-meats in omelettes or make wilk-soup with them. They would be boiled and some of the juice kept with the meats, to which would be added a handful of oatmeal and an egg broken into the soup and 'swirled' so that it formed particles through the mixture. 'I cou'na take them,' May said. 'Never could take them. They would always leave me sick.' [May McDougall, 2003]

Carragheen

The naturally gelatinous seaweed *Chondrus crispus*, in Gaelic *carraigean*, and anglicised as 'carragheen', was gathered from certain tidal rocks along the coast of Gigha and dried for use in puddings. As Donald MacDonald remarked: 'Aye, it was fine with the dinner, after yer potatoes an everything, a plate o carragheen.' [1978] Mary Menzies' mother, Catherine McSporran (p 15), belonged to Gigha and would bring back dried carragheen after a visit to the island. Mary herself remembers visiting Gigha as a child and seeing the seaweed drying on white sheets spread on the ground. She still makes carragheen pudding, when she can obtain the seaweed, and considers it a very satisfying cold sweet in summertime and beneficial to those with stomach ailments. The following is her recipe: '1 teacup carragheen, 5 teacups milk. Soak carragheen in water for a short time to soften. Add carragheen to milk and slowly heat until back of spoon is coated. Strain through muslin. An egg, optionally, can be switched through the mixture at this stage. Rinse pan. Put strained carragheen back in pan. Add 4 tablespoons sugar and slowly dissolve. Pour into dish and leave to set. When cooking, carefully watch pan doesn't burn.'[1] Dulse (*Rhodymenia palmata*) was also gathered as a food by the islanders, and teething babies were given the tough stalk of a tangle (*Laminaria*) to chew on. [Angus MacAlister, 2003]

Brallach

The *brallach* or *brollach*, the sand gaper *Mya arenaria**, was dug from the mud in Tarbert harbour with spades, for both food and line-bait. 'He puts up this feeder up through the ground an he'll haul it doon through a hole, lik a rabbit in a burra,' Hugh MacFarlane remembered. 'They wir great bait, but they wirna good at stickin on the hook.' [1976, 1978] Dugald MacFarlane agreed: 'Good bait, an it's damn good tae eat if ye wir stuck for a meal. Ye winna go far wrong wi it. Many a feed o it A had, but afore this big dose o sewage.' [1978] Robert Ross, as a boy, collected them using the iron hoop of a barrel trailed along like a rake. The brallach meat – which resembled that of the cockle – was used for hand-lines, and codling were fond of it. [2003]

*Anachan *in Gaelic of South Kintyre*.[2]

Fish and soup

When the McBride children in Carradale returned home from school, their mother would often have fish frying in a big iron pan, sometimes herring and other times *stanelock*, cut in squares. Once a week, her mother would do a big washing at an outside boiler, fuelled by long sticks which had to be constantly 'poked in'. 'It wis some day when she washed. Everythin wis turned upside-down. An yet she wid have the two big pots o soup on, one on each side o the fire.' One pot would contain, in season, rabbit soup, to which one of Annie's brothers was partial, while the other would contain gigot (leg of mutton) soup. Left-over rabbit would be fried for breakfast. [Annie McBride, 2003]

Dookers

In Tarbert, the dooker – which is the guillemot *Uria aalge* – was a regular source of food in winter, so much so that the collective nick-name for the Tarbert people is 'Dookers'.

Archie Carmichael first went dooker-shooting with his grandfather, also Archibald Carmichael, a Gaelic-speaking fisherman. The birds were shot from a 'punt', and, in a breeze, the hunters would often be 'soakin wet'; but Archibald the elder 'always wis lookin for a breeze o win tae save him rowin'. They would stop in the middle of Loch Fyne and put out a lure, which was usually liver-oil. Saithe livers were kept in a perforated tin, which would be dipped into the water. Then the hunters would withdraw to leeward and await the arrival of gulls to form the screaming 'cavvy'* which would, in turn, bring in the dookers. When asked how many birds he would be looking to shoot in a day, Archie's reply was: 'As many as ye could get.' If livers were unavailable, the hunters would row after the birds.

Every Tarbert fishing-boat carried a gun and in every house occupied by a fishing family there would be a gun hung above the fireplace 'tae keep it dry'. A twelve-bore shotgun was the standard equipment, but when Archie was very young he saw muzzle-loaders in use. Birds and gun would be carried home inside the boat's sail, because licenses were not commonly held in those days. 'Ye wir learnin tae shoot when ye wir maybe aboot twelve year old,' Archie recalled. The birds would be plucked and singed with a red-hot poker, then made into 'dooker soup' or else pot-roasted on the open grate; but, as Archie remarked: 'Ye had'ae waatch in case a lump o soot wid go intae the pot; ye had'ae be quick wi the lid.' Dookers would be sent by post, wrapped in paper and with a label round their necks, to uncles and aunts in Glasgow, who might send a bag of potatoes in return, from their allotments there. An uncle, John MacPhail, who captained a 'steamer', brought the potatoes to Tarbert. After the guillemot became a protected species, the custom of shooting them declined. [Archie Carmichael, 2003]

*Also 'cavag' and 'cavach' in Tarbert. Latimer McInnes, in his Dialect of South Kintyre, defines 'cavag' as, 'The call and flurry of seabirds over an eye of herring', and suggests a derivation from Gaelic cabhag, 'haste, hurry'.

Katie and Mary Jackson recalled 'the big black pot o dooker soup' their mother made. They also recalled the distinctive smell when their father, having plucked the birds, would take a red-hot poker from the ribs of the fire and go out the back door to singe the down off the carcasses. The soup itself consisted of typical broth ingredients – peas, barley, carrot, turnip and leek – with a bunch of kail suspended in the pot on a length of string. That kail was lifted out and served as a vegetable with potatoes and the dookers themselves. As children, Katie and Mary found the dooker rather too 'strong' in flavour for their taste, but they got used to it and, in any case: 'We had tae eat it.' [Katie and Mary Jackson, 2003]

Rabbits

When Nan McKay was growing up in Dalintober, the family – she had three sisters and a brother – 'lived on rabbits an fish'. Her father, Alexander, a plumber, was friendly with the farmer at Baraskomel and was permitted to trap rabbits there. He kept a dog and two ferrets. Nan was encouraged to assist with the muzzling of the ferrets – 'Catch it!' her father would insist – but she hated handling them. She became adept, however, at skinning and cleaning rabbits: 'Me father had us taught tae dae everythin.' Her mother would cook the rabbits 'every way'. They would be boiled and onions added to the stock to make a soup; the meat, after cooling, would be fried and served with mashed turnip and potatoes; they could also be stewed or stuffed and roasted. An old traveller woman, camped at Maidens Planting, showed Nan how to bake rabbits in the earth. A pit would be dug and a fire lit in it, then the rabbits, encased in clay, would be placed in the fire and the pit covered in. After the rabbits had cooked, they would uncovered and broken out of the clay.

Her mother, who trained as a dressmaker, made coats trimmed with rabbit-fur for the children, and Harry Finn made fur gloves. On one memorable occasion, a visiting relative, 'Uncle Jim', accompanied Alexander McKay to the hill. Jim was to return the following day and collect the snared victims. He duly set off with a suitcase, but when he got there he discovered that couldn't bring himself to kill the rabbits, so he put them in the case alive and brought them back for Alexander to kill! When Nan turned 21, in January, 1944, she asked one of her friends and two submariners – Campbeltown was a Naval base during the War – to the family home for a birthday tea, 'an it wis rabbit-pie!' She worked in the Creamery at the time and was able to obtain some cream with which to make cakes, 'but there wir nae such thing as a praisant (present) though'. [Nan McKay, 2003]

Eggs

Katie Jackson's maternal grandparents, the Kennedys, farmed Barfad, on the north side of East Loch Tarbert, and she and her siblings went about the farm at week-ends and during holidays, helping with potato-lifting, hay-making and much else. At certain times of the year, the hens would 'lay out', and Katie had the job of walking round the farm, finding the nests and bringing in the eggs. Once, past the barn, she came on a nest, but a stone had rolled into it and smashed the eggs which had been 'clocking', or incubating. The 'bloody mess' that confronted her there created such a strong impression on her imagination that she was 'violently ill' for weeks afterwards and not only never ate another egg, but wouldn't eat a bit of bacon that her mother had fried in the same pan as an egg, and was ill once after inadvertently sampling mayonnaise. [Katie Jackson, 2003]

Barter

At the onset of winter, Willie Jackson would cure half-barrels of herring for farming acquaintances on Islay and Gigha, who, in exchange, would send him beef or lamb; but his children tended to be 'fussy' over that bartered meat. 'Sometimes we wirna pleased tae eat it because it wisna bought in a butcher's shop.' The farmer at Kilchamaig, near Whitehouse, a Miss Turner, would send the Jacksons, by Alex Blair's taxi, pheasants, hares and rabbits. This was in exchange for Mary Jackson's hospitality to Miss Turner's drovers when they brought cattle to the sale. The Jackson house, Conchra, was adjacent to the cattle-mart and Mary would 'make tea' for the men. [Katie Jackson, 2003]

Christmas puddings

The Edinburgh-based architect and artist, Archie MacAlister, was born in Glasgow, but belongs to a long-established Tarbert family. His grandfather, also Archie, was a fisherman, and his father, Peter, fished for a time before crewing on the herring steamer *Gael* and then going 'deep sea'. Archie's grandmother, Margaret Smith MacAlister, had a house in Tarbert and his early memories 'are as much, or more, of Tarbert than anywhere else'.

From 1946 to 1951, he spent his summers on Archie MacCaig's *Seonaid*, which neighboured the *Sweet Marie* at ring-netting. The youngest crew-member was Archie 'Ja' McDougall, one of whose responsibilities was the provisioning of the boat. One bright August Monday, 'Ja' delegated that task to young Archie, who duly set off for the chandler's store with a quay trolley and money in pocket. Having filled the trolley with plain loaves, tea, sugar, tinned milk, etc., he discovered that there was about £1 to spare. Since he had been instructed to use all the money, he looked around the shelves and decided on the purchase of a box of Christmas puddings.

That evening, awaiting dusk in Buck Bay, he prepared the 'first bite of the night'. The pudding cans were brought out from the locker and the instructions carefully read: 'Simmer for 5 minutes and cover can as you open.' As the skipper was at the tiller, puffing on a pipe, Archie took his mug of tea, toast and Christmas pudding aft to him. MacCaig took one look at the offering and asked what it might be. 'A Christmas pudding, Mr MacCaig,' Archie explained. After a momentary silence, MacCaig let out a roar: 'But this is the fucking month of August!'

'I got below as quick as possible, to the great amusement of the crew, who had foreseen the likely reaction whenever they saw me, bull-headed opener and can in hand. Well, Archie [McDougall] told me that whenever there was a "fishing" and any extra pennies, the *Seonaid* sailed with Christmas puddings from that day on.' [Archie MacAlister, 2003]

References
1. Mrs Mary Menzies, Campbeltown, 1992 and 2003.
2. L McInnes, *Dialect of South Kintyre*, Campbeltown 1934, p 9.

Childhood

For many people, particularly as they enter middle or old age, childhood memories become a refuge from the realities of a fast-changing world.

The Currans and the 'Cockle Wife'

Close to Brae House, Tarbert, where Archie Carmichael was born and brought up, there lived a family of general dealers, the Currans. They had an old-fashioned motor-lorry – entirely open and with candles for headlights – which invariably required to be push-started. They travelled the countryside in that lorry, but, the engine being as it was, 'there was no such thing as stoppin'. Archie and four or five other young fellows would help push it out in the morning, and at night would wait on the road near Stonefield for its return and climb into the back of it, among the rags and rabbit-skins, for the final downhill stage of the journey. 'It wis a great thing tae get a lift in a lorry.' [Archie Carmichael, 2003]

Droving

Another childhood pleasure was to accompany, stick in hand, a cattle-drove on the road north through Tarbert. At about Meall Dubh, one of the drovers would say: 'Now, A think ye's are far enough, boys. Turn back. Away ye go home.' The drovers were 'only too pleased' to have the boys' help for a time; and for the boys, 'It wis a great thing tae go away wi the cattle.' [Archie Carmichael, 2003]

The McBrides

The family home of the McBrides was at Pirnmill on Arran, across the Kilbrannan Sound from Carradale*. Lawrence McBride met his future wife, Helen Sharp, when she was at Pirnmill in service with a family holidaying there. She belonged to Longriggend, Airdrie, and had no fishing background. The fishermen's wives at Pirnmill were dismissive of her, saying that she couldn't bait lines; but she decided to 'show them' and did indeed become proficient at baiting. When Lawrence wanted to build himself a house, he couldn't get a plot of land at Pirnmill, so he built instead at Port na Cùile, Carradale, and did much of the work himself, including the surrounding wall, which he worked at every week-end he was home. He employed two slaters from Campbeltown to roof the house, but when he came home one day he found the men 'lyin sunnin themselves on the roof', so he sacked them and finished the job himself. When moving house, he rowed a punt backwards and forwards from Pirnmill to Carradale with furniture and other belongings.

He once bought a punt in Irvine and, to make the trip worthwhile, loaded it with a ton of coal and alone rowed boat and cargo home to Carradale, only breaking the journey to have a drink of water at the Cock of Arran.

While his parents, William and Annie, were in life he would spend occasional week-ends at the family home, Annfield. He would take the steamer across, accompanied at times by his daughter Ellen, and land from the ferry-boat that came out from Pirnmill. Sometimes, however, they would land at Lochranza, and Ellen recalled travelling in a horse-drawn buggy with her Grandmother. The old woman gave her a big bag of hazelnuts to eat, but the nuts hurt her teeth so much that she surreptitiously dropped them, one by one, through a hole in the floor of the buggy 'the whole way from Lochranza tae Pirnmill'. Annie recalled being rowed to Pirnmill by her father to attend family weddings and the like.

Uncle Willie in Seahome, Pirnmill, kept hens, and McBride relatives who were grain-merchants in Glasgow would send two bags of corn each week to feed them. The hens frequently invaded an adjacent 'churchyard', which caused 'objections' among some of the neighbours, and Ellen recalled being present, at 6.30 one morning, when the hens each had a wing clipped with scissors to curb their wanderings. 'Och, it only lasted a wee while an the wings grew an they wir over the wall intae the churchyard agane.' [Ellen and Annie McBride, 2003]

*The family originated in Ayrshire. William McBride was born in Troon and his wife, Ann Lamb, in Irvine.

Net-mending

Lawrence McBride taught all his children to mend nets in the dining-room at Helendale. The netting would be tied to a door-handle while each child practised, and Lawrence would judge which one had made the best job. In bad weather, if a net needed mending, he would pull it through the big window and stretch it out in the dining-room, where he could work on it in comfort, assisted by the children, who would repair the small holes. 'Would people have a net in their dining-room now?' Annie asked. 'No! No!'

Lawrence was keen on making netting-needles and would sit at the fireside by night whittling wood. He gave the needles freely to other Carradale fishermen and made one for his daughter Annie's husband, Eddie Martindale (p 183), a gamekeeper, for weaving rabbit-nets. Annie still has that needle. [Ellen and Annie McBride, 2003]

'The Net'

In Tarbert, the 'setting up' of a new ring-net was something of a community event. Some days, when school came out, word would go round, 'There's a net the day!', and the children would run off to find out where the net was being assembled. Katie Jackson's father set up his nets near the Bowling Green, but he would never say to his family, so it was always a surprise when she came out of school and found him and his crews at work. For the village children, there would be a quarter-cran basket filled with buns and bottles of lemonade, and for the men jars of whisky and bottles of beer. 'It was the war cry, "There's a net,"' Katie recalled. 'An everybody knew what it meant – it meant ye got buns and lemonade.' [Katie Jackson, 2003]

Gaelic

Nan McKay's maternal grandparents, John McGeachy and Isabella MacNeill, came to Dalintober from Gigha. John was a fisherman and owned the skiff *White Heather*. Nan has no memory of him, but an older sister, Mary, who was born in 1916, remembered speaking Gaelic with her grandparents when she was small and being forbidden to address her grandfather other than as 'Shennar' (Gaelic *seanair*, 'grandfather'). [Nan McKay, 2003]

May McDougall's father was a Gaelic-speaker, but her mother wasn't, and he never spoke Gaelic at home except when his brothers Neil and Alistair would visit. 'We never had a word of Gaelic, none of us,' May said. 'We weren't interested in Gaelic.' Her father could read Gaelic and would bring home, on Sundays, a church magazine which contained a

'Gaelic page'. When he had finished with the magazine, he would take it up to a Gaelic-speaking woman, Katie Cameron, who lived in the Row at Port Righ. His brother Neil was more interested in the language. He spoke it at home, was a member of the Carradale Gaelic Choir and went to the Mod (an annual Gaelic festival). [May McDougall, 2003]

A travellers' wedding

When she was 11 or 12 years old, Annie McBride and her elder sister, Ellen, were asked by the Rev Argyll Baker – who both christened and married Annie – to attend a travellers' wedding at which he had been asked to officiate. The wedding took place at Port Righ crossroads. 'Oh, it wis great. So, there naw many can say they wir at a tinkers' wedding. My, what a feast we had!' Sandwiches, dumpling and cakes were eaten around a big fire at the encampment. [Annie McBride, 2003]

Rabbit-skins

A dealer from Campbeltown came to Carradale to buy rabbit-skins. If he had enough money, he would come by bus; if not, he walked. He paid 3d a pair for the skins and, if there was a 'black mark' on the underside of any skin, he would remark: 'Aw, these rabbit-skins is naw as good.' He slept in the cave at Black Port, sometimes in 'freezin' conditions. 'Ma mother used tae be that sorry, him goin away over tae the cove, sleepin jeest wi the cloes he had on.' Helen McBride always gave him a hot meal and four salt herring to take home with him. She would feed his dog, too, with a big bowl of 'saps': bread, hot water, sugar, butter and some milk. He had a young son with him once, and some one gave the boy a bantam cock, which disappeared. 'An, here, the state he wis in, lookin for that banty cock.' [Ellen McBride, 2003]

Colin 'Grogport'

Colin Campbell was known as 'Colin Grogport' because he kept a small shop there early in the twentieth century. It was just a 'lean-to' beside the road 'down from the inn', but Ellen McBride remembered it as 'a lovely wee shop'. She and her companions would walk from Carradale to Grogport – a distance of some six miles – just for the 'novelty o a shop against the wall'. It was open winter and summer and sold groceries and sweets. Colin also took provisions to Carradale in a buggy, calling, as he did his rounds: 'Syrup an treacle! Sausages an cream crackers! Dae ye waant any?' [Ellen McBride, 2003]

'Oakies'

There was a Campbeltown man who came to Carradale to fish for salmon. He lived in an old boat hauled up on the foreshore near Port na Cùile, and when he'd be asleep by day and the boat's scuttle open, Ellen McBride and a companion would gather all the 'oakies', or acorns, they could find, and, from the high ground above the shore, throw them down through the scuttle and 'get him on the face'. 'Oh, he would've killed us,' Ellen recalled. 'He wid seh tae me: "A'll gut ye like the way A'd gut a *gleshan*!" He wis that cross.' These 'oakies' also served as crude pipes when bored to take a hollow stick and lit. [Ellen McBride, 2003]

A character

Another character at Port na Cùile lived in a wooden hut with a 'poor roof' which was held down by chains laid on it. He used a length of chain to clean his chimney. 'When we wid hear the thing rattlin, we knew fine the fire had been smokin,' Annie McBride recalled. To keep the wind from blowing through the planking of the hut, he would paste sheets of newspaper over the gaps using margarine. His hut caught fire once and he was 'nearly burned tae bits, keepin all them buttery papers'. He was evidently easily annoyed. As Annie recalled: 'We used tae crack nuts an he used tae come out an give us the awful doin for makin a noise wi crackin nuts on the shore.' He and a friend sometimes walked to the inn at Sunadale and drank more than was good for them. Returning to Carradale, they might 'sleep for a while up on the hill' before completing their journey home. Once, when the McBride children, Alec, Willie and Ellen, were gathering wilks on the shore and saw the two of them returning from Sunadale Inn, Willie advised: 'Hide behind the rock – don't let them see ye or they'll come down.' [Ellen and Annie McBride, 2003]

Sabbath

Certain activities were discouraged in the McBride household, as in many others, on the Sabbath. Knitting was one of them and listening to the radio was another, though the children would sometimes sneak the radio away to a secluded upstairs room and listen to it with a coat over their heads. [Annie McBride, 2003]

The North

When May McDougall was a girl, her father would be absent from home for weeks at a time during the summer herring-fishing in 'the North'. Uig and Portree, in Skye, were familiar names to her. It was in Uig, she thought, that her father's sciatica forced him ashore. He was both unfit to work and to travel home, and lodged with a local family until he recovered. That family was very kind to him and he 'kept up' with them for many years, writing to them and sending them Christmas presents.

She remembered the large quantities of hard 'butter-biscuits' that were carried North in the boats (p 158). These biscuits were sometimes bought from Joe Black, the baker in Campbeltown, but the local baker also made them. Paterson's biscuits were of the rimmed variety and when newly baked would be spread with butter or jam or sprinkled with sugar. She 'loved them'. Her mother would make a clootie dumpling for the crew to take to the North (p 158). [May McDougall, 2003]

Chickenfeed

When Mary McGeachy was a young girl she would watch barley being unloaded from carts at Scotia Distillery in High Street. Sometimes a sack would burst as it was being hauled up by pulley and chain to the hoisting-door of the malt-loft, and grain would spill on to the street. The workers would never bother to sweep up the spilled grain and, when the carts left, Mary would gather it into 'big *pokes*', or bags, which she'd then sell to neighbours who kept hens. One of her customers was an old woman known as 'Katie Whippy', who stayed in Woodland Place and had a henhouse there. One day Mary hid under one of the fishermen's ferry-boats which had been hauled ashore for repair. She found three eggs there and took them to her mother, but her mother was annoyed and said: 'That wumman's tae work hard for her livin.' Mary, however, was defiant and answered: 'She got a loat o grain for thruppence.' [Mary McGeachy, 2001]

The Schoolmaster's hens

Mr MacInnes, the schoolmaster at Carradale, and his wife kept a large number of hens. Ellen McBride and Peter 'Pinkie' McMillan would go early to the school and play tricks with the birds in order to alarm Mrs MacInnes. 'We used tae catch the hens an shake them, an then we put thir head under thir wing, an then leave them down an they would lie there for a good while. An the old woman came oot. When she saw the hens all dead… they wirna dead at all. They jeest lay a certain time an then got up an away.' [Ellen McBride, 2003]

Awaiting the fleet's return

When the Dalintober fleet would return from a week's fishing, children would gather at the quay to welcome their fathers. Carol McAulay was just three years old when her father, Neil, died at the age of 34, in 1926, of malaria contracted in Salonika, whence he had been posted towards the end of First World War. One day, she and her brother Duncan went to the quay as the skiffs arrived, looking on from the rear of the crowd and feeling very much isolated; but when her Grandfather, Duncan Martin, came around the corner he put both arms out to greet them and they ran into his arms. Afterwards, they went to the quay with the rest of the children and felt as though they belonged there. [Carol McAulay, 2003]

Holidays

Holidays were uncommon in May McDougall's childhood. They would go to Glasgow to stay with a maternal aunt who had married a Glasgow fish-buyer, John MacFarlane, and lived in Mount Florida. From a back window of that house, a corner of Hampden football-park could be seen. She was taken once to spend a holiday with another maternal aunt, who had married in Port Bannatyne, Bute. [May McDougall, 2003]

One of Jean Martin's earliest memories concerned a trip to Invergordon to visit her mother's parents, Henry Dunn and Ann Grant, when she was approaching her fifth year. Her father was 'away fishing' at the time and her mother decided to return to her native place. They went by boat to Gourock and from there by train to Central Station, Glasgow. To get to Buchanan Street, whence the north-bound trains ran, a 'conveyance' was necessary, and, 'It wis a horse an carriage – that wis the taxi'. Some acquaintances to whom Jean related the story were incredulous. 'They winna believe me, an A said: "Aye, A remember it fine." So that wis a wee experience A got.' [Jean Martin, 2003]

Walking

Annie and Ellen McBride thought little of walking the 16 miles to Campbeltown from their home in Carradale. On one occasion, it was to see the film 'Ben Hur'* in the Picture House. They walked in flat shoes, but carried fashionable 'high heels' with them in a bag and changed into these before they reached town. The journey took them almost three hours and Annie developed a painful blister on a heel. Their brother, John, who was at Campbeltown Grammar School and who subsequently became a minister in Kelso, had a Morris Oxford car and drove them back to Carradale at night. [Annie McBride, 2003]

*Released in 1925.

A lift in a baker's van

Once, when Ellen McBride was returning to Carradale from Glasgow, the weather was 'that stormy' the steamer couldn't call at Carradale and she was ferried ashore at Saddell. She was faced with an uncomfortable six-mile walk home, but, by good fortune, got a lift in a baker's van from Campbeltown. The driver, Dougie McMurchy, warned her: 'Well, ye can come wi me, but ye'll have tae go tae every farm aweh up the Glen.' She was 15 or 16 years old at the time and recalled: 'A think it wis near night-time afore A come home.' [Ellen McBride, 2003]

Games

When May McDougall was growing up in Port Righ, there was a total of about 20 children from the four houses there. 'I can never mind o any fighting or anything. We all seemed tae get on very well together.' They played *peevers* (hopscotch), 'skipping ropes' and, among the rocks, 'wee houses' and 'shops', the latter stocked with stones, shells, bits of coloured glass and the grain-like seeds of dockens, stripped by the handful from the stalks. [May McDougall, 2003]

In Tarbert, the hoop that children rolled along the streets was called a *rawlin*. The local blacksmith would make one 'in a meenit' from a bit of old iron. He would also make the *cleep*, which was the iron hook by which, rather than hitting it with a stick, the hoop could be kept in motion. Pavements would be marked with *bawbeds* for playing hopscotch, which was mainly a girls' game, but in which boys would sometimes join. [Archie Carmichael, 2003]

The children – there were 13 of them – of Willie and Mary Jackson had 'plenty of room' at Conchra, the family home in Tarbert. The lawn could be converted into a putting-green, but, as Katie said, 'We got a row when Father would come back an see the holes...' In wintertime, 'peever beds' would be chalked on the kitchen linoleum. Conchro was one of those houses where young folk tended to collect, which hardly pleased Willie Jackson when he was trying to sleep after being out at the fishing all night. 'Dae they think this is a playground?' he'd enquire. [Katie and Mary Jackson, 2003]

Numerous games were played on the streets and pavements of Dalintober: dodge the ball, rounders, beds, jecks, jarries, smugaleerie, hide and seek. North Shore Street, where Jean Martin played, was practically car-free and the rare car that did appear would be a talking-point. In those days, Jean believed, adults were 'very tolerant' of children at play. Nowadays, she said, it's: 'Ye canna play there... Ye canna dae this... Ye canna dae that.'

If a wet day, the girls would sit playing guesses – a version of I-Spy, but without visible objects – on the tenement stairs of the Red Land. Scraps, which were bought for a ha'penny or a penny a sheet in stationery shops, would be exchanged, 'maybe a big angel for two or three other wee [ones]'. In summer, Jean and a couple of girlfriends would walk to Kilchousland to swim. The swimming continued after she began work as a shop assistant, but by then she had a second-hand bicycle, which her mother 'sacrificed' to buy, for 10 shillings, in the County Garage. Jean and her friends were thus able to travel farther to swim, and Southend was often their destination. [Jean Martin, 2003]

When Davie MacFarlane was a boy in Tarbert, he and his companions would get a cabbage-stock, hollow it out until left with only the 'crust', pack it with tarry netting – 'lik the wey ye'd fill a pipe' – and light it. When smoking well, an end of the stock would be placed against a keyhole and the smoke puffed, from the other end, into the victim's house. 'Smock them oot! Oh, we wir devilage when we wir wee. We wirna as bad as they are now, all the same.' [David MacFarlane, 1978]

Picnics

Carol McAulay's maternal grandfather, Duncan Martin, wouldn't take his skiff the *Fame* to sea on Sundays for picnicking purposes, but let his sons do so. On most fine Sundays in summer, there would be upwards of 30 people – fishermen, their wives, children and other relations – crowded on to the skiff for excursions to Davaar Island, Lochranza, Blackwaterfoot or Saddell Bay, which was a favourite picnic beach. The skiff would be anchored and her passengers rowed ashore. There would be a fire going on the beach for brewing the tea that was in constant demand, and a meal for the company – perhaps steak pie, potatoes and peas – would be cooked aboard the skiff and ferried ashore in the punt. If there was a potato or turnip field nearby, it would be raided.

One day, a party of picnickers – including Carol, who was just a child – had a terrible fright when the weather turned. They set off for Saddell on a 'beautiful day'; but the men saw that a change was coming and left early for home. Duncan Martin also saw the change in the weather and became frantic with worry, pacing the floor and looking out on to Campbeltown Loch from the attic window of Gayfield Place. 'There's goin tae be a storm and they're still out there wi the women an weans,' he'd repeat to his wife. The *Fame* reached her moorings at Dalintober without mishap, but all aboard her were badly shaken and one of her crew, Henry Martin, was occupied the following day cleaning vomit off the boat's sides.

After the *Fame* was sold in 1935, the family instead hired a bus to Southend or Westport. 'It ran oot tae aboot sixpence each an the weans got for naethin,' Carol recalled. [Carol McAulay, 2003]

Kilchousland, three miles north of Campbeltown, was 'the one and only' picnic beach for Nan McKay, as for most other Dalintober folk. As a girl, she and her friends would walk there and back, though on one memorable occasion they travelled part of the way in a car. They had stopped at Miss Lloyd's Well, on the roadside past Baraskomel steading, and were drinking from the chained metal cup. When they heard the car coming, the cup was thrown into the well. The driver stopped for them and they completed the journey seated in the back. It was the first time that Nan, who was about 10 at the time, had ever been in a car. A jam or jelly *piece* was the usual picnic fare, though a few cold fried herrings might be shared. These were left-overs from the breakfast Nan's mother cooked for her lodgers (p 182). A pin served to extract a gathering of boiled winkles from their shells, and a turnip might be lifted from a field, skinned on barbed wire and eaten on the road home. [Nan McKay, 2003]

Margaret McBride's father, Willie, occasionally took parties of visitors on picnics across the Kilbrannan Sound. Regularly, between the wars, a group of boys from Quarry Brae School in Glasgow came to Pirnmill, Arran, to camp for a fortnight in the grounds of the local school. On an arranged day, Willie would ferry them and their teachers to Saddell or Skipness. Fires would be lit on the shore and kettles boiled for tea. [Margaret McBride, 2003]

Sweetie money

Lawrence McBride was generous to his children, particularly after a successful week's fishing; but he was careful not to let his wife know what he was giving them. 'I remember when they had a fishing we used tae put our hand out for money on the Saturday tae go up for sweeties, up tae the Bungalow that wis there. That wis our sweetie place. An he wid say, "Ma barra's broke. No money this week." – "Ach, well," A said, "we'd better away then if we're naw gettin anythin."' Lawrie, however, would wait until his daughters were 'round the turn' of the Shore Road, then call Annie back and give her half-a-crown. [Annie McBride, 2003]

Schooling

May McDougall's father, Charlie, would walk from South Dippen to Achnasavil and back, attending school. May herself had less far to go to the school – itself now replaced – opposite Semple's shop. At the well, she and her companions would turn off the Port Righ road and take the farm-track to where the Village Hall now stands and meet up with children coming from the eastern end of the village. When she left the village school, it was to Campbeltown Grammar School she went, travelling to town on Monday morning by bus and returning home on Friday evening. Carradale secondary pupils, in common with other country pupils, lodged in Campbeltown during school weeks. May and her cousin, Flora 'Flossie' McDougall from Dunvalanree, stayed at 1 Castle Park with a Campbeltown fisherman, John Durnin (p 25), his wife and two young daughters. The two Carradale girls shared a bedroom there and received their meals from Mrs Durnin. Dick, Peggy and Mary Galbraith also lodged in Castlepark, with a Mistress Sillars, and the two groups would visit each other at their lodgings. Occasionally they'd go out and buy a bag of chips at the 'Tally's' – an Italian café – and occasionally, too, would walk along the railway towards Machrihanish. Once, she and her companions travelled to Machrihanish by train (which ceased to run in 1932) and walked home. [May McDougall, 2003]

When the day came for Jean Martin to go to Dalintober School, her brother Harry – who was a year older – held her hand and walked her there; but he also 'terrified' her by telling her that the school was 'lik a dungeon, a big dark horrid place'. When she got there, she was 'so surprised – A saw this lovely school wi the sun shinin through the windows'. Back home, she complained to her mother: 'That Harry frightened me – A dinna want tae go tae the school.' – 'A'm sure ye know he's always tormentin ye,' her mother replied.

Donald Fisher was headmaster at Dalintober and Jean liked her teachers, particularly Miss Findlay, whom she described as 'a gem'. 'She wis a great teacher. Everybody loved her.' Miss Findlay lived in Killean Place and brought up the infant daughter of a brother, who worked in a Clydebank shipyard and whose wife had died. Jean's father, Angus, had been 'pally' with Findlay in his youth and salted down a firkin of herring for him every year. When he came back to Campbeltown on holiday, he would bring the empty firkin to be refilled in the back-end. [Jean Martin, 2003]

Shopping

In the mornings, before she went to school, Jean Martin would go into town to shop for her mother. From James Girvan's butcher's shop in

Longrow South she would buy 'something for the dinner' and a bone for soup, and from Agnes McKay in Cross Street sixpence worth of vegetables. She 'went messages' – ran errands – for others too, including a grand-aunt, Sarah Martin, who lived in an old property in Dalintober. Sarah always gave her a penny, but, 'If ye got a penny, ye gied it tae yer mother for the gas'. In the Depression years of the 1920s, her father gave up fishing and had to work 'on the roads' for 10 shillings a week. Jean – then 'a wee lassie in the school' – would be sent with a jug to the soup-kitchen at the Christian Institute. 'That was a bad time.' [Jean Martin, 2003]

Line-fishing

After the spawny herring fishery ended in March, Jean Martin's father went to small line fishing, a demanding occupation which involved the whole family. Angus Martin had three *trochs* of lines to bait, and his wife would leave the house at about three o' clock in the morning and go to the net-store opposite Dalintober Quay to cut up bait herring, for which Angus had already been out fishing with a small ring-net. If herring were unobtainable, Jean's brothers would help gather mussels from a bed on the shore below Tangy Place. These mussels – which were imported in the skiff – would then have to be shelled. When her father and his crew returned from fishing, they had to '*redd* all these lines an bait them agane'. Jean's job was to tidy up the net-store and wash the *trochs* with a deck-scrubber. If her father could not sell his fish in the market, he put them on a net-barrow and went round the streets with them. 'A mind it wis sixpence for a cod. Two pounds o whitins wis about sixpence or some-thin lik that. So he cou'na get tae his bed when he came in wi the fish. Aye, it wis a hard life, but we wir happy. An we all helped if we could.' [Jean Martin, 2003]

Spout-fish

In spring-time, when Margaret McBride's father, Willie, went to small lines, her regular job, which she 'hated', was to gather withered grass for laying between the layers of hooks in the trough to prevent fouling. She also helped her father gather 'spout-fish' (p 142) which were abundant in the tidal sand-banks from the jetty at Pirnmill south to Whitefarland. Remarkably, her brother Angus could 'pull them up with both hands at the same time', and, when the tide didn't suit for gathering by hand, he had a home-made 'spoutfish-catcher' – a simple but effective wooden-handled rope-operated metal grab – with which the shellfish could be collected from a small boat providing the sea was calm enough to see the bottom. Spout-fish would be gathered by the quarter-cran basketful and the 'tongue' – or foot – of the opened shellfish cut up for bait. These 'tongues' were also chopped or minced and turned into a tasty soup with milk and butter. Lucrative commercial diving on the Pirnmill spout-fish beds in recent years, however, has catastrophically depleted the resource. [Margaret McBride, 2003]

Christmas

There was little enough to put in the Christmas stocking – an orange and perhaps a 'chocolate figure' – but one year Jean Martin received a doll with 'a nice china face' from an aunt, Jeannie Martin, who kept house for an elderly lady in the West End of Glasgow. 'A still remember the day A got the doll. It was wonderful – A got a doll for ma Christmas!' [Jean Martin, 2003]

On Christmas Eve, the McBride children in Carradale would be told: 'Now, ye'll need tae get tae bed early or ye'll get nothing – he'll maybe leave a poke o ashes.' 'He', of course, was Santa Claus. Some time through the night, Annie would say to her older sister, Ellen, 'We'll go an see what's left', and they would rise and feel the stockings hung at the fireplace. 'He's been!' Then they would find big dolls in boxes waiting for them. Their brother John saw a black doll in a shop window one year and decided: 'That's what A want from Santa.' He 'loved' that doll and had it 'for ages'. Christmas concerts were held in the Mission Hall. [Annie McBride, 2003]

New Year

At New Year, Jean Martin and her brothers would be taken to visit relatives. Her mother's sister, Maggie McDougall, who lived in Bolgam Street and was married to a prosperous fisherman, Hugh McLean, always gave them sixpence each. 'That wis a great thing, a sixpence, in these days.' Maggie had no family, but was fond of her sister's children. She was 'very clever with her hands' and crocheted doilies and tablecloths. On January 2nd, the family was always served a meal of salt herring, which was believed to 'clean yer stomach' after the over-indulgence in ginger wine and pastries and other sweet stuff. [Jean Martin, 2003]

Nan McKay's 'Ne'erdays' were memorable for the 'big feast' the family had. Her father, being friendly with the farmer at Baraskomel (p 162), received a share – chops, perhaps – of the 'beast' killed to mark the New Year. Meat – in the form of mince or boiling beef, which was cooked in a big pot of broth and afterwards served in the soup-plate along with potatoes and perhaps turnip – was ordinarily a rarity on the table. New Year was a time for visiting friends and relatives, and in Nan's mother's youth it wasn't unusual, when visiting, to take a big umbrella along and secrete uneaten cake and other sweetstuffs in it for later consumption. 'A suppose they dinna have much.' [Nan McKay, 2003]

Glasgow Fair

When Jean Martin was a girl, on the first Sunday of Glasgow Fair she and her friends would go to Maxwell's Park – a level field by the shore beyond Maidens Planting – to count the number of camps there and 'there wis always over a hundred'. She considered the tents 'aafu close together – A winna've liked it mesel, but we wir aye curious tae know how many tents wis there'. Jocky McLean, who ran a lorry in Campbeltown, always met the steamer when it arrived and drove all the camping gear to the site. [Jean Martin, 2003]

Pinching a boat

Jean Martin and her friend Margaret Johnston spent much of their childhood around Dalintober Quay. One of their pastimes was to 'pinch a boat' which the fishermen kept for ferrying crews to and from the skiffs which lay at moorings offshore. Margaret was 'great at scullin'. One day, they took a punt, which belonged to Jock Taylor, across to the Old Quay at Campbeltown. Jock appeared on Dalintober Quay shouting and cursing at them: 'A'll kill ye's when ye's come in here!' The sequel, however, proved to be an anti-climax: 'He wis that gled we came back safe that he dinna say anything.' [Jean Martin, 2003]

Willie Jackson

Willie Jackson, whose nick-name was 'Baillie', was one of the best-fished of the Tarbert skippers, a reputation of which his family was not unaware. He skippered his first boat at the age of 21 and died, of heart failure, on 26 January, 1953, at the age of 56. That day was also his youngest child's sixth birthday, and Willie's last words were to ask his wife to go and mix Kenneth's birthday dumpling. When Mary Jackson returned to her husband's bedside, he was dead. [Katie Jackson, 2003]

It was Willie Jackson's custom to *wheck* – 'whack', or divide among his crew the proceeds of the week's fishing – in the Tarbert Hotel on a Saturday, and when he had the first *Village Belle* built by William Reekie of St Monans in 1932, the hotel's owner, Mistress MacArthur, gave him, as hansel, a brass bell in the form of a lady in a crinoline dress. The gift had a double significance – a bell for a belle – which played on the boat's name. When, after wartime service – Willie and his brother Tommy were engaged with the *Belle* in retrieving live mines in the Clyde – the boat was sent by the Ministry of War Transport to Sierra Leone, Katie Jackson asked her father: 'Where's the bell that was on the *Village Belle*?' His answer was: 'Oh, we don't touch it. It's away. It goes wi the boat.' Katie remembered her father, during the War, weaving nets he had himself designed for lifting mines. These would be attached to a handle of the big chest-of-drawers behind the kitchen door. [Katie Jackson, 2003]

Willie Jackson kept in his purse a 'double nut' – two hazel nuts joined – given to him by his father-in-law, Neil Kennedy, at Barfad. He had it for years and it was dark with age, but he finally lost it. He was able to replace it with another double nut, but the next one didn't carry the same significance for him.

Whenever he would meet a red-headed woman, 'Mary Kellar', on his way to the fishing, he would return home, remove his cap and sit in his chair for 'a wee while' before setting off again for the harbour. His family would say to him, 'Don't be so stupid!', but no rational argument would alter his belief in the unluckiness of red-haired women.

He would never turn a 'tinker' away from the door of the house, but always gave the caller something. 'A giein hand's a gettin hand,' he'd say. [Katie and Mary Jackson, 2003]

Sometimes when Willie Jackson had a few drams in him he would put a familiar question to his children – 'Have ye ever been lost in a snowstorm?' – and answer it himself with the story of how, in the 1930s, he came to be stranded at Muasdale. Having urgent business with his lawyer in Campbeltown, Archibald Stewart, Willie hired Hughie McNab's taxi. Meantime, a snowstorm arose and, on the way home from Campbeltown, Hughie's taxi got no further than Muasdale, where he and Willie were forced to take refuge in Maggie Watson's inn. The hospitality must have been of the best because Hughie and Willie stayed at the inn for several days before a means of escape suggested itself. The idea succeeded. They walked the shore to Tayinloan, took the ferry to Gigha, boarded the Tarbert-bound Islay steamer there and at last arrived home none the worse for their adventure. [Katie Jackson, 2003]

Women in the Fishing Community

The presence of 'women in the fishing community' has so faded that it now seems like a dream. Fishing communities themselves are dissolving, as stocks decline, beaurocratic restrictions multiply, earnings drop, fleets contract, astute skippers seek steady wages in other employment and intelligent young men reject the once-irresistible allure of family tradition.

What constituted the core vitality of the fishing industry was its communities, each one distinct, with its own speech and traditions, its complex tangle of interrelated families, and its own sense of self-worth and self-determination. These qualities have been so eroded in the course of a generation, that the very concept of the fishing community as a recognisable cultural entity within the broader social frame has ceased to mean much.

The diminution of the role of women in the fishing community goes back farther. With, for example, the decline of small-line fishing between the wars, the wives and sisters and mothers who hitherto had shelled mussels and baited lines, lost those burdens. Women, anyway, had enough to do, not least the rearing of (usually) large families, for much of the year as virtual 'single parents', since most of the men would be pursuing herring in distant fisheries.

Against all that, the traditional fishing community was self-sustaining. Families lived close to one another and neighbours were neighbourly, in the old sense. If a household ran short of any commodity, some other household would supply it. Neighbours were sociable and visited one another far more than is the case now that television, videos and computers have mesmerised the general populace. In times of crisis, relatives and friends were there to provide comfort and practical assistance. Such intimate association had its disadvantages, certainly, but these, on balance, did not outweigh the stabilising factors.

In common with the generality of women, fishermen's wives no longer content themselves with a purely domestic role, not least because that role has become economically unsustainable. Many wives, particularly those with professional qualifications, now earn as much, or more, than their husbands, and the 'feast or famine' philosophy that once governed the finances of fishing families has become unacceptable in this age of rampant materialism.

Stewardess on the *Davaar*

At about the age of 16, Mary McGeachy got a job as stewardess on the SS *Davaar*, which ran between Campbeltown and Gourock, with stops along the way. Her Uncle, Sam Campbell, had the catering contract for the steamer, her sister Jane was cook, and another sister, Kate, head stewardess, so it was 'a family affair'. She had a cabin aboard the steamer and, on Monday mornings, would rise in time for the sailing at 3.45, perhaps after playing rounders for hours on a picnic beach the day before.

Passengers would begin to appear for breakfast at about 5 a m, then, about 2 p m, 'they'd come for their lunch; in fact, they wid get a meal any time'. When a meal was ready, Jane – who was alone in the kitchen – would 'whistle down', and one of the stewardesses would collect and serve the food. On stormy days, they'd speculate among themselves: 'How can they folk eat wi this storm?' A stewardess's weekly wage was 15s – 'Ye could dae quite a lot wi fifteen shillins' – supplemented by tips.

Having arrived at Gourock, the steamer would lie a while there, and sometimes, when the Clyde was busy with traffic, Captain Galbraith from Saddell – 'a very careful man' – wouldn't leave to berth at Broomielaw until the river was quiet. One morning, the *Davaar* put to sea in a snow storm, and, with visibility deteriorating, Captain Galbraith ordered the anchor dropped until the blizzard cleared. The only time off that Mary and her sisters had was when the *Davaar* would be laid up for her annual overhaul in January. Then, come 'rain, snow or blow', she and Kate would get 'happed up' and take long daily walks as relief from being 'cooped up' in the heat of the ship's saloon. It was aboard the *Davaar* that Mary met her husband-to-be, Duncan Blair, who, when herring-fishing in and around Loch Long, would take the steamer home at week-ends. [Mary McGeachy, 2001]

Cattle

Prior to the mid-twentieth century, practically everything that came into and left the West Coast of Scotland was carried by sea. On one occasion – memorable for the wrong reasons – a crew-member on the *Davaar* drove some cattle towards the galley while Mary McGeachy was there, and a cow actually charged in and trapped her. 'The crew thought it wis a good laugh,' she said, 'but it near knocked me silly. I'd tae climb up on the coo's back, an they hauled me oot. Me uncle gied them a wild tellin off aboot it. I wis frightened for cattle.' [Mary McGeachy, 2001]

Stuck to the deck

When Annie McBride was a member of Carradale Gaelic Choir, they used to sing at concerts in Lochranza, Arran. Willie Galbraith, a choir-member, took them across on his fishing-boat, the *Cluaran* (Gaelic, 'Thistle'). They would return home after the concert, in the 'clear nights' of spring, with the funds nicely boosted. 'We made a lot o money in Lochranza. They fair turned out.' During one trip across Kilbrannan Sound, there was a mishap. The choir-members, in their 'nice kilts', sat on the deck to enjoy the crossing; but the *Cluaran* had been beached for her annual spring-clean and the deck varnish wasn't 'right dry'. The kilts stuck to the varnish and 'wir never right after that'. The choir's Gaelic tutor was Maggie Paterson, who belonged to North Uist. 'Ye never forget songs ye've learned,' Annie said. 'If A hear them, A know every word.' [Annie McBride, 2003]

Summer letting

As May McDougall recalled: 'I canna say that we had a poor upbringing, that we wanted for anything. We wir brought up tae save. When ye got it, ye saved it, because ye never knew when it was goin tae stop. We always managed withoot really a struggle.' For many families in Carradale, the summer letting of their houses provided extra income. Her parents, when the family was young, let both Braemar and the cottage at the back, from June until September, and themselves moved into a converted wash-house. Later, as the children grew up, only the big house was let and the family lived in the cottage throughout the season. About £30 a month would be realised, between the wars, by letting. The other houses at Port Righ – Dunvalanree, Dunolly and Dunalastair – were also seasonal boarding-houses. 'They all depended on the letting for their income.' [May McDougall, 2003]

At Seahome, Pirnmill, across the Kilbrannan Sound from Carradale, the 'front house' would likewise be let and the family move into a smaller 'summer house' at the back. The rent, between the wars, was £18 for the entire month of July and £20 for August, by no means a fortune, but, as Margaret McBride remarked, 'it helped', given that fishing tended to be 'a hunger and a burst'. [2003]

Nan McKay's mother took in lodgers during the Greenock Fair, Glasgow Fair and Paisley Fair. During those six weeks, the McKays lived in the two big attic boxrooms while two families of lodgers – for whom her mother cooked breakfast and dinner – occupied the rooms downstairs. One morning, Flora McKay cooked no fewer than 40 herrings for lodgers. [2003]

Poverty

On North Shore Street, Dalintober, in a building long since replaced by the Davaar Bar, an old couple, James and Janet MacPherson, lived. Known as 'Jamie the Hoose', he was a native of Skye* and was reputed to be so unlucky a fisherman that no crew would take him unless forced by necessity. 'Jamie the Hoose cou'na make tuppence' was the popular verdict on the poor man's fortunes. 'Red Jinny', his wife – a local MacLean – would go across to the Old Quay early in the morning, when coal-boats were unloading, and gather, 'for her own fire', the lumps of coal that fell from the swinging buckets. [Chrissie Black, 2003]

*He was born in the Parish of Sleat, c. 1866, son of Donald MacPherson, fisherman, and Mary MacDonald, and died in the Poor House Hospital, Campbeltown, in 1927.

Knitting

Until the 1960s, a fisherman's main distinguishing feature was his blue hand-knitted, tight-fitting jersey. He'd generally have at least two, one for work and the other – his 'good jersey' – for wearing ashore. These jerseys were at once functional and decorative. The commonest motifs were the vertical cables, or 'ropes', six or eight of them, on the body of the jersey, and the 'moss stitch' and 'fern', or 'tree of life', on the upper sleeves. Some women made jerseys for fishermen who didn't have a knitter in the family.

Chrissie Black knitted for her cousin, Duncan 'Spotty' Martin. She bought her wool from Miss Hyndman in High Street Post Office, Dalintober. In Campbeltown, it was not uncommon to see women knitting while they walked. In Chrissie's younger years, much of the town fishing community lived in and around Shore Street, and when the men went off to the herring fishing on a Monday, the womenfolk would 'go down to see them away' and take their knitting with them.

In Dalintober, by contrast, the women generally knitted only at home. Aggie McLean, who was married to Jock McKinlay and lived at the top of the Red Land on North Shore Street, kept a clothes-basket beside her in which to keep her current knitting in good order. 'When she'd be knittin, she'd be sittin at the window an she wid see everybody backwards an forwards on the Esplanade an she wid drop the knittin into the cloes-basket an push it under the bed an she knew she jeest had tae pull oot the basket.'

Aggie could also be seen engaged in another form of knitting – net-mending. She was the only woman in Dalintober that Chrissie Black ever saw mending with the men. Jock McKinlay generally repaired damaged nets at the foot of the Free Church Brae, where the torn parts would be suspended from nails in the wall, and it was there that his wife could be seen standing with needle in hand. [Chrissie Black, 2003]

Flora McGeachy, Nan McKay's mother, was in the habit of knitting 80 'cuts', or hanks, of wool annually when her brothers were young. These had to be turned into balls and it was usually a child's job to sit with the hank extended on the outstretched arms while the knitter wound off the wool. It was a tedious and tiring service, which Nan would perform for her mother, but not without complaint: 'Oh, hurry up!' Flora knitted jerseys on two needles and sewed back, front and arms together, but jerseys were mostly knitted seamlessly 'in the round'. She might manage to knit for 'a wee while' in the afternoon, but most of her work was done by the fireside in the evening. 'Fether wid sit on the wan side wi the newspaper an Mother wid be sittin knittin at the other.' [Nan McKay, 2003]

Annie McBride remained at home after she left school; she was needed there. 'I wis always at home – I did the baking and knitting.' She was taught to knit at school by one of the teachers, Mrs McIntosh, who took a class for an hour every afternoon. Stockings were Annie's speciality. 'She taught me tae turn the heel, an ever since that A knitted.' When interviewed in April 2003, at the age of 92 Annie was still knitting and had three pairs of socks, in varying stages of completion, laid out on a table. She averaged some 50 pairs a year, most of them given away to male family members, particularly at Christmas. The best-known wearer of Annie's socks was the late singer and comedian, Andy Stewart, for whom she knitted white 'kiltie hose'. She also knitted women's stockings, which reached above the knees and were held up by suspenders, and boys' suits and trousers, before these garments went out of fashion. Her father regularly bought wool in Ayr, when fishing there. [Annie McBride, 2003]

Marriage to a gamekeeper

When Annie McBride married, in 1938, she chose a husband outwith the fishing community. Eddie Martindale had come to Carradale Estate from Dumfriesshire at the age of 17. He had seen an advertisement in the *Glasgow Herald* for a kennel boy and applied successfully for the job.

When he arrived by steamer with his box of belongings, the unfamiliar sight of blue-jerseyed fishermen crowding the quay so intimidated him that his immediate reaction was: 'Gosh, A'm goin away back home.' One of those fishermen, however, took charge of him and escorted him to the bothy at the Sawmill, which was to be his home. Walter Shaw was the fisherman's name and he helped Eddie adjust to his new surroundings and later became a friend. Both Annie and Eddie would 'go over the road at night' with friends, boys in one group and girls in the other, and met in that way.

Before Eddie's father, William, had gone off to the First World War, he had said to him: 'Now, if A don't come back, you look after the other two.' His father did not come back, but was killed at the age of 32 on 24 October, 1918, while serving with the Royal Garrison Artillery; and when his mother died, Eddie brought his brother John and sister Peggy to Carradale and gave them a home at Brackley Lodge, in which he was by then installed as 'second keeper'. Annie herself spent 10 months in Brackley Lodge before Eddie was appointed head keeper and they moved to The Kennels, in the grounds of the Estate, which had by then passed into the ownership of Dick Mitchison, a barrister, and his wife, the author Naomi Mitchison.

When Eddie soon afterwards went off to the Second World War, as an anti-tank gunner, Annie was left with her daughter Helen, son William and 16 dogs to care for. Naomi Mitchison would 'come down from the Big House' and sit with her at night, and if she couldn't manage, would send some one else. She used to fill Naomi's basket with 'wee banty eggs… She wis that pleased; she used tae bring scraps down.' They were good eggs, with rich yellow yolks, but Annie herself wouldn't eat them – she always bought eggs – nor could she kill and eat a hen of her own.

When Eddie came home at the end of the War, his son William didn't know who he was and would say to Annie: 'A don't know when that man's goin away. He seems tae be never goin away.' Eddie came through the War unscathed, despite active service with the 51st Highland Division, first in North Africa, then in Sicily, then up through Italy and into Austria. 'He used tae like to sit at the fire afterwards an tell me all his escapades… all about where he was.' When he finally retired, he had been 64 years with Carradale Estate, employed first by Major Austin MacKenzie and then by the Mitchisons. [Annie McBride, supplemented by information from Mrs Helen Togneri, her daughter, 2003]

Shop-keeping

When Jean McDougall Martin's grandfather, John Martin, died in 1933,

Jean took to spending nights with her widowed grandmother, not only to keep her company, but also because the family home in North Shore Street was merely a room and kitchen and Jean had three brothers. Jean's grandmother was Jane McDougall, after whom she was named. The old woman kept a shop in Princes Street, Dalintober, and Jean helped there. At the back of the shop there was a big kitchen, with two 'set-in beds', and a bedroom, which was occupied by Jean's uncle Johnny. On Saturdays, Jean would serve in the shop while her grandmother cleaned the kitchen and bedroom, and she was also put to work weighing out and bagging in the back-shop. There were two sets of brass scales there, one large and one small, along with scoops. Such basics as oatmeal, flour, lentils and sugar came in sacks and had to be weighed and filled into thick blue paper bags holding various amounts, half-pound, pound, quarter-stone, half-stone, etc. There was a knack to closing the bags. 'It was a certain way ye folded it in an turned it over, each side, an that kept it sealed.' Customers would regularly ask for empty sacks, which would be cleaned and bleached and turned into pillow-slips, etc. (p 158). 'When her shop wis shut on the Sunday, an anybody wis needin anything, they jeest went round tae her kitchen window an knocked an she gave them what they wanted oot the window.'

When Jean's uncle Johnny opened a fish and chip shop at the head of Longrow, Jean went to work there too, on Saturday nights and also on certain Mondays when he attended meetings at the Masonic Lodge. Saturday nights were busiest and the shop and adjoining tea-room remained open until midnight to cater for the crowd that emerged from the dance at the nearby Templars' Hall, locally known as the 'Bowery'. Jean's parents would always meet her at the shop at midnight and accompany her home through Kinloch Green to Low Askomil. 'They dinna think A should be comin oot at that tim o night masel. It's jeest A wisna very big. It wis a walk for them too.'

Jean's first job, outwith the family, was with a tobacconist in Longrow South, Archie McNeill. He had been blinded in the First World War and she had to collect him in the morning from his home at Grianan and accompany him to the shop, where he remained all day. His other shop-assistant, Margaret Thomson, took him home after the shop closed. Jean's wage was seven shillings a week, from which her mother gave her a shilling back, and she was 'quite happy wi that'. Jean next moved to the City Warehouse for a better wage, of 18 shillings, and finally got employment in the Courier Office for a still better wage of 25 shillings. She was there when she married a Navyman, Joe Crowther from Jersey, during the Second World War. [Jean Martin, 2003]

Confidential messages

Katie Jackson's first job was in the Telephone Exchange at Tarbert, and, occasionally, while on duty, she would receive a confidential message from one of her father's contacts in Minard or Loch Caolisport, saying: 'Tell yer father there's signs o herrin.' At that time, neither her father nor her Uncle Tommy had a telephone at home. 'They wid go away quietly an come in wi hundreds o baskets,' she recalled. [Katie Jackson, 2003]

Leezie Campbell

Opposite the counter in Ellen Munro's grocer's shop at 37 High Street there was a 'lovely wee room'. On a Saturday morning, some of the Dalintober crews went into that snug to 'divide' the week's money. Ellen's shop being licensed to sell spirits, they would have their first drink there, then move next door, to Ellen Adams's at number 41, or to Leezie Campbell's at number 23, and continue drinking. Leezie – 'a wee woman wi a long grey skirt doon tae her heels an a wee white mutch' – was very strict with her customers and didn't tolerate excessive drinking. One night a fisherman, whose wife had been delivered of a baby that day, came into Leezie's pub and announced: 'That's me fifth the day.' Leezie at once came round the counter and 'put him tae the door', saying: 'Well, aweh ye go oot o here – ye're naw gonny get a sixth fae me!' As Chrissie Black explained: 'She thought he wis speakin aboot the pints, an it wis his baby. So it wis a standin joke.' [Chrissie Black, 2003]

The *Cailleachan*

Cailleachan, in Gaelic, has the meanings, among others, 'women, old women'; but in Tarbert it had a particular meaning: 'the women's night before a wedding'. Traditionally, in Tarbert, weddings were held on a Wednesday and the *cailleachan* took place on the preceding Monday. Those who were giving wedding-presents went to the bride's house in the evening. Their presents were added to the display and they were given a drink and a meal accompanied by home baking. Village children, having heard that there was 'a Cailleachan on', would go to the windows of the house and shout: 'The leg o the juck!' They wouldn't get a duck's leg, but some one would come out with a treat for them. Around the 'back of eleven', the women would disperse to the Templars' Hall to attend the 'Cailleachan dance', which would continue until two or three o' clock in the morning. Local musicians, such as Sarah Hay, Willie Richmond, Adam Barbour and Jack Dawson, would form the dance-band, and there were always singers, such as Isobel Black, whose party-piece was 'This Old House', to vary the entertainment with impromptu renditions. If the boats were in harbour, owing to weather, the fishermen would join in the 'ploy'. In the final decades of the last century, however, the custom declined. The cost of food and drink became prohibitive to some families and the event itself – traditionally confined to one night – began to spread inconveniently over several nights. [Katie Jackson, 2003]

Sea-phosphorescence

One night, when Betty MacNeill was returning from a fishing trip to Cath Sgeir with her father Malcolm and a cousin John MacNeill, as the rowing-boat approached the jetty at Cuddyport, on the west side of Gigha, the sea turned brilliant with phosphorescence.* 'The sea was just a mass of stars in the water... like fairyland,' Betty recalled. 'It was absolutely gorgeous, absolutely fantastic. A'll never forget it.' [Betty MacNeill, 2003]

*Losgadh, *'burning', in Gaelic.*

Appendix

Peter Whyte's evidence to the Royal Commission, 1892

Peter Whyte was born at Taigh-an-achaidh in Aird, but his father left to work elsewhere, returning to 'the old croft' when the family had grown up. There were more than 31 crofting families on that estate, but after Sir John Orde (p 148) got possession of it, all were evicted in three batches and 'scattered to every part'. The land, which they had been 'very sorry to leave', was 'under rabbits, sheep and every sort of trash: you would hardly think anyone had ever lived on it'.

When asked what circumstances these crofters had been in, Peter replied: 'At that time there was neither poorhouse nor anything else in Lochgilphead, and the people did not want anything to help them. If there was one in need of help, there were people to help him...' The tenants, he said, had not been in arrears of rent and were evicted for no other reason than to create a large land-holding. The houses had been built by the tenants themselves. Taigh-an-achaidh had caught fire one night and burnt down. 'We paid for the carting of the stones and paid for the wood and built the house of our own accord, and did not get a penny for it when we left.'

His holding at Silvercraigs was on the estate of Mr Graham Campbell of Shirvain, which supported about 35 families of 'crofters and cottars' and one large holding, Castleton, occupied by a tenant-farmer. The crofts, which 'used to be far bigger', were now between an acre and an acre-and-a-half in size, along with 'a cow's grass'. Rent was paid to the landlord, but if crofters kept more cows than their own ground could sustain, some would be put out on hill ground and a rent – of from 30s to 40s, for their six months' summer grazing – paid to the tenant-farmer.

The Whytes themselves kept three cows and 'followers' (calves). 'This is the stock we ought to keep, but we are curtailed,' Peter explained. 'Sir John Orde has put a march between himself and Shirving; that march was cut straight and it cut a great deal of land from the crofters. And again, there was one Captain Cole, who was a farmer or a manager in Castleton, and he has taken from them the peat moss that was there and has made it into a big park. So that the township now is curtailed, and it will not keep half the stock they ought to have. But you would never dare say a word when paying your full rent to the laird, or else you were away.'

Asked about cultivation of crofts in the district, Peter said: '... We take more crop off our crofts than the farmer takes off his holding, in proportion'. Asked, 'Do you find that the large farmers now allow their land to get back into a state of nature?' he replied: 'A great many of them, because they do not work them but look to sheep. The ground that was worked for the good of the people is now under sheep... They allow it to lie in a state of nature... rushes and brackens and moss.' He agreed that large farms were 'more favourable' for hunting and shooting: 'When people are on the land, they are counted as vermin and spoiling the sport.'

The enquiry then turned to his occupation as fisherman. He said his croft was 'about 20 or 30 yards' from the sea and that there was a natural harbour there. He was primarily a herring-fisherman – 'It is all trawl-nets (ring-nets) that are worked here' – but he also fished with lines for white fish. Among the 31 crofters whose evictions he detailed comprehensively by family-name and location, there were fishermen, but the old men did not fish much: 'The young people went to the fishing while the old people looked after the crofts.' It was from the money earned at fishing that crofters were able to 'pay such an exorbitant rent for their small bits of ground that would yield them very little'.

He himself 'would rather have a big croft and pay rent for it than a small one that would yield next to nothing. If I had a croft and was able to stock it and keep it, I would rather have a croft that would support a family than a small croft, even if I got it for nothing... I get some work in the winter, whereas if I had no land I would have to go to every quarter of the world seeking work.' *Report of the Royal Commission (Highlands and Islands, 1892)*, Edinburgh, 1895, pp 837–41.

Glossary

A I
aa all
aafu awful
aathegither altogether
aboot about
afore before
agane again
aheid ahead
aweh away
aye yes, always

back en late autumn
barra barrow
bey bay
birled turned
birth berth, space
bittie a little
bob a shilling
bonny lovely, beautiful
bothy a farm-building for housing unmarried male workers
bow buoy
brash a burst of activity
braw fine, splendid
breck break
breid bread
burd bird
burning sea-phosphorescence
burra burrow

cam came
canna cannot
canny cautious, careful
chowin chewing
cloes clothes
coo cow
coorse coarse, course
cou'na couldn't

dae do
deh day
devilage devilish
dhan marker-buoy, with pole and flag, at outer end of seine-net ropes

dinna didn't
divide a share, specifically of a boat's earnings
doon down
dose a large quantity
dreg a drag, a tow or haul of a net
dridge a (clam-)dredge
droadge as above

efter after
emdy anybody
erm arm
ett ate
eye a shoal of fish

fadom fathom
fae from
fella fellow
femily family
fether father
fry a meal (of fish)
furst first

gan going
gether gather
gie give
gied gave
gled glad
gonny going to
grett great
grip a seabed obstruction or 'fastener'
grun ground

haal haul
had'ae had to
haev have
hame home
han hand
hanna hadn't
happed wrapped
heid head
hert heart
hervest harvest
hoora whore of a, i.e. terrible

190

hoose house
hoot what
hopper-net a trawl equipped with heavy-duty rollers on its sole-rope for bouncing over hard ground

intae into

jeest just

kinna kind of
kinnle kindle

laik like
lift the quantity of fish in the cod-end of seine-net or trawl able to lifted aboard by winch
lik like
loast lost
loat lot

ma my
male meal
masel, mesel myself
mash mesh of net
mashed enmeshed
me my
meenit a minute
merr more
mind remember
moarnin morning
mooth mouth

naething, naethin nothing
naw no, not
nawthin nothing
neebor neighbour, or partner, in a fishing combination
nee'na needn't
nesty nasty

o of
och anee an expression of weariness, despair, etc.
oot out
ould old
ower over

paling a fence-post
peyed paid
piece sandwich
pletform platform, or decking, on skiff
ploy a light-hearted plan for one's own amusement
poke a bag
puckle a little
pun a pound weight

rasher a meal of fish
redd clear, tidy
rid red
roon, roond round

saalt salt
seeck sick
sehin saying
sell sail
sherp sharp
shot to shoot, or set, fishing gear; a catch of fish
sile herring fry
smock smoke
smockin smoking
snood short hook-bearing line attached to main line
sookin sucking
sou south
spot a shoal of fish
stabby jaggy
stey stay
steyed stayed
stravaiger one who roams around
streetch stretch

tae too
teemed poured
tell tail
they these, those
thir their
thon that
totie tiny
touch a lucrative catch
trauchle an exhausting business
troch trough, the container for small lines
twinty twenty

waash wash
wae with
wan one
wance once
watter water
wean child
weel well
werena weren't
wey way

wheen   a quantity
wherr   where
whoot   what
wi   with
wid   would
wile   wild, very, terrible
win   wind
winna   wouldn't
wir   were
wirna   weren't
wis   was

wisna   wasn't
wou'na   wouldn't
wrang   wrong
wreck   wrack, seaweed
wumman   woman

ye   you
yer   your
yersel, yersilf   yourself
yin   one

Amendments to Previously Published Books

I wish to make the following corrections to my previous books published by House of Lochar.

The North Herring Fishing (2001)

Jim Tarvit, Anstruther, points out that the skipper of the *Manx Rose* PL 48, named on p 90 as 'Lachie Horsburgh', was in fact Lockie Horsburgh, 'a native of Pittenweem who married a Manx lass and settled in the Isle of Man'. He later skippered and owned *Signora* PL 15 and *Signora II* PL 27. The Christian name 'Lock', Mr Tarvit says, is 'fairly common in the Horsburgh family of Pittenweem'. He believes that the original name was 'Lockhart', which was shortened to 'Lock', of which 'Lockie' is presumably a pet-form. A Manx contact, Michael Craine, who gave me the name, had it correct – Lockie – but I decided that this form, hitherto unknown to me, must be a mistaken rendering of 'Lachie'. I, however, was the one who was mistaken. I am a firm believer in the saying, 'The man who never made a mistake, never made anything', and take comfort from the fact that not only do I now know that the name was 'Lockie', but I know why!

The *Fiona* was not bought by Jim and Denis Meenan in 1963 (p 168), but in the following year. Since Jim died on 6 October, 1967, the brothers therefore had three years neighbouring each other in the North with the *Fiona* and *Stella Maris*.

Lachie Paterson points out that Willie Anderson's *Prospector*, referred to on pages 67, 76 and 85 in relation to events in the 1960s, should be the *Jasmine*, because the *Prospector* – the first, and only, square-sterned ringer – was not built until 1973.

The word *bargin* – which I glossed as 'packing' – has apparently never existed except in my own transcription of Johnny Munro's account (p 74). He, and everyone else whom I all too belatedly asked, is unfamiliar with the word. It is, therefore, an unwitting lexical invention of my own, which may henceforth be completely disregarded.

Ian Main, Hopeman, was particularly interested in the story of the

Harvest Queen's obtaining her position at sea from the *Undaunted* (p 91) because the *Undaunted*'s skipper was his father, William John Main of Hopeman. 'At that time,' Mr Main writes, 'there was seven of a crew and five of them had the first name William.'

Mr Main thinks that the Lossiemouth seine-net skipper, whose nickname was 'Boysie' (p 141), must have been Daniel More of Hopeman, who had the *Alert* INS 287.

Herring Fishermen of Kintyre and Ayrshire (2002)

My 'correction' of Mungo Munro's information (p 3) that fisherfolk colonised Newton-upon-Ayr not from Rosehearty, as he said, but from Pitsligo, was extremely ill-judged, because Rosehearty is in the Parish of Pitsligo.

In the Index of Fishermen, three references to Archie Kerr, Tarbert, appear. There were, however, two skippers of the name involved and the Archie Kerr mentioned on p 64 in a footnote was the one known as 'Young Cook'.

Index

Where possible, registration numbers have been matched with fishing boats, but some blanks remain owing to doubt or lack of information. Also, some scientific names have, for better or worse, undergone revision in recent decades, therefore in the interest of consistency M Pritchard's *Fresh and Saltwater Fish*, Glasgow, 1986, has been adopted, except in a very few cases, as the standard authority. When informants' names are mentioned only in brackets, as sources, these names are not included here.

Aberdeen, 85
Aberdeenshire, 21, 24, 62, 129
Acacia (CN 56) 22
Achalephin/Ach' an leth-Pheighinn, 137, 148
Achnaba, 64, 77, 119, 121, 137
Adams, Ellen, publican, 186
Adoration (BA 238) 131
Adriatic (H 190) 65
Ailsa Craig, 79, 83, 89, 113, 134
Aird, 137, 188
Airdrie, 165
alcohol, 8, 42, 95, 119, 124, 166, 168, 178, 186
Aliped, 140
Alison, 63
Allan's – see Feochaig
Allan, Willie, Gigha, 4
Alliance (CN 187) 122, 134
Allt a' Chrè, 151
Allt Oigh, 137
Altair (CN 292) 122
anglerfish *Lophius piscatorius*, 101–2, 134
Annie (CN 37) 62
Annie (CN 178) 19, 117
Aquaculture, Department of, Stirling University, 63
Arbroath, 18
Ardfern, 68

Ardkinglas Estate, 118
Ardlamont, 84
Ardminish, 66, 133
Ardnaherir, 137
Ardrishaig, 20, 137, 139, 140, 141, 142, 148, 149,
Ardrossan, 133, 134
Arran, 25, 35, 68, 77, 78, 80, 84, 87, 92, 100, 106, 113, 116, 125, 128–9, 135, 165, 173, 175, 181
Arranman's Barrels, 11, 91, 132
Auchenhoan, 12, 15, 17, 24, 76, 89, 90
Auchindrain Museum, 54, 95, 143
Ayr, 16, 67, 78, 81, 85, 89, 114, 116, 122, 183
Ayrshire, 16, 21, 52, 78, 80, 94, 97, 108, 116, 120, 133, 134, 140, 165 (fn.)

bag-net, saithe, 53
bag-net, salmon, 118, 119
Baile Beag, 137
Baile Mór, 137, 138, 146, 147
bait: fish, 3, 49, 54–7, 62, 64–5, 111, 121, 141, 160, 175; lobster, 4–5, 6, 7, 28, 30–32, 36, 39, 43; ground, 53, 56, 57; hole, 53, 57
Baker, Rev Argyll, 167
Ballantrae Banks, 80, 128, 134, 140
Balnabraid Glen, 28
Balvicar, 68
Bangor, Ireland, 125
Baraskomel, 162, 173, 176
Barbour, Adam, Tarbert, 186
Barbour, Cissie and Elsie, Southend, 13
Barbour, James, farmer, 13
Barfad, 162, 178
Barmore, 80
Barr, Silvercraigs, 147
basking shark *Cetorhinus maximus*, 106–10, 120
bass *Dincentrachus labrax*, 41
Beakie (buoy), 75, 77
Beattie, Alastair, Southend, 60–1
Beauty (CN 93) 62

195

Bede, Cuthbert, 27–8, 62
bee-keeping, 10, 11, 148
Bee (CN 83) 62
Bell, Margaret – see MacVicar
Bella (CN 145) 65
Bellochantuy, 36, 52, 65, 103
Bengullion (CN 229) 19
Ben Gairn (A 508) 85
Bennan, 68
Bettess, Richard, Fleetwood, 65
Betina (KY 212) 39
Betty (CN 260) 98, 128
bib – see pouting
Billingsgate, 37, 113, 125, 127
birthdays, 157, 162, 177
biscuits, sea-, 140, 141, 158–9, 169
blacksmiths, 86, 95, 125, 126, 171
Black, Chrissie, Dalintober, 182–3, 186
Black, Isobel, Tarbert, 186
Black, Joe, baker, 169
Black, John, Tarbert, 93
Blackstock, Peter, Bellochantuy, 36
Blackwater, 75, 172
Blair, Archie, Tarbert, 92
Blair, Billy, yachtsman, 97
Blair, Dugald Jr., Campbeltown, 24
Blair, Duncan, Campbeltown, 180
Blair, Jane, Silvercraigs, 137, 144
Bloody Bay, 12
Bluebird (CN 125) 19, 24–25
bodach, 59
bodach glas, 59
bodach ruadh, 59, 61
Bogha a' Chrùbain, 49
Bonnie Lass III (CN 126) 132
Boy Stewart (CN 9) 134
Bradley, Edward – see Bede, Cuthbert
Brainport, 95
brallach, brollach – see sand gaper
Brierly, Jack, Bangor, 125
Brig, 19, 90 (fn.), 136
Brighter Hope (LK 502, CN 16) 130, 132, 134
Brighter Morn (CN 151 etc.), 82, 88
briosgaidean – see biscuits
Brodick/Bay, 128, 129, 134
Brodie, Jock, Campbeltown, 18, 24
Brodie, Malcolm, Campbeltown, 24
Brown Head, 39, 80, 98, 129
Brown, Andrew, Campbeltown, 17, 19
Brown, Janet McMillan, 5
Brown, Joe, Campbeltown, 138
Brown, Kenny, Tarbert, 117

Brown, Peter, Tarbert, 131
Brownie, Fred Sr., 129
Brownie, Fred Jr., Carradale, 130, 133
Brownie, Ronnie, Carradale, 51, 129–30, 132, 133, 134
buckie – see whelk
Buckie, 71
Buck Bay, 163
bullhead, freshwater *Cottus gobio*, 102
burning – see phosphorescence
Bute, 73, 91, 170
butter, 124, 140, 142, 143, 158, 169, 176
buttermilk, 60, 143

Cailleach, 146
Cailleachan, 186
cailleach bhàn, 59
Cairnbaan, 141
Caledonia (TT 17), 131
Caledonia (TT 34) 117
Cameron, Archie, Southend, 44–45, 59, 60
Cameron, Archibald D, Southend, 52, 61
Cameron, Charlie, Sanda, 10, 91 (fn.)
Cameron, Hugh, Port Ellen, 66
Cameron, John 'Dog', Southend, 90, 91 (fn.)
Cameron, John Sr., Southend, 91 (fn.)
Cameron, Katie, Carradale, 167
Campbell family, Silvercraigs, 137–49
Campbell, Alan, Ardrishaig, 148
Campbell, Alexander of Auchindarroch, 149
Campbell, Colin, Carradale, 83–4, 134
Campbell, Colin, Grogport, 167
Campbell, Dugald Coutts, Carradale, 109
Campbell, Graham, of Shirvain, 188
Campbell, Hughie, 121
Campbell, Jessie, Silvercraigs, 137–49
Campbell, John of Shirvain, 148
Campbell, Johnny, Carradale, 22
Campbell, J, Bowmore, 66
Campbell, Leezie, publican, Dalintober, 186
Campbell, Maggie, Silvercraigs, 137–49, 150
Campbell, 'Mistress Jock', Shirvain, 148
Campbell, Sam, Campbeltown, 180
Campbeltown, 5, 15, 16–19, 20, 21, 23, 28, 30, 48, 51, 62, 65, 69, 71, 75, 76, 79–80, 82, 87, 90, 97, 98, 99, 105,

117, 122, 125, 126, 127, 138, 162, 167, 169, 170, 174, 177, 178, 180, 182
Campbeltown Courier, 1, 31, 45, 74, 79, 110
Campbeltown Loch, 26, 39, 40, 46, 74, 75, 119, 127
Campbeltown Shipyard, 17
Cape Wrath, 111
Cara Island, 33, 122
card schools, 20
Carmichael, Agnes, Dalintober, 18
Carmichael, Archie, Tarbert, 53, 126, 127, 157, 160, 164
Carmichael, Archibald, Tarbert, 160
carrachan a' chinn mhóir – see gurnard
Carradale, 22, 51, 52, 62, 76, 85, 86, 108, 109, 110, 125, 129, 132, 157, 158, 159, 160, 165, 166, 167, 168, 169, 170, 171, 173, 174, 176, 181, 183–4
Carradale Bay, 71, 76, 92, 118
Carradale Gaelic Choir, 167, 181
Carradale Water, 119
carragheen *Chondrus crispus*, 159–60
Carrick Castle, 93
Carskey, 31, 32
Castlebay, 79
Castleton, 137, 138, 143, 145, 146, 150, 188
Catacol/Bank, 25, 81, 129
Cath Sgeir, 187
Catriona (TT 24) 20
cattle, 143, 145, 146, 163, 164, 180, 188
cavvy, 161
ceiteanach, 52
Ceol na Mara (CN 699) 46
Charlotte Ann (TT 49) 19, 25, 73
chat hake, 82
cheese, 15, 145, 158
Christmas, 169, 176, 183
Christmas puddings, 163–4
clabba/clabby doo – see mussel, horse
Clabbadoo Bank, 76
Claits, 113
clam – see scallop *Pecten maximus*
Clan McDougall (CN 9) 158
Claonaig, 81, 83, 111
Clark, Colin, Tarbert, 83
clay, 144, 151, 153, 162
cleeban, clibean, 58, 59
Cleit, 36
Clio (AG 67) 141
Cluaran (CN 240) 181

Clydebank, 138, 174
Clyde Fishermen's Association, 136
cnòdan – see gurnards
coal, 127, 133–4, 147, 165, 182
'Coasters', 12
Cock of Arran, 109, 120, 128, 165
cockle *Cardium edule*, 1, 63, 77
cod *Gadus morhua*: 19, 58–69, 77, 84, 89, 91, 134, 135, 141, 142, 152–3, 160, 175; 'Pan', 'red', 'rock', 13, 41, 58, 59, 61–3, 77; salting of, 60, 63, 64, 67, 122, 142, 153; farming of, 63
coinean mara – see sea-urchin
Colonsay, 112, 126, 131
Colville, Willie, Machrihanish, 1, 3, 4, 5, 6, 8
Commissioners and Trustees for Fisheries, Manufacturers and Improvements in Scotland, 107
conger eel *Conger conger*, 42, 99, 112–4
Connell, D, fish-buyer, 68
Cook, Angus, Carradale, 129 (fn.)
Corriegills, 128, 129
Cossack Inn, 137
Cour, 80
Cowal, 113, 148
Cowper, James and Margaret, Southend, 13
crabs: edible *Cancer pagurus*, 2, 4, 8, 36, 37, 48–50, 63; snaring of, 4, 7–8; hermit, 41; shore *Carcinus maenas*, 31, 39, 41; velvet swimming *Portunus puber*, 30, 31, 33, 39, 40, 41; in general, 30, 31, 36, 41, 113
Craignish, 51, 103
crawfish *Palinurus elephas*, 41, 45–6
creagag, creggach, creggag, craigach, criggach – see wrasse, ballan
Creag an Airgiod – see Silvercraigs
Creag an Airgiod (Muasdale), 49
Creag Dhomhnuill Mhóir, 9
creag dhubh – see anglerfish
Creag Ruadh, 14
crechan, creachann, creachal – see scallop, queen
creels and creel-making, 11, 28–30, 33, 35, 40, 64, 65, 141
Creggan, 158
Crimson Arrow (CN 30, built 1927), 17
Crimson Arrow (CN 30, built 1970) 86, 109, 117
Crinan, 38, 131, 140
Crinan Canal, 131, 140, 141, 149

197

crofting – see Silvercraigs
crooban, cruban – see crab, edible
Crossaig, 42, 80, 82, 120
Crossibeg, 77
Crowther, Joe, 185
cudainn, cuddie, cuddin, 52, 53, 56, 71, 142
Cuddyport – see Port nan Cudainnean
Culzean Bay, 128
Culzean (BA 172) 23–24
Currans, general dealers, Tarbert, 164
Currie, John, Pirnmill, 128
cuttlefish, 121

Dalintober, 51, 76, 138, 139, 162, 166, 169, 171, 172, 173, 174, 175, 177, 182, 183, 185, 186
Dalriada, PS, 85
Dalriada (TT 77) 72, 73, 81, 83, 93, 131
Dan Mann's Port, 9
Danish anchor-seiners, 16, 80
dannie, 70
Dansey, Jack, Hull, 104
darras, darrows, 31, 116
Davaar Island/Lighthouse, 18, 22, 26, 74, 77, 83, 89, 91, 114, 125, 172
Davaar, SS, 180
Davidson, Alexander, Bangor, 125
Dawn Carol (CN 30) 109
Dawson, Jack, Tarbert, 186
dealers, 164, 167
Dearg Sgeir, 55
Dempsey, Daniel, Sanda, 32
Denmark, 111
Destiny (TT 42) 131
Dewar, Johnny, Inveraray, 54
Dickson, Willie, Tarbert, 101
Dippen, 173
dogs, 55, 64, 159, 162, 167, 184
dogfish, greater spotted *Scyliorhinus stellaris*, 96, 112
dogfish, lesser spotted *Scyliorhinus caniculus*, 42, 96, 110, 112
dogfish, spurdog – see spurdog
Doirlinn, 75 (fn.), 77
dolphins, 2, 110
dookers, 160–1
Doos' Cove, 2
Douglas, Robert, Campbeltown, 11
driftwood – see wood-gathering
drift-net, 37, 52, 62, 78, 139, 152
drovers, 163, 164
drowd, 58
Druimyeonmore, 29

Drumlemble, 2, 4
Drum Fuar, 137
Duart, 103
Dubh Chaol-linn, 63, 94
dulse *Rhodymenia palmata*, 160
Dumfries-shire, 183, 184
dumplings, clootie, 157, 158, 167, 169, 177
Dunadd, 68
Dunan Hole, 134
Dunaverty, 13, 59, 60, 62
Dunaverty Bay – see Machribeg Bay
Dundalk, 3
Dunmore East, 25
Dunn, Henry, Invergordon, 170
dunny (see also skate, common), 85, 97
Dunoon, 146
Dunure, 23, 129 (fn.)
Durnin, Charlie, Campbeltown, 19, 25
Durnin, James, Campbeltown, 25
Durnin, John, Campbeltown, 25, 174

eagach – see lines, long
Eaglesome, Thomas, Peninver, 84, 118
earnings, 12, 13, 15, 22, 24, 72, 80, 111, 118, 122, 127, 128, 129, 132, 177, 180, 185, 186
easgann – see conger eel
East Coast fishermen, 16, 19, 20–21, 27, 39, 68–69, 71, 72, 87, 97, 103, 113, 131
echo-sounder, 34, 39, 69, 71, 77, 133
Edward VII, King, 87
eggs, 7, 151, 156, 159, 162, 169, 184
Eilean Dubh, 38
Eilean Mór, 38, 39
Eilean Port a Chaolais, 67
Elf, 111
Elizabeth Campbell (CN 186) 22
Ella (RO 62) 128
Ellary Estate, 38
Elma (CN 25) 22, 110
engines, 17, 38, 39, 56, 80, 99, 113–14, 125
Enterprise (CN 256) 19
Erines (Tarbert), 106
Erines Bank, 77
Eriskay, 53
Escart, 80, 82
Ettrick Bay, 91
Eyemouth, 131

Fairlie Sound, 94

Fairy Dell, 116, 129
falaisg, 147, 153
Falcon (CN 97) 19
Fame (CN 118) 90, 172–3
feeling-wire, 34
Felicity (CN 64), 69, 72, 93, 94, 104, 135
Feochaig, 11, 91, 99
ferrets, 162
Fifies, 20, 24
file fish, 42
Findlay, Miss, schoolteacher, 174
Findochty, 98
Finn, Cecil, Campbeltown, 19, 21, 22, 26, 72, 73, 74, 80, 82, 83, 86, 87, 88, 89, 92, 93, 94, 98, 99, 102 (fn.), 104, 127
Finn, Harry, 162
Finn, Tommy, Campbeltown, 74, 111
Fionnaghal (TT 65) 19
Fionnaghal (TT 106) 131
Fionnaghal (TT 104) 100
First World War, 13, 15, 108, 148, 151–2, 170, 184, 185
Fisher, Donald, headmaster, 174
fish-cakes, 4, 51, 56
flatfish (in general), 13, 24, 71, 75, 135
Fleetwood, 65, 78, 79, 100, 104
Florian (CN 2) 23–4
flounder, freshwater *Platichthys flesus*, 93, 94–5
flounder – see plaice
flour-bags, 57, 127, 144, 158, 185
fluke – see plaice
fluke, freshwater – see flounder, freshwater
food, 3–4, 5,-6, 9, 39, 51, 53, 54, 56, 57, 60, 63, 80, 93, 100–1, 104, 105, 106, 115, 122, 124, 140, 141, 142, 143–5, 153, 155, 156–64, 166, 167, 172, 176, 180, 184, 186–7
France, 122
Fraserburgh, 71
Fraser, Dugald, mason, 45
Fraser, Rev William, Gigha, 56, 57
French hake-trawlers, 80
Frigate Bird (TT 137) 100
Furnace, 74

Gael, herring steamer, 163
Gaelic language, 14, 61, 68, 138, 147, 150, 151, 152, 166–7
Galbraith, Captain, 180
Galbraith, Dick, Peggy and Mary, Carradale, 174

Galbraith, D, Jura, 97
Galbraith, Lizzie, Drumlemble, 4
Galbraith, Willie, Carradale, 181
Galdrans, 1, 4, 5, 6, 32
gambling, 20
games, children's, 50, 171–2
gannets, 30, 59, 60, 134
Garbhard, 147
Gardener's Rock, 9
garfish *Belone belone*, 116
Garland, 90
Garrion (CN 474) 62
Garroch Head, 122
geàrr bhodach, 59
Geelot, 133
gibearnach – see squid
Gigalum and Cottages, 29, 67
Gigha, 4, 15, 21, 29, 30, 31, 32, 33, 37, 38, 39, 41, 42, 45, 46, 53, 55, 56, 57, 58, 59, 64–8, 85, 86, 94, 95, 99, 100, 112, 117, 126, 130, 133, 159, 162, 166, 178
Gigha, Sound of, 33, 65, 111
Gilchrist brothers, Pans, 45, 62
Gilchrist, Alistair, Campbeltown, 117
Gilchrist, Billy, Campbeltown, 104
Gilchrist, Donnie, fish-merchant, 25, 47, 117
Gilchrist, William, Campbeltown, 117
gildee – see pout
Gillies, Robert, Campbeltown, 46, 77, 100, 105, 112, 134
Gillies, Valerie, Campbeltown, 134
Gillon, John, Southend, 13
Gillon, Captain John, 13
Gillon, Richard 'Dick', Southend, 13–14, 31, 59, 60, 95
giomach cuan – see crawfish
Girl Ann (CN 66) 132, 133
Girl Eileen (CN 38) 136
Girl Seona (TT 37) 93
Girvan, 18, 128, 140
Girvan, James, butcher, 174
Girvan, Dan, Campbeltown, 77
Glacknabay, 73
Glad Tidings (PD 300) 19
glasan, gleshan, 13, 51, 52, 54
Glasgow, 17, 37, 52, 73, 84, 85, 86, 97, 117, 118, 124, 132, 161, 163, 165, 170, 171, 173, 176
Glasgow Fair, 82, 83, 140, 177, 181
Glas Eilean, 77
Gleaner (PD 336, CN 41, TT 2) 19, 20,

25, 70–1, 74, 101
Gleaner (CN 284), 99
Gleaner (CN 222) 111
Glemanuill, 59, 60–1
Glen, Mary Ann, 6
Glenacardoch, 42, 54
Glencreggan, 27
Glenehervie, 87
Glenramskill, 77
glibe, glipe, 58
Glunimore, 132
goats, 2, 98 (fn.), 139
gobach odhar (see also skate, common), 97
gobag – see spurdog
Golden Chance (CN 18) 72
Golden Fleece (CN 170) 114
Golden Hind (CN 199) 104
Golden Promise (KY 278) 111
Golden Sheaf (CN 7) 135, 136
goose feathers, 55, 56
Gourock, 37, 170, 180
Grahams, Silvercraigs, 140
Graham, Alasdair, Gigha, 29
Graham, Archie, Peninver, 10, 11, 21, 28, 29, 30, 31, 33, 34, 44, 120
Graham, Margaret Buchanan, Peninver, 34
Grant, Ann, Invergordon, 170
Gratitude (CN 114) 18
Graveyard Rock, 9, 49
Greencastle skiffs, 59
Greenock, 84, 124, 138, 147, 153, 181
Green Pastures (BF 4) 71, 87
Grimsby, 118
Grips, 26, 74
Grob, 57
Grogport, 80, 167
groundkeepers, 61, 92
ground-net, 97, 152
Grumoli, Leo, Campbeltown, 122
guillemot *Uria aalge* – see *dookers*
gulls and eggs of, 6, 55, 56, 71, 144
Gundry, Joseph & Co, 21
gurnards *Eutrigla gurnardus* and *Aspitrigla cuculus*, 41–42, 103–5

haddock *Melanogrammus aeglefinus*, 21, 22, 24, 25, 64, 70–5, 77, 78, 91, 102, 134
haddock, golden, 74
haddock, spotted, 74
hake *Merluccius merluccius*, 16, 22, 40, 78–84, 92, 114
halibut *Hippoglossus hippoglossus*, 84–6

Hall, Jimmy, Campbeltown, 77
Hamilton, Dan, Ardrishaig, 141
Harbour, Big and Wee, 140, 142
Hardy, Sir Alister, 109
hares, 157, 163
Harmony (BF 158) 20
Harmony (TT 24) 20
Harpoon at a Venture, 108
Harvester (CN 200) 34
Harvest Home, 146
Harvest Queen (CN 167) 22, 23
Harvison, Bill, Pirnmill, 77
hawking fish, 13, 52, 60, 62, 153, 175
hay, 36, 145, 162
Hay, Sarah, Tarbert, 186
Hay, William & Co, Tarbert, 124
hazel/nuts, 28–9, 35, 54, 64, 165, 168, 178
heather, 28, 147, 153
Helen (CN 36) 62
Henderson, Eoghann, Gigha, 30, 67
hens, 7, 146, 151, 162, 165, 167, 169, 184
Heron (BCK 71) 19
herring *Clupea harengus*, and fishery of, 6, 24, 36, 51, 59, 64, 66, 79, 80–1, 83, 116, 119, 121, 127, 128, 129, 131, 139, 140, 141, 151, 156, 160, 173, 175, 179, 180, 186
herring, cured, 39, 53, 141, 156, 157, 163, 167, 174, 176
Herring Industry Board, 23
Highland Division, 51st, 184
holidays, 138, 170, 181–2
Holy Isle, 134
honey, 13, 148
Horning (GY 1106) 25
housing, 28, 139, 153, 181, 185
Hull, 65, 104
huts, fishermen's, 60–1, 62, 120
Hyndman, Miss, Dalintober, 182

Iceland, 85, 104
Imachar, 77
Inch(marnock), 26, 82
ink(fish) – see squid
Innellan, 91
Inveraray, 54, 118, 143, 149, 153
Invergordon, 170
Inverkip, 94
Ireland, 13, 16, 23, 25, 59, 60, 61, 64, 105, 106, 125, 127, 130
Irene (RO 43) 116, 121, 128, 129

Irvine, 65
Isabella, 'Sanda Lugger', 52
Isabella (CN 668) 24
Islay, 21, 41, 60, 63, 66, 68, 126, 130, 131, 162, 178
Islay fishermen, 60–1
Islaymen's Port, 9, 49, 60
Isla Ross, 90, 133
Isle of Man, 80, 111, 130
Italian community, Campbeltown, 122, 174
Italy, 122

Jackson family, Tarbert, 80, 131, 186
Jackson, Katie, Tarbert, 161, 162, 166
Jackson, Kenneth, Tarbert, 177
Jackson, Mary Kennedy, Tarbert, 163, 171, 177
Jackson, Mary, Tarbert, 161
Jackson, Tommy, Tarbert, 178, 186
Jackson, Willie, Tarbert, 163, 171, 177, 178
Janet (CN 49) 37
Janet Lang (CN 84) 17, 24, 47
jellyfish, 34
Jenny Lind's Bay, 92
jerseys, fishermen's, 140, 182–3
Jessie (CN 194) 17, 39, 40, 74, 102
jigs, jigging (lines), 30, 64, 111, 116
Jinks, Lt. Sydney, 104
Johnson, Angus, Tarbert, 20, 104, 131
Johnson, Donald, Tarbert, 115
Johnson, Malcolm, Tarbert, 73, 83, 93
Johnson, Margaret McGougan, Tarbert, 25
Johnson, Ronnie, Tarbert, 25, 101, 108, 131
Johnston, Jackie, 131
Johnston, John, Eriskay, 53
Johnston, Margaret, Dalintober, 177
John Dory *Zeus faber*, 118
Jura, 38, 68, 97, 110, 112, 126, 130, 131

kail, 145, 158, 161
Kames, Loch Fyne, 150–5
'Katie Whippy', Dalintober, 169
Keil, Southend, 9, 13, 49, 90, 95
Keills, Gigha, 15, 37
Keith, Archibald, Campbeltown, 118
Kelso, 170
Kennedy, James, Irish seaman, 3
Kennedy, Neil, farmer, Barfad, 178
Kerr, Archie, Tarbert, 81

Kerr, Willie, Lochranza, 128
Kerry Shore, 128
Kia-Ora (BA 110, CN 62, BA 190) 17, 18
Kilberry, 35, 37, 100, 117
Kilbrannan Sound, 24, 71, 74, 75, 82, 88, 90, 109, 120, 125, 173, 181
Kilchousland, 172, 173
Kildalloig, 62, 76, 84
Kilfinan, 81
Killean Bay, 133
Kinerarach, 57
King, John, 131
King Bird (CN 264) 23, 24
King William Bank, 111
Knapdale, 37
knitting, 182–3
Kyles of Bute, 73, 130

Lady Charlotte (CN 175) 127
Lady Edith (CN 174) 127
Lafferty, Teddy, Campbeltown, 12, 31
Lagan, 126
Lake, The – see Leac Bhuidhe
Lamlash, 129, 134
Lammas Fair, Ballycastle, 60
landmarks in fishing, 25–6, 34, 47, 54, 67–8, 72, 75, 76, 77, 89, 91, 133
Lang, Duncan Sr., Campbeltown, 17
Lang, Duncan Jr., Campbeltown, 17, 24, 47
Lang, John, Campbeltown, 17, 47
Lang, Neil, Campbeltown, 17, 47
Largs, 97, 134
Lassie (BF 318) 19, 98
Law, Angus, Ardrishaig, 148
Leac Bhuidhe, 1–9, 41, 43
Leim, 57
leister – see spear, fish-
Lendalfoot, 134
limpet *Patella vulgata*, 1, 4–6, 53
limpet hammers, 5
lines: hand, 59, 62, 63, 64, 75, 76–7, 106, 109, 118, 128, 142, 160; long, 'big', 'small', 25, 58, 62, 63, 64–7, 78, 80–1, 98, 99, 100, 105, 111–12, 113–4, 121, 134, 141, 165, 175, 179, 189
ling *Molva molva*, 41, 105
lion-scrìobaidh, 53
Liverpool, 113
Lizetta (CN 15) 13
lobster, *Homarus gammarus*: 2, 7, 8, 11, 26–44, 104, 113, 132; creels, 28–30,

35, 40; rearing of, 42–44; snaring of, 4, 7–8
lobster, American, *Homarus americanus*, 28
Lochgair, 140, 150, 151, 152
Lochgilphead, 137, 147, 148, 153, 188
Lochie (BF 295) 87, 92
Lochinver, 22
Lochranza, 25, 106, 116, 128, 129, 134, 135, 165, 172, 181
Loch Boisdale, 140
Loch Buie, 127
Loch Caolisport, 38, 93, 186
Loch Craignish, 38
Loch Fyne, 20, 63, 70, 74, 77, 84, 108, 109, 115, 116, 121, 124, 137, 138, 161
Loch Fyne Skiffs, 23, 37
Loch Goil, 93, 94
Loch na Keal, 38
Loch Lomond, 94
Loch Long, 93, 180
Loch Melford, 131
Loch Stornoway, 38, 100
Lodan, Loaden, 19, 48, 76, 77, 80, 84, 89, 102, 126, 127
London, 27, 36, 37
Lovie, Francis and Willie, Ardrishaig, 20
Luce Bay, 16
lugworm *Arenicola marina*, 77, 95
lythe – see pollack

Machribeg/Bay, 13, 95
Machrihanish, 2, 4, 29, 30, 35, 42, 43, 45, 49, 62–3, 120, 130, 131, 174
Machrihanish Bay, 2, 39, 41, 104
Machrihanish Colliery, 2, 5
Machrihanish Marine Farms Ltd, 63
Machrie Bay, 86, 90, 109
mackerel *scomber scombrus*, 30, 56, 79, 111, 115–16
MacRingan's Point, 33
Madelaine Ann, wreck of, 3
Maidens, 78, 122
Maireared (TT 113) 81
Maireared (TT 135) 115
Mairi Elspeth (CN 116) 19
Maisie (TT 83) 81
Mallaig, 22, 23, 79
Maol Dubh, 81, 91, 108, 164
Mara, fisheries research vessel, 126
Margaret Rose (CN 115) 10, 21
Mari-Dor (BA 217) 15
Marie (BA 211) 23

Marine Research Laboratory, Torry, Aberdeen, 74, 13
Martin, Angus, Dalintober, 174, 175
Martin, Duncan 'Naiser', Dalintober, 170, 172
Martin, Duncan 'Spotty', Dalintober, 182
Martin, Harry, Dalintober, 174
Martin, Henry, Dalintober, 89, 92, 126, 127, 172
Martin, Jean, Dalintober, 170, 171, 172, 174, 175, 176, 177, 184–5
Martin, Jeannie, Glasgow, 176
Martin, John 'Scatarach', Dalintober, 51
Martin, John 'Boachal', Dalintober, 184
Martin, Johnny, Dalintober, 185
Martin, Sarah, Dalintober, 175
Martindale, Eddie, Carradale, 166, 183–4
Martindale, Helen, Carradale, 184
Martindale, John, 184
Martindale, Peggy, 184
Martindale, William, 184
Martindale, William, Carradale, 184
Mary, skiff, 17
Mary Sturgeon (BA 40) 129 (fn.)
Mayflower, yacht, 48
Maxwell, Gavin, 108
Maxwell's Park/Planting, 127, 177
Meanders in South Kintyre, 49
meat, 143–4, 160, 162, 163, 176
Meenan, Denis, Campbeltown, 18, 83, 138
Meenan, Jock, Campbeltown, 18
Meenan, Tommy, Campbeltown, 98
Menzies, Mary, Campbeltown, 159
'mermaid's purses', 96
Merrilees, Marion, 10
methylated spirit, 89, 110
Midge (CN 679) 13
milk, 12, 143, 145, 157, 159, 163, 176
Miller, J N, St Monans, boat-builder, 17
miller's thumb – see anglerfish
Milloy, Archie, Gigha, 57
Minard, 151, 186
Minches, 19, 22, 37, 64, 131, 140, 158, 168
Mingary, 6
Minna, FC, 68
Mitchell, Ian, Campbeltown, 17
Mitchison, Dick, 184
Mitchison, Naomi Haldane, 184
Moil – see Meall Dubh

202

mole, black – see flounder, freshwater
'monk' – see anglerfish
monkfish *Squatina squatina*, 101
moorlach – see dogfish, lesser spotted
Morning Dawn (CN 252) 46, 86, 105
Morrans, James 'P O', Campbeltown, 102
Moscardini, Gioni, 25
Muasdale, 14, 28, 36, 37, 41, 49, 54, 56, 59, 63, 65, 68, 178
Mull, 62, 63, 103, 126, 131
Mull of Kintyre, 32, 34, 44, 45, 59–61, 91, 120, 132
Munro, Ellen, grocer, Dalintober, 186
Murrays, Kames, 152
Murray, Robert, mason, 45
mùrlach – see dogfish, lesser spotted
music, 79, 146, 181, 186
mussel *Mytilus edulis*, 54, 175, 179
mussel, horse *Modiolus modiolus*, 41, 76, 90, 142

MacAlister, Angus, Gigha, 12, 15–16, 76, 111
MacAlister, Archie 'Snesie', Tarbert, 163
MacAlister, Archie, Edinburgh, 163–4
MacAlister, Archie, Gigha, 15, 32, 35, 42, 46
MacAlister, John, gamekeeper, 15
MacAlister, John, grandson of above, 15, 111
MacAlister, Margaret Smith, Tarbert, 163
McAllister, Neil, Tarbert, 20
MacAlister, Peter, Tarbert, 163
McAllister, Phemie, Southend, 60–1
McAllister, Ronald, shepherd, Southend, 60–1
McAlpine, Duncan, Tarbert, 115
McAnsh, Donald, Torrisdale, 51, 128
MacArthur's Island, 98
MacArthur, Archibald, farmer, Castleton, 145
MacArthur, Hughie, Baile Mór, 139
McArthur, Robbie and Campbell, Campbeltown, 77
McAulay, Carol, Dalintober, 169–70, 172–3
McAulay, Duncan, Dalintober, 170
McAulay, George, Glasgow, 132
McAulay, Neil, Dalintober, 170
MacBrayne family of Campbeltown, 138

MacBrayne, Colin, Ardrishaig, 138
MacBrayne, Mary, Campbeltown, 138–9
McBride family, 160, 165
McBride, Alec, Carradale, 168
McBride, Angus, Pirnmill, 121, 128–9, 175
McBride, Annie Lamb, Pirnmill, 165
McBride, Annie, Carradale, 166, 167, 168, 170, 173, 176, 181, 183–4
McBride, Ellen, Carradale, 165, 167, 168, 169, 170, 171, 176
McBride, Helen Sharp, Carradale, 165, 167
McBride, John, Carradale, 170, 176
McBride, Lawrence, Carradale, 165, 166, 173
McBride, Lawrence, Carradale, 122
McBride, Margaret, Pirnmill, 77, 100, 173, 175, 181
McBride, William, Pirnmill, 128, 165
McBride, Willie, Pirnmill, 87, 173, 175
McBride, Willie, Carradale, 168
McCaffer, Gorrie, Tarbert, 63
McCaffer, Willie, Tarbert, 63
MacCaig, Archie, Tarbert, 163–4
MacCall, Calum, Silvercraigs, 140
MacCall sisters, Silvercraigs, 139
McCallum, Janet, Muasdale, 14
McCallum, Peter, Campbeltown, 46
McConnachie, A, Blasthill, 68
McConnachie, John, Carradale, 76, 133
McCourt, James, Patrick and John, Irish seamen, 3
McCrindle, Howard, Maidens, 108, 109
McCrindle, J Turner, Maidens, 78
MacDonald, baker, Ardrishaig, 140
MacDonald, Donald, Gigha, 53, 55, 58, 95, 159
McDonald, Frank, Dunmore East, 25
Macdonald, James, Campbeltown, 24, 75, 86, 104, 109, 117, 122, 135, 136
MacDonald, Murdo, Baile Mór, 139, 150
McDonnell, James, Greencastle, 13
McDougall, Alistair, Carradale, 166
McDougall, Archie 'Ja', Tarbert, 163, 164
McDougall, Archie 'Poogie', Tarbert, 93
McDougall, Archie 'Tar', Tarbert, 91, 99
McDougall, Archie 'Tom', Tarbert, 81
McDougall, Charlie, Carradale, 158,

173
McDougall, Donald, Tarbert, 19, 51, 80, 116, 128
McDougall, Duncan 'Tar', Tarbert, 19, 25, 73, 131
McDougall, Duncan, Tarbert, uncle of above, 25
McDougall, Flora, Carradale, 174
McDougall, Jane, Dalintober, 185
McDougall, Maggie, Campbeltown, 176
McDougall, Mary McKinlay, Carradale, 158
McDougall, Matthew 'Matha', Carradale, 22
McDougall, May, Carradale, 157, 158, 159, 166, 168, 170, 171, 173, 181
McDougall, Neil, Carradale, 166
McDougall, Neil 'Donna', Carradale, 22
McDougall, Peter, Tarbert, 69, 109, 131
McDougall, Willie, Tarbert, 73
McEachran, George, Campbeltown, 90
MacEwans, Silvercraigs, 139
McFarlane & Jackson, fish-salesmen, Tarbert, 111
MacFarlane, Davie, Tarbert, 73, 172
MacFarlane, Dugald, Tarbert, 116, 160
MacFarlane, Hugh, Tarbert, 98, 99, 105, 106, 160
MacFarlane, John, fish-buyer, 170
MacFarlane, Sandy, Tarbert, 40, 98
McGeachy, Flora, Dalintober, 156, 182, 183
McGeachy, James, Campbeltown, 86
McGeachy, Jane, Dalintober, 180
McGeachy, John, Dalintober, 166
McGeachy, John Edward, Dalintober, 156
McGeachy, Kate, Dalintober, 180
McGeachy, Mary, Dalintober, 156, 169, 180
McGeachy, Minnie, Gigha, 57
McGeachy, Sweeney, Dalintober, 156
McGee, George, fishery officer, 65
McGougans, Silvercraigs, 139
McGown, Dunky, Machrihanish, 33
MacInnes, Mr, schoolmaster, 169
MacInnes, Duncan, Eriskay, 53
McInnes, Latimer, Campbeltown, 121, 161 (fn.)
McIntosh, Denis, Carradale, 130
McIntosh, Donald, Carradale, 76, 108
McIntosh, Gilbert, Carradale, 129 (fn.)
Macintyre, Dugald, naturalist, 7, 62, 63

MacIntyre, Jackie, Feochaig, 11
McKay, Agnes, greengrocer, 175
McKay, Alexander, Dalintober, 162
McKay, Eddie, Campbeltown, 85
McKay, Jessie, Campbeltown, 104
McKay, Mary, Dalintober, 166
McKay, Nan, Dalintober, 156, 162, 166, 173, 176, 181, 183
McKellar, Robbie, Campbeltown, 72, 74, 102
MacKenzie, Major Austin, Carradale, 184
McKerral, Duncan, Campbeltown, 104
McKerral, John, Peninver, 42, 47, 132
McKillop brothers, Dalintober, 76
McKinlay, Jock, Dalintober, 182, 183
McKinney & Rafferty, fish-salesman, 85
McKinnon, Iain, Tarbert, 88
McKinven, Charles, Campbeltown, 85
MacKinven, Hamish, journalist, 79
McKinven, James, Campbeltown, 82, 93
McLady/McLardy, Malcolm, Campbeltown, 76
MacLarty, Mary, Silvercraigs, 137
McLean, Aggie, Dalintober, 182–3
McLean, Allan, Feochaig, 91 (fn.)
MacLean, Archie, Campbeltown, 62
McLean, Donald, Campbeltown, 76
McLean, Hugh, Campbeltown, 176
McLean, James, Campbeltown, 17
McLean, Jocky, Campbeltown, 177
MacLean, John – see 'Tobermory'
McLellan, Flora, Campbeltown, 23
Macleod, Alasdair, Achnaba, 64, 109, 121
Macleod, Donald, Castleton, 77, 109, 115, 119, 121, 150
McManus, Jack, 125
McMillan, Archie Bob and Helen, Carradale, 117
McMillan, David, Campbeltown, 8
McMillan, Dugald, Machrihanish, 62
McMillan, James, Campbeltown, 17, 18
McMillan, James, Machrihanish, 29, 30, 33, 61
McMillan, John, Dalintober, 16, 17
McMillan, Johnny, Carradale, 158
McMillan, Malcolm, fish-buyer, 117
McMillan, Neil L, Campbeltown, 18
McMillan, Peter, Carradale, 169
McMillan, Willie, Drumlemble, 4, 5, 6, 8
McMillan, William, Campbeltown, 8
McMurchy, Dougie, Campbeltown, 171

McNab, Hughie, Tarbert, 178
McNab, Iain, Tarbert, 93, 131
MacNeill, Archie, Muasdale, 68
McNeill, Archie, tobacconist, 185
MacNeill, Betty, Gigha, 37, 57, 187
MacNeill, Calum, Campbeltown, 113
MacNeill, Dougie, Gigha, 37
McNeill, Douglas, Tarbert, 20
MacNeill, Duncan Sr., Gigha, 37
MacNeill, Duncan Jr., Gigha, 37, 40, 42
MacNeill, Isabella, Dalintober, 166
McNeill, James, author, 49
MacNeill, John, laird of Gigha, 64
MacNeill, John, Gigha, 187
MacNeill, Kenny, Gigha, 37
MacNeill, Malcolm Sr., Gigha, 37–9, 40, 66, 85, 187
MacNeill, Malcolm Jr., Gigha, 37
MacNeill, Mary MacColl, Gigha, 37
MacNeill, Neil, farmer, Dunamuck, 68
McNicol, Donald, Carradale, 22
McNiven, Mary, 57
MacPhail, John, Captain, 161
MacPhee, Alick, Machrihanish, 2, 3, 4
MacPhee, Mary, Machrihanish, 2, 3, 5, 6, 8
MacPhee, Mary Glen, Machrihanish, 44
McPherson, Charlotte, Gigha, 15
MacPherson, James and Janet, Dalintober, 182
McPherson, John, Tarbert, 111
McPherson, Robert, fish-salesman, 69
McShannon, Alex, 1
McShannon, Captain Hugh, Southend, 13, 59–61, 95
McShannon, Jamie, 59
McSporran, Catherine, Gigha, 15, 159
McSporran, Captain George, Southend, 14, 49
McSporran, George, Campbeltown, 1, 9, 49, 77
McSporran, John, brother of above, 49
McSporran, Johnny, farmer, 15
McSporran, Willie, Gigha, 29, 31, 35, 46, 55, 56, 57, 112
McTaggart, William, artist, 1
MacTavishes, Kames, 152
McVicar, Davie, Machrihanish, 2, 5, 7, 8, 29, 31, 33, 35, 40, 41, 42–4
MacVicar, Donald, Kames, 150–5
McVicar, Helen MacPhee, Machrihanish, 43, 44
MacVicar, Janet, Kames, 152

MacVicar, John, Kames, 151
MacVicar, Margaret Bell, Kames, 150, 151, 152, 155
MacVicar, Mary, Kames, 151
McWhirter, John, Campbeltown, 89, 90, 113, 126

Nancy Glen (TT 10) 69, 81, 111, 131
NATO Jetty, Campbeltown, 31
Natural History Museum, London, 96
needles, netting-, 166
Nellie (CN 475) 62
Nephrops norvegicus – see 'prawns'
net-mending, 135, 166
Newfoundland, 85, 111
Newlands, George, Campbeltown, 85, 104
Newlands, Jeannie Hamilton, Campbeltown, 104
Newlands, Malcolm, Campbeltown, 48
New England, 97
New Orleans, 10, 11, 12, 28
New Year, 176–7
Nicolson, Miss, Tarbert, 53
Niven, Flory, Southend, 49
North – see Minches
North Uist, 181
Numora (CN 136) 133
nursehound – see dogfish, greater spotted

oats, oatmeal, 6, 14, 53, 144, 145, 146, 156, 158, 185
oatcakes, 144, 158
Oban, 127, 131, 149
octopus *Eledone cirrhosa*, 40, 121
oil of fish, 51, 106–7, 111, 161
oil as shark repellent, 109
Onyx (CN 40) 62
Orde, Sir John, 148–9, 188
Oronsay, 52
Orr, Neil, Gigha, 39
otter *Lutra lutra*, 40, 114
Otterard/Buoy, 74, 75, 76, 128
Otter Ferry, East, 138, 146, 147
Otter Ferry, West, 146, 150
Otter Spit, 64, 73, 77, 81, 115, 124
Our Lassie (PD 199, TT 8) 74, 131
owdan – see gurnard
oyster *Ostrea edulis*, 1, 124

Paisley, 181
Pans – see Machrihanish,

Paterson, bakers, Carradale, 157, 167
Paterson, Archie, Carradale, 22
Paterson, Dugald, Carradale, 22
Paterson, Lachie, Carradale, 84
Paterson, Lachlan, Carradale, 97
Paterson, Maggie Ferguson, Carradale, 181
peasemeal, 143, 158
peat-cutting, 146, 151, 154
peat-torch, 154
Peninver, 30, 118, 132, 133
Pennant, Thomas, 106
Pentland Firth, 98
Peterhead, 20
phosphorescence, 121, 126, 187
picnics, 3, 172–3, 180
pigs, 143
piocach, 'pyoochky', 'pyoochty', 31, 52, 53, 56, 57, 142
Pioneer (CN 226) 16, 18
Pioneer, PS, 68
Pirnmill, 70–3, 77, 87, 88, 106, 127, 135, 136, 165, 173, 175, 176, 181
plaice *Pleuronectes platessa*, 90–3, 134, 136
plowt – see flounder, freshwater
Pluck, 81, 121
podlie, 52
pollack *Pollachius pollachius*, 3, 4, 31, 41, 54, 55–6
Polly Cook (CN 6) 129
porridge, 156
Portknockie, 71
Portnahaven, 60
Portree, 168
Port nan Cudainnean, 53, 58, 95
Port na Cùile, 76, 86, 168
Port Righ, Carradale, 24, 51, 76, 90, 157, 167, 171, 174
Port Righ, Gigha, 57
Port Righ Beag, 159
Port of Rush, 105
Port Wemyss, 60
potatoes, 4, 6, 56, 128, 141, 142, 143, 144, 145, 105, 151, 157, 161, 162, 177
potato-growing, 144–5, 158, 162
pouting *Trisopterus luscus*, 105
'prawns' *Nephrops norvegicus*, 22, 46–8
Prentice, Jimmy, Tarbert, 73
Prentice, Neil, Tarbert, 118
pronnan, 56
Psyche (RO 55) 20, 101, 104
puffers, 68, 83

Puritan (CN 408) 85

Queen Victoria, 149
queenie – see scallop, queen

rabbits, 6, 7, 14, 36, 59, 76, 156, 160, 162, 163, 164, 166, 167
Radiance (BA 289) 131
Rae family, 62
Rae, Donald, Kildalloig, 10
Rae, James, Kildalloig, 84
Rae, James, Pans, 120
Rae, Jimmy, Ugadale, 120
Rae, Maggie, 10
Ralston, Tommy Sr., Campbeltown, 23
Ralston, Tommy Jr., Campbeltown, 23, 114
Ramsay, John, Carradale, 135
Ramsey, 111
Ranger (TT 73) 20
Ranger (BA 290) 131
ray, blonde *Raja brachyura*, 100
ray, spotted, *Raja montagui*, 100
ray, thornback *Raja clavata*, 100, 111
razor-fish *Solenidae*, 77, 142, 155, 175–6
Red Land, Dalintober, 172, 182
Red Wharf, 101
Reekie, W, boatbuilder, St Monans, 177
Reid, Janet, Southend, 13
Reid, William, Southend, 60
religion, 36, 74, 79, 138, 147, 166, 168
Rhu-na-Gal (CN 163) 24
Richmond, Willie, Tarbert, 186
ring-netting, 10, 16, 17, 18, 19, 22, 24, 25, 76, 79, 80, 93, 109, 110, 115, 119, 121, 122, 126, 128, 139, 166, 175, 189
Rioch, John, fishery officer, 117
Ritchie, Alexander, Sanda, 52
Rob McB (PW 30) 35
Robertson, Andrew, Campbeltown, 18, 92
Robertson, Davie Sr., Campbeltown, 19
Robertson, Davie Jr., Campbeltown, 117
Robertson, James, Campbeltown, 16, 18
Robertson, John, Campbeltown, 20, 25, 69, 71, 93, 135
Robertson, Lawrence, Campbeltown, 18, 20, 21, 25, 69, 70–1, 74, 92, 99, 135
Robertson, Robert, Campbeltown, 17
Roc a' Chaisteil, 64
rocklings, bearded *Gaidropsarus vulgarus*,

Ciliata mustela etc., 41, 43
rock fishing, 3, 4, 56–7
rods, fishing-, 3, 4, 7, 8, 13, 32, 46, 54–7, 95, 142
roker – see ray, thornback
ron's egg – see sea-urchin
Rona, SS, 85
Ross, Robert, Tarbert, 25, 72, 73, 81, 82, 83, 88, 91, 93, 101, 104, 105, 106, 110, 115, 118, 131, 160
Rothesay, 48, 130, 136
Roxana (CN 221) 16, 17, 18
Royal Burghs (CN 72) 102
Royal Commission on the Highlands and Islands, 1892, 139, 188–9
Royal Garrison Artillery, 184
rushes, 51, 145, 146, 153
Russell, John, Glenramskill, 77
Russell, Johnny, Kildalloig, 76
Ru Stafnish, 26, 89, 92, 99, 104, 122

Sabbath observance, 125, 147, 168, 172
Saddell, 171, 172, 173, 180
Saffron (BA 182) 122
saithe *Pollachius virens:* 13, 30, 31, 32, 41, 50–5, 59, 60, 61, 142, 161; salting of, 52, 53, 77
sail-fish – see basking shark
St Catherine's, 70
St Monans, 17, 18
salmon *Salmo salar*, 10, 11, 12, 31, 32, 34, 62, 118–20, 168
Salt Pans – see Machrihanish,
Sanda, 10, 22, 32, 34, 39, 52, 60, 75, 77, 80, 104, 134
Sanda, Sound of, 13, 33, 34, 87, 98, 117, 132
sand gaper *Mya arenaria*, 160
Sapphire, 132
scallop *Pecten maximus*, 41, 124–33
scallop, queen *Chlamys (Aequipecten) opercularis*, 124, 126, 134–6
scallop-dredging, 42, 69, 80, 125–36, 135
Scarba (AG 93) 141
Scarlett, Colonel J W, Gigha, 159
scarts, 40, 160–1
schools, schooling, 138, 151, 173–4
Scotia (BCK 37) 71
Scotia Distillery, 169
Scotnish, 93
Scott, Archibald, fish dealer, 84
screenge-net, 32, 52, 90

seals, 102 (fn.), 120
seaweed, 32, 34, 92, 93, 146, 151, 155
sea-anemones, 43
Sea-mar's egg, mar's egg – see sea-urchin
sea-perch *Sebastes marinus*, 56
sea scorpion, long-spined *Cottus bubalis*, 121
sea trout *Salmo trutta trutta*, 31, 32, 119, 120–1
sea-urchin *Echinus esculentus*, 41
Sea My Hunting Ground, The, 108
Sea Nymph (CN 70) 17
Second Waters, 19, 28, 89, 90 (fn.), 136
Second World War, 17, 18–19, 39, 51, 98, 104, 113, 116, 151, 157 (fn.), 162, 178, 184, 185
seine-netting, 16–26, 46, 47, 68–9, 70–5, 77, 78, 81–3, 87, 89, 91, 92, 93, 98, 99, 101, 104, 117, 118, 125, 135, 136
Selene Packet, 48
Seonaid (TT 32) 163–4
'Sgeir an Neich', 38
Sgeir Mhór, Machrihanish, 32, 45
Sgeir Mhór, Muasdale, 54
Sgeir an Trì, 56, 65
Sgolaig, 82, 83, 91, 111, 132
Shaw, Walter, Carradale, 184
Shepherd, Jack, Campbeltown, 79
Shetland, 57, 130
shopkeeping, 167, 184–5
Short, John Sr., Campbeltown, 23, 24
Short, John Jr., Campbeltown, 23, 24
Short, Neil, Campbeltown, 17, 18, 19, 23, 24, 79
Showls/Shoals, 20
Showl Meith, 74
Sillars, Mistress, Campbeltown, 174
Sillars, Robert, blacksmith, Machrihanish, 45
Silvercraigs, 137–48, 150, 155, 188
Silver Chord (KY 124) 100
Silver Cloud (CN 267) 133
Silver Craig (AG 2) 139, 140
Silver Fern II (CN 76) 83–4, 134
Silver Line (BF 52) 118
Silver Spray (TT 33) 131
Silver Spray (TT 65) 109
Sincerity (BF 39) 7
Sinclairs, Silvercraigs, 139, 140
Sinclair, Jackie, Tarbert, 81
skate, 'barndoor', 97
skate, 'blue', 97

skate, 'grey', 97
skate, common *Raja batis*, 22, 65, 91, 96–100, 134
skate *Raja laevis*, 97
Skelmorlie Bank, 134
Skipness, 74, 92, 101, 104, 109, 115, 173
Skipness Bay, 69, 91, 126, 134
Skye, 55, 64, 103, 168, 182
smacks, 63, 152
Smith, Bob, 54, 70, 94–6, 120
Smith, John H, 115
Smith, Willie, Tarbert, 83
sole, black – see Dover
sole, Dover *Solea solea*, 88
sole, lemon *Microstomus kitt*, 88–90, 134
sole, red – see lemon
Solway Firth, 131
soup, 6, 57, 153, 157, 159, 160, 161, 162, 175, 176
soup-kitchen, 175
Southend, 9, 13, 15, 29, 31–32, 44, 49, 52, 59–61, 68, 95,172, 173
Spain, 105
spear, fish-, 13, 94–5, 118, 119
splash/plash-net, 32, 52, 106, 119, 121
spout-fish, spoot-fish, spooties – see razor-fish
spurdog *Squalus acanthias*, 30, 36, 42, 110–12
squat lobsters *Galathea strigosa, G squamifera*, 41
squid, 40, 121–2
stanelock, 51, 52, 59, 61, 142, 160
starfish, 40
Star of David (BA 258) 108, 109
Stella Maris (CN 165) 19
Stella Maris (CN 250) 83
Stewart, Andy, 183
Stewart, Archibald, lawyer, 178
Stewart, Gilbert, Southend, 31
'stoker', 22, 47
Stonefield, 38, 164
Stornoway, 53, 151
Strachan, Charlie and Jimmy, Peterhead, 20
Strachan, Grace, Peterhead, 20
Stratford, 38
Stronachullin, 77
sturgeon *Acipenser sturio*, 116–8
sturgeon *Acipenser huso*, 117
Summer Rose, 39
Sunadale, 168
Sunshine (CN 76) 130, 134
superstitions, 25, 112, 119, 140, 157, 178, 182
Sutherland, Sandy, Findochty, 98
Swedish hake-seiners, 16, 79–80
sweets, 156, 173, 176, 177
Sweet Marie (TT 105) 163

tàbh – see bag-net, saithe,
Taeping (TT 79) 108
Taigh-an-achaidh, 188
tangle *Laminaria*, 160
tangle-nets, 46
Tarbert, 19, 20, 25, 28, 37, 41, 53, 54, 58, 59, 63, 64, 68, 73, 74, 78, 81, 82, 93, 94, 97, 98, 101, 104, 106, 108, 109, 110, 113, 118, 124, 127, 134, 136, 157, 160–1, 162, 163, 164, 166, 171, 172, 177, 178, 186
Tayinloan, 68, 111, 112, 178
Taylor, Capt James, 13
Taylor, Jock, Dalintober, 177
Tayvallich, 37, 38, 68
tea, 3, 12, 18, 20, 48, 58, 102, 141, 152, 154, 163, 172, 173
Templars' halls, 185, 186
thatch, thatching, 145, 146, 151, 153
Thomson, Don, 6
Thomson, Hector, Muasdale, 14
Thomson, Hector, Muasdale, grandson of above, 54
Thomson, James, fishmonger, 25
Thomson, Malcolm, 1
Thomson, Margaret, Campbeltown, 185
Thomson, May, Muasdale, 36, 56
Thomson, Neil, Muasdale, 14–15, 30, 31, 32, 36, 41, 52, 54, 56, 61, 63
Thomson, Neil, Drumlemble, 3
Tobermory, 131, 159
'Tobermory', 13
Togneri, Ronald, Campbeltown, 122
Toll a' Choilich, 118
Tòn Bhàn, 1, 2, 6
tope *Galeorhinus galeus*, 42
Torrisdale, 51, 76, 128
Tor Mór, 76, 88
Tour in Scotland and Voyage to the Hebrides, A, 106
trammel – see ground-net
transport, 14, 16, 17, 20, 22, 37, 52, 54, 68, 73, 85, 120, 129, 133, 140, 164, 165, 167, 170, 171, 172, 173, 174, 177, 178, 180, 184
travellers ('tinkers'), 152, 162, 167, 178
trawl: otter, 89–92; pair, 47, 52, 84;

pelagic/mid-water, 74, 78, 84, 88, 108, 118, 119; prawn, 46–8, 86, 93, 99, 100, 109, 117, 122, 125; queenie, 126
trawlers, damage to lines caused by, 65–6
Tris, 57
Troon, 165 (fn.)
trout *Salmo trutta fario*, 142–3
True Love (188 AG) 139, 140
Trustful (A 370, TT 79) 68, 99
turbot *Scophthalmus maximus*, 87–8, 91, 134
Turners, Kames, 152
Turner, Edward, Hull, 65
Turner, Miss, Kilchamaig, 163
Tyrell, Arklow, boat-builder, 23

Ugadale/Point, 62, 84, 90, 120
ugh ròin – see sea-urchin
Uig, 168
Uisead, 44, 63
Urquhart, Hector, gamekeeper, 118

vans, travelling, 144, 157, 171
vegetables, 145, 158, 161, 175
Victoria and Albert, Royal Yacht, 87
Vigilant, Fishery Cruiser, 65
Village Belle I (TT 34) 126, 127, 131, 177, 178
Village Maid (TT 25) 131

walking, 138, 141, 147, 167, 170, 171, 172, 173, 174
Wareham, Billy, Campbeltown, 35, 39, 40, 41, 42, 134, 136
Wareham, Hamish, Campbeltown, 39
Wareham, James, Campbeltown, 84
Wareham, James 'Puggy', Campbeltown, 17, 102
Wareham, Jock, Campbeltown, 39
Wareham, Willie, Campbeltown, 39, 102
water, 2, 142–3, 145, 147, 151, 165
Waterfoot, 76
Watkins, Anthony, 108
Watson, Alex, Southend, 13
Watson, David, Muasdale, 36

Watson, Lachie, Muasdale, 36
Watson, Maggie, Muasdale, 178
Watson, Margaret, Southend, 13
Watson, Willie, Muasdale, 14, 36, 41, 54, 56
weddings, 165, 167, 186–7
Wee Bank, 87
Weir, John, Tarbert, 106
Weir, Neil, Tarbert, 118
wells, 2, 142–3, 151, 173, 174
West Bank, 91
West Loch Tarbert, 21, 33, 34, 41, 68, 105, 124
West Shore, Tarbert, 40, 81, 83, 106, 128
whelk *Buccinum undatum*, 41, 62, 64–5, 112, 141
whins, 147
Whitehaven, 80
Whitehills, 20, 92
Whitestone Bank, 76
White Heather (CN 101) 166
White Heather (B 208) 125
whiting *Merlangius merlangus*, 21, 22, 24, 25, 30, 64, 70, 75–7, 175
Whiting Bay, 116, 129
Whyte family, Silvercraigs, 139, 143, 145, 147–8, 188
Whyte, Peter, Silvercraigs, 139, 188–9
winkle *Littorina littorea*, 1, 6, 56, 128, 142, 151, 155, 159, 168, 173
witch *Glyptocephalus cynoglossus*, 22, 94
witches, 157
wood-gathering, 2, 6, 12, 138, 147
Wotherspoon, Hughie, Gigha, 55
Wotherspoon, John, Gigha, 65
wrack, *wreck* – see seaweed
wrasse, ballan *Labrus bergylta*, 4, 41, 105–6
Wylie, Marjory Rae, New Orleans, 10, 11, 12
Wylie, Robert, New Orleans, 10–13, 15, 28, 29, 30, 33, 34, 120
Wylie, Robert, boat-builder, 10
Wylie, Thomas, joiner, 10
Wyre (FD 196) 65

Yonge, C M, 41, 44